UNEQUAL

The Central Park Jogger Trials

VERDICTS

AMERICAN LAWYER BOOKS

SIMON & SCHUSTER

NEW YORK

LONDON

TORONTO

SYDNEY

TOKYO

SINGAPORE

UNEQUAL

The Central Park Jogger Trials

VERDICTS

Timothy Sullivan

AMERICAN LAWYER BOOKS/
SIMON & SCHUSTER
SIMON & SCHUSTER BUILDING
ROCKEFELLER CENTER
1230 AVENUE OF THE AMERICAS
NEW YORK, NEW YORK 10020

PUBLISHED BY AMERICAN LAWYER BOOKS/SIMON & SCHUSTER INC.
AMERICAN LAWYER BOOKS ARE PUBLISHED BY
AM-LAW PUBLISHING CORPORATION.
SIMON & SCHUSTER AND COLOPHON ARE REGISTERED TRADEMARKS
OF SIMON & SCHUSTER INC.
THE AMERICAN LAWYER IS A REGISTERED TRADEMARK OF
THE AMERICAN LAWYER NEWSPAPER GROUP, INC.
DESIGNED BY CARLA WEISE/LEVAVI & LEVAVI
MAP BY DAVID KORALEK
MANUFACTURED IN THE UNITED STATES OF AMERICA

1 3 5 7 9 10 8 6 4 2

LIBRARY OF CONGRESS CATALOGING-IN-PUBLICATION DATA
SULLIVAN, TIMOTHY (TIMOTHY JOHN)
UNEQUAL VERDICTS: THE CENTRAL PARK JOGGER TRIALS /
TIMOTHY SULLIVAN.
P.   CM.
INCLUDES INDEX.
1. CENTRAL PARK JOGGER RAPE TRIAL, NEW YORK, N.Y., 1990.
2. TRIALS (RAPE)—NEW YORK (N.Y.) 3. TRIALS (ASSAULT AND BATTERY)-
-NEW YORK (N.Y.)   I. TITLE.
KF224.C435S85 1992
345.73'02532—DC20
[347.3052532]   92-1688
CIP
ISBN: 0-671-74237-X

In memory of my father,
the Honorable Timothy John Sullivan,
Justice of the Supreme Court
of the State of New York

Acknowledgments

THIS IS A BOOK ABOUT A HANDFUL OF TRIAL LAWYERS AND HOW THEY dealt with one of the most explosive criminal cases ever to hit the New York courts.

The cooperation of the lead prosecutor, Elizabeth Lederer, and her co-counsel, Arthur "Tim" Clements, was crucial to my understanding of how the two Central Park Jogger trials developed. Without their patient and candid assistance, I could not have hoped to analyze adequately this complex case. Another assistant district attorney in Manhattan, sex crimes chief Linda Fairstein, was also helpful.

Among the defense lawyers, those who shared their time and experience were Michael Joseph, Elliot Cook, Colin Moore, Howard Diller, Jesse Berman, William Kunstler, C. Vernon Mason and Natasha Lapiner.

I was fortunate enough to have the input of many other lawyers during the writing of this book. Among them I owe a special debt to Roger Parloff, a friend and colleague who reviewed the manuscript to excise error. He bears no responsibility for flaws that may exist despite his efforts.

On Justice Thomas Galligan's staff, I was assisted by his law secretary, Dennis Boyle (now a Criminal Court judge), and clerk Sandra Martin.

Private investigators Evrard Williams and Roland Thomas were also helpful.

Anyone who has tried to analyze a jury verdict knows it cannot be done properly without the cooperation of those whose deliberations produced it. I am therefore indebted to jurors George Louie, Harold Brueland, Ronald Gold, Richard Peters, Earle Fisher, Migdalia Fuentes, Rafael Miranda, Charles Nestorick and, from the second trial, Steve Gilliam, Eric Roach and Victoria Bryers.

Among the supporters of the defendants, I am grateful for the assistance of William Perkins, Elombe Brath, Nomsa Brath, Lamont Radcliff, Grace Cuffee, Angela Cuffee and Sharonne Salaam.

Several teachers and counselors also helped me learn something about the lives of black and Latino youngsters in New York: John Bess, Abiodun Oyewole, Dr. Vera Paster, Larry Saposnick, Julia Rivera and Joyce Duncan.

Several friends provided welcome counsel and support. First among these is Felipe Luciano, without whose vision and guidance I would never have been able to see this story. On matters of reportage, Ellen Joan Pollock's advice was much appreciated.

It is not possible to list all of those journalists whose work made mine easier. But I would, at least, like to credit Emily Sachar, Guy Trebay, Erica Munk, Sam Maull, Lizette Alvarez, Ronald Sullivan, Vynette Price, Mike Pearl and Mary Murphy.

The pretrial reporting of Michael Stone, Timothy Clifford, Rick Hornung and Barry Michael Cooper was also important.

Several excellent editors deserve as much credit as thanks. Steven Brill's endorsement, as well as his flexibility as an employer, went a long way toward making this book a reality.

Alice Mayhew was an attentive, direct and enormously supportive instructor. Her ability to see the essence of things, and to bring organization to sometimes scattered material, rescued me from quicksand of my own making.

Ari Hoogenboom's editing and encouragement were always appreciated.

My agent, Ethan Ellenberg, ably protected my interests throughout this project and provided sound feedback on the manuscript.

I would like to mention a few of the many books that contributed to the development of my thinking during the two years I spent report-

ACKNOWLEDGMENTS

ing and writing this one. I am glad that James Kunen wrote *How Can You Defend Those People?* and that Robert Katz wrote *Naked by the Window.* A few others deserve mention: *The Autobiography of Malcolm X* by Alex Haley, *The Fire Next Time* by James Baldwin, *Black Robes, White Justice* by Judge Bruce Wright, *Wasted* by Linda Wolfe, and *The Hundred Percent Squad* by E. W. Count.

To the people who spoke to me on the condition that they remain anonymous, I again say thank you.

Any words I could include here as an acknowledgment of the vast contribution of my wife, Margy, would prove woefully inadequate. She has always been a frank, insightful critic of my writing. I hope I may someday have an opportunity to return the enormous favor she has done me.

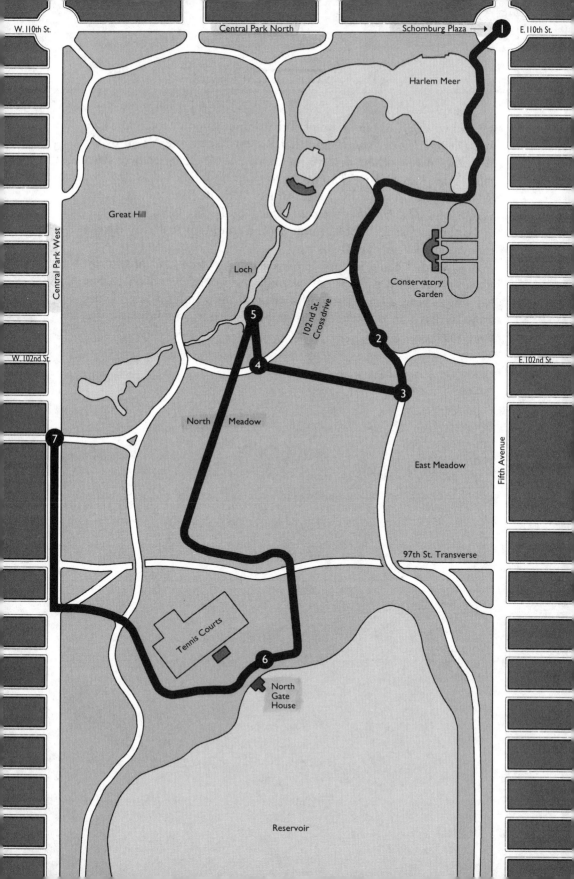

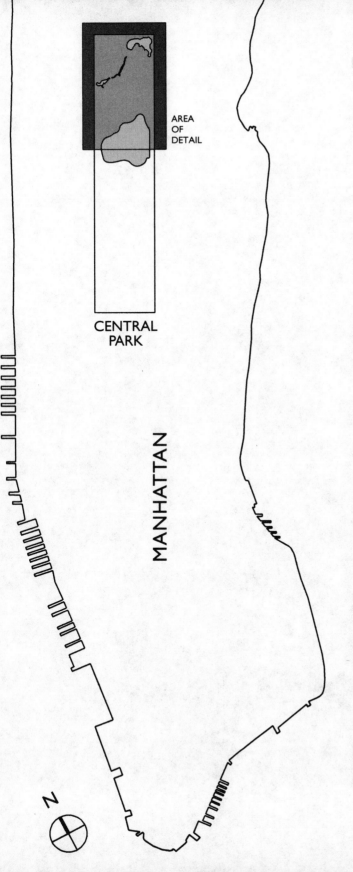

AREA
OF
DETAIL

CENTRAL
PARK

MANHATTAN

N

1. Schomburg Plaza. A gang of about 33 teenagers gathers here at about 8:30 P.M. to discuss where to go wilding. They choose Central Park and enter through the gate across the street.

2. The gang first encounters Antonio Diaz, 52, whom they all later describe as "the bum." He is knocked down, punched and kicked by several boys. Diaz, nearly unconscious, is dragged into the bushes so he won't be discovered. A passing police car disperses the gang into several smaller groups.

3. In this area, several cyclists are harassed but escape unharmed.

4. A group of about 10 to 12 boys attacks a lone female jogger on the 102nd Street Crossdrive.

5. After dragging the woman 300 feet into a damp ravine, the assailants beat her unconscious. She is repeatedly raped beside a footpath on the edge of the Loch, where she is left bound and gagged.

6. Having regrouped in the North Meadow, the larger gang walks south to the reservoir, where several male joggers are attacked, including John Loughlin who is left unconscious.

7. At about 10:15 P.M., police officers who have been searching for the gang spot at least a dozen boys on Central Park West near 100th Street. [Most of the teens break and run when they see the police.] Five boys are caught and charged with unlawful assembly and the assault of John Loughlin. The female jogger is found 3 1/2 hours later.

Contents

Foreword

A HORRIFYING CRIME MAKES NATIONAL HEADLINES. POLICE AND prosecutors give it their highest priority. Arrests come quickly, and those arrested look guilty. They even confess.

That is not the end of the story, nor should it be. Doing justice in a country committed to the presumption of innocence and due process is harder than it looks. The process is messy, complicated, and as imperfect as the people and the evidence involved.

The story of what became known as the "Central Park Jogger case" reveals just how messy, complicated, and imperfect it all can be. *Unequal Verdicts* is a journey through that process.

We confront a series of haunting "what if's?" What if the teenage defendants had had the sense to keep quiet when first questioned? Or had had the advice and the money to hire the best lawyers from the beginning? What if such a tough-minded judge had not been especially selected to handle this case? What if the victim had not been white and middle class? If the lawyers had been shrewder and the prosecutor less skilled? Suppose the plea bargaining had been seriously pursued at the start. Or that one of the holdout jurors had been excluded originally by the lawyers.

15

We all recognize that life is filled with uncertainty. Yet we expect our system of crime and punishment to be precise and certain, predictable, as clear as the law as it is written in textbooks. The fact that the legal system doesn't work that way shouldn't surprise us. Nor disappoint us. It is people, not some perfectly calibrated "justice machine," who operate the system. It is people—the jurors—who make the ultimate decisions of guilt or innocence. So, yes, the process becomes a kind of game, in which luck, skill, and the resources, or "tricks," one can bring to the game all count, much the way they count in anything else that involves people.

This is not meant to belittle the judicial system; and indeed Tim Sullivan's wonderfully textured account of the Jogger case presents a system that is neither capable of—nor guilty of—machinelike precision.

To read the story that follows and to understand these *Unequal Verdicts* is to understand what we can expect from the system. And what we can't. We can expect a system that tries to be fair, that has rules that are supposed to apply to everyone, and that cherishes freedom so much that it battles long and hard before it takes it away.

STEVEN BRILL
President and Editor-in-Chief
The American Lawyer and *Court TV*

THE
PRELUDE

Part One

CHAPTER 1

THIS IS MY FIRST RAPE

—

"STEVE RIPPED HER PANTS WITH HIS KNIFE. THAT'S WHAT MADE HER mad. And then, that's when she start scratchin', uh, what's-his-name? Kevin. She was yellin' pretty loud. Yusef closed her mouth, because he had bigger hands than us."

Kharey "Polo" Wise, sixteen, was talking to Elizabeth Lederer, a senior homicide and sex crimes prosecutor in the Manhattan district attorney's office. It was about 3:30 on the afternoon of Friday, April 21, 1989, thirty-nine hours after the horribly beaten body of a young woman had been found in the northern woods of Central Park, nude except for the bra pushed up above her breasts. Lederer had been interrogating suspects in front of a video camera for fourteen hours. As soon as she finished taking one statement the cops would bring her another kid with a story to tell.

This was Lederer's second video session with Wise, and she was beginning to worry about the credibility of the case. He had given detectives two contradictory written statements before Lederer had arrived at the precinct, and his story was still changing. How was a jury to know which version to believe? Lederer would have preferred a clean case; one written confession, one video from each defendant. But this case wasn't going that way.

She knew from experience that a suspect will admit what he has to and deny what he can. But Wise was more slippery than the other teenagers Lederer had interviewed that day. He went off on tangents and created completely implausible explanations for the myriad contradictions in his tale. Yet Wise's account of the wild spree he and approximately thirty other kids had taken through Central Park two nights before was also rich in detail and highly incriminating.

"So we was lookin' at her, and I felt kinda bad," said Wise. "This is my first thing I did to any type of female in the street. This is my first rape. I never did this before, and this is gonna be my last time doin' it."

———

Linda Fairstein, an ambitious career prosecutor who enjoyed an investigation as much as a trial, got the news at about 9:00 A.M. on Thursday, April 20, from Sergeant Robert Fiston of the Manhattan Sex Crimes Squad. A nearly nude woman, bound, gagged and within an inch of death, had been found at about 1:00 A.M. in a muddy ravine below the 102nd Street Crossdrive in Central Park. She was apparently the victim of a large gang of East Harlem youths who had rampaged through the park the previous night, mugging joggers and harassing cyclists and cab drivers. The cops were questioning a group of juvenile suspects and would need a DA to come uptown later and videotape their statements. The victim was in intensive care at Metropolitan Hospital and still unidentified.

As chief of the twelve-lawyer Sex Crimes Prosecution Unit, Fairstein, forty-one, didn't try many cases herself anymore. Her last trial, the notorious Preppy Murder Case of 1988, had raised her to a level of celebrity beyond the considerable status she had achieved in criminal justice and feminist circles for championing the aggressive prosecution of hitherto hushed-up crimes. That trial had ended in disappointment when she accepted Robert Chambers's plea to manslaughter for the killing of Jennifer Levin. The jury was stuck in its ninth day of deliberating a murder charge at the time.

No media spotlight gets as hot or as bright as that which burns in New York City, and the media love nothing more than a case like *The People* v. *Robert Chambers*. Chambers, twenty, killed Levin, eighteen, behind the Metropolitan Museum of Art, in a part of the park that serves as playground for respectable Manhattanites, from the rich and powerful of Fifth Avenue co-ops to the intellectuals of Central Park West. Regardless of who this victim turned out to be, Fairstein reasoned, a violent rape in Central Park would attract a lot of media. The case should go to somebody who could not be intimidated or rattled by the city's hypercompetitive press corps.

Two other aspects of the case influenced Fairstein's choice: the possibility that the victim would die and the fact that she had apparently been gang-raped. In any sex crime an effective prosecutor must establish a meaningful rapport with the victim, who may be unwilling or afraid to cooperate. If this victim died, however, the prosecutor would have to be able to get the same kind of cooperation from her family, in order to present the deceased to a jury as a real person. Second, the likelihood of gang-rape meant multiple defendants, which, in turn, portended a complex investigation and a team of opposing counsel. So, in addition to a good trial lawyer who could handle the media, Fairstein needed an experienced investigator whom victims and their kin would instinctively trust. She called Lederer.

Meanwhile, Nancy Ryan, deputy chief of the Trial Division, had heard about the Central Park assaults on the radio. The first thing she did when she arrived at work that morning, even before making contact with the detectives running the investigation, was assign the case to Peter Casolaro, one of the office's top homicide prosecutors. A few months earlier, Casolaro had proven his ability to overcome the distractions of the media and win a difficult circumstantial case when a jury convicted lawyer Joel Steinberg of the manslaughter of his six-year-old, illegally adopted daughter. The killing of Lisa Steinberg had shocked the public, exposing a middle-class household in which the deranged Steinberg and his battered companion, Hedda Nussbaum, had horribly mistreated the girl and a surviving, two-year-old adopted boy.

When Fairstein heard that Ryan had assigned the Central Park case as a homicide, she rushed to her colleague's office, ready for a turf war. The woman was not dead, said Fairstein, but she was very obviously the victim of a rape. Moreover, she continued, Lederer had proven time and again her ability to establish firm relationships with victims and their families, which would undoubtedly become crucial in this case. Fairstein was confident that District Attorney Robert Morgenthau would settle the argument in her favor if Ryan chose to take it that far. But Ryan did not.

The conflict downtown in Morgenthau's office was similar to a contest that was taking shape uptown among rival detective squads, whose members also smelled printer's ink all over the case. When detectives from the Manhattan North Homicide Squad began arriving at the Central Park Precinct shortly after 9:00 A.M. to assist in the investigation, the small parking lot was already crowded with print and broadcast reporters elbowing one another for a piece of the story. And inside, the converted nineteenth-century stable was packed not only with suspects and their relatives but with Sex Crimes detectives and Central Park precinct regulars.

A team of experienced investigators from Homicide was often called in when a precinct detective squad had to solve a difficult murder or other major felony. The Sex Crimes Squad assigned teams to the appropriate cases in the same manner. Standard procedure dictated that the precinct where the crime occurred would maintain official control of the case, a fact signified by the designation of a local detective as arresting officer. That officer, in this case Detective Humberto Arroyo of the Central Park Precinct, was responsible for coordinating the paperwork and guiding the case through the NYPD's red tape.

The dispute in Morgenthau's office was settled by administrators relying on bureaucratic procedures and personal clout, whereas the rivalry among the cops was resolved by immediate performance. With dozens of potential suspects, the size of the case dictated that several teams from Homicide and Sex Crimes would assist the Central Park detectives. The cops who got the best results soonest would end up running the case. The Central Park and Sex Crimes squads had little chance, therefore, against the wizened veterans of the Manhattan North Homicide Squad, each of whom had been chosen by the unit commander, Lieutenant Jack Doyle, because of demonstrated success as an investigator.

The police finally called Lederer to say they were ready for the video crew at about 8:00 P.M. By that time the brass had moved the investigation from the tiny Central Park stationhouse to the much bigger facilities of the Twentieth Precinct on West Eighty-second Street. Lederer called Fairstein, who offered to meet her at the precinct to help out.

By the time Fairstein and Lederer arrived, the Central Park detectives and the Sex Crimes Squad had essentially been bumped by the homicide specialists. That elite crew had been more successful in convincing the families of the juvenile suspects to cooperate and had conducted a series of interrogations producing the written confessions that would serve as prelude to Lederer's videotaped interviews. Their tactics were time-honored and unarguably effective, but would later be challenged by every defense lawyer in the case as coercive, deceptive, manipulative, improper and illegal.

The prosecutors' first order of business was to get a briefing from the cops, to learn as much as the detectives knew about what had happened in Central Park the previous evening. As Lederer listened to the police officers and read the written statements of a few suspects, the picture began to come into focus.

A group of about fifteen boys had gathered in front of Schomburg Plaza, a government-subsidized housing complex across Fifth Avenue from the northeast corner of Central Park. They were joined between 8:30 P.M. and 9:00 P.M. by another group of about fifteen boys who had come across 110th Street from the Taft Houses project on Madison Avenue. The gang went into the park, some scouting for cyclists whose bikes they could steal, some hoping to mug pedestrians and joggers for money or cassette players. They surrounded a young Latino man, but somebody in the group knew him, so they let him pass. They approached a couple with the idea of beating up the man until somebody said, "Yo, he's with his girl." Some twisted sense of chivalry prevailed and they left the couple in peace. Next the boys came upon an old Latino man, apparently drunk, carrying a bag of food and several bottles of beer. The man, whom they all later described as "the bum," was beaten and left unconscious. On the park's East Drive the boys threw rocks and bottles at taxicabs and tried unsuccessfully to dismount several cyclists, including a couple on a tandem bike. After having been dispersed by a cruising police car, the gang split up.

This was the point at which the accounts Lederer was reading began to differ significantly. Most of the boys described a series of assaults on men jogging around the large reservoir in the middle of the park. But there was disagreement about the timing of those attacks. Among the few boys who admitted participating in the rape and beating of a female jogger near 102nd Street, some said it happened after the reservoir muggings, while others claimed it was earlier.

As the prosecutors brought themselves up to speed on the sprawling investigation, the detectives continued interrogating a relentlessly growing list of suspects. The state's case against each defendant would inevitably have its share of holes, but none seemed so vulnerable in the early going as that of Yusef Salaam. The circumstances surrounding his interrogation, conducted on the third floor of the Twentieth Precinct while Lederer studied the statements of other suspects on the second floor, would become a *Rashomon* in which no two characters agreed on anything.

Thomas McKenna, a second-grade detective with the Manhattan North Homicide Squad, would later testify that when he questioned Salaam at about 11:15 P.M. on Thursday, April 20, he did not know other suspects had claimed that Salaam played an especially violent role in the reservoir assaults and the rape. But McKenna and his partner had interviewed Al Morris, who said he and Salaam had gone into the park with a large group of kids, one of whom suggested, "Let's wild some joggers." So when Salaam, sitting opposite McKenna in a third-floor office, said he had never gone to Central Park the previous night, the detective believed the boy was lying. And to McKenna's way of thinking, the kid wasn't walking out of that room protected by a lie.

I know you were in the park, said McKenna, because other people who were there told me so. But Salaam, tall and confident, looked him in the eye and again said the cop was wrong. This standoff lasted for a while, with Salaam coolly denying two or three more times that he'd been in the park.

A detective for twenty years, McKenna embraced the common investigative premise that an innocent person will not falsely incriminate himself. He decided, therefore, to run a ruse on the boy.

"Look," said McKenna, "I don't care if you tell me anything. I don't care what you say to me. We have fingerprints on the [female] jogger's pants. They're satin, they're a very smooth surface and we have been able to get fingerprints off of them. I'm just going to compare your prints to the prints that we have on the pants, and if they match up, you don't have to tell me anything. Because you're going down for rape."

To which Salaam exclaimed, according to McKenna, "I was there but I didn't rape her."

"Well, why don't you just tell me what did happen then," said the detective. "If you were there, you tell me what did happen, and we'll see what happens from there."

Salaam casually responded, said McKenna, with a story that was quite similar to that of the other defendants. In Salaam's version of the assault on the female jogger, as recounted by McKenna, he admitted hitting her twice with a pipe and fondling her breasts. The victim was then "fucked," said Salaam, by Kharey Wise, Kevin Richardson and two other boys whom he did not know.

If the kid had not gone for the fingerprint angle McKenna would have tried something else. He was in no hurry. He figured he had all night to get the kid talking, to get the story straight, to get as much information as possible about who did what to whom before committing the statement to paper and having Salaam sign it.

That was where the wily cop was wrong.

An hour into the interrogation, at about 12:30 A.M., Detective John Taglioni knocked on the door and told McKenna that Salaam's mother was downstairs, claiming the boy was only fifteen years old. "Don't tell me that," said McKenna, "he's got identification that he's 16!" McKenna looked again at the student subway pass Salaam had shown him earlier, with his date of birth listed as February 27, 1973. He held the pass up to Salaam. "Is this you?" he asked.

"Yes," said Salaam.

"How old are you?"

"Fifteen."

"Can't you count?" said McKenna. "This makes you 16."

"No, no. I'm only 15," said Salaam, explaining that he used the card to pass himself off as sixteen to impress girls.

McKenna was livid. If the kid he'd questioned without a parent or guardian present was only fifteen, the admissions he had made might never get into court. Not only that, Taglioni had more bad news: There was a lawyer downstairs inquiring about Salaam.

—————

Fairstein had been in the Twentieth Precinct squad room about an hour earlier when a detective came in and told her there was a lawyer in the lobby asking for Yusef Salaam. Fairstein and Lederer, now on the scene for more than three hours, were still sorting out the case, dashing in and out of impromptu meetings, hurrying up and down the stairs, with Fairstein, at five feet seven inches, towering over the petite Lederer. The defendants, still waiting for the videotape sessions to begin, had taken to calling them "the Big One and the Little One."

Before going downstairs to meet the attorney, Fairstein wanted to know what the cops had on Salaam, so she sent a detective upstairs to check on the status of the interrogation. He returned with McKenna's notebook, in which Fairstein read that Salaam was sixteen years old and admitted hitting the female jogger twice with a pipe.

The presence of a lawyer inquiring about Salaam troubled Fairstein. The prosecutors and detectives were proceeding as though this were a murder investigation—a doctor at Metropolitan Hospital had told Fairstein that the comatose victim could not live. As far as Fairstein was concerned, they had the killer, he was being interrogated by a skilled detective and he was incriminating himself. Salaam was the last kid she wanted to see represented by a lawyer at that point.

The lawyer in the lobby was David Nocenti, who worked in the civil division of the U.S. attorney's office in Brooklyn. Nocenti, a bachelor, was in the Catholic "Big Brother" program and had been paired with Salaam about four years earlier, shortly after the boy's parents divorced. Salaam's mother had called him a half-hour earlier and asked him to meet her at the stationhouse.

It was not the first time Ms. Salaam had asked Nocenti to help get her son out of a jam. Nocenti had represented his "little brother" the previous November at an administrative hearing concerning Salaam's suspension from LaGuardia High School, a highly competitive performing arts school where the boy studied painting. Salaam was suspended after a ninja star (a Chinese martial arts weapon) and a butcher knife with a nine-inch blade were found in his locker. Salaam said he carried the weapons for protection from two gangs, the Decepticons and Public Enemy, whose members often fought at or near the school.

Testifying later, Fairstein and Nocenti would disagree about many of the details of their conversation at the Twentieth Precinct, but the essential points were clear. Nocenti, being a federal prosecutor, was precluded by Department of Justice regulations from representing Salaam. He was there, he said, to assist Ms. Salaam as a friend of the family, and in that capacity, he wanted to see Yusef.

Fairstein was within her rights to refuse his request. If Salaam was sixteen he was an adult under the law and the authorities did not have to permit him to have visitors before he was questioned. And if he was fifteen (a fact of which Fairstein says she was unaware at the time) the police were only required to give access to a parent or guardian.

Fairstein considered Nocenti's presence a breach of professional ethics and she demanded a phone number at which she could reach his supervisor to complain. When Nocenti declined to give her the number she called her husband to get the phone number of Andrew Maloney, the U.S. attorney for the Eastern District of New York. Fairstein's husband suggested that, it being after midnight, perhaps the call could wait until morning. Fairstein later testified that an intimidated Nocenti had confessed to being "in over his head" and begged her not to call Maloney.

If Fairstein was appalled at the young prosecutor's bad judgment in inserting himself into the defense side of a criminal matter, she was at least relieved at Nocenti's ignorance of criminal law. Instead of insisting on seeing Salaam and asking the detectives questions about the investigation, all Nocenti had to say was: "I'm calling a lawyer for him now, so you can't question him further." If he had done that, said Fairstein later, she would have stopped the interrogation. Instead, Nocenti huddled with Salaam's relatives on the sidewalk and, apparently distracted by Fairstein's threats, tried to answer their questions. In the meantime, upstairs, McKenna continued questioning Salaam, who was adding more incriminating details to his story about wilding in the park.

———

Sharonne Salaam, Yusef's mother, arrived at the precinct at about midnight. Like her son, she was tall and thin, dark-skinned with fine features and intense eyes. After conferring with Nocenti on the sidewalk, Ms. Salaam told Fairstein, in a cultivated southern accent, that her son was only fifteen and she didn't want him questioned.

Fairstein was not inclined to believe Ms. Salaam. The prosecutor had seen plenty of cases in which parents claimed their older teenagers were minors, hoping they'd be released on simple summonses to appear in Family Court. Fairstein asked Ms. Salaam if she had any identification that proved her son was fifteen. She did not.

To resolve the issue, said Fairstein, she would send for the detectives who were questioning Yusef. In a few minutes the women were joined by detectives Taglioni, who had brought Salaam to the precinct from Schomburg Plaza earlier that night, and Rudy Hall, who had been sitting in on the interrogation. McKenna, meanwhile, remained upstairs with Salaam.

The detectives and Ms. Salaam debated the boy's age for perhaps ten minutes. Fairstein then took the detectives aside and told them that, for the sake of protecting the case, they should accept Ms. Salaam's word that her son was fifteen and tell McKenna to stop the interview. A few minutes later, at about 12:30 A.M., Ms. Salaam told Fairstein she was getting a lawyer for the boy. Somebody had finally said the magic words Fairstein had been dreading for the past hour.

Ms. Salaam's assertion of her son's right to counsel may have been too late to protect him from self-incrimination, but it did throw a serious curve at the prosecution. There was now no hope of getting Salaam to sign a written statement, let alone sit for a videotaped interview with Lederer. Unless the lab technicians were able to link him physically to the crimes, Salaam would be in a position to deny any participation whatsoever.

CHAPTER 2

MAKING THE VIDEOTAPES

BOBBY AND LINDA MCCRAY HAD BEEN WAITING MORE THAN SIX HOURS for a district attorney to take a videotaped statement from their fifteen-year-old son, Antron, about Wednesday night's horrendous events in Central Park. It was nearly 1:00 A.M. on Friday, more than thirteen hours since four cops had come to their Harlem apartment and asked them to bring "Tronny" to the Central Park Precinct for questioning. In the meantime, the McCrays, both in their mid-thirties, had twice been moved to other stationhouses and had unhappily signed a confession the boy had given to detectives, incriminating himself in the rape.

Now the McCrays were at the Twenty-fourth Precinct on West 100th Street, crowded into a little room in a corner of the first floor that had been partitioned out of the busy main lobby by barriers made of metal and frosted glass. The partitions were about seven feet high, which made them about five feet too short to reach the ceiling. The pale green room, the only one in the building that the courts had approved as appropriate for the questioning of juveniles, was perhaps ten feet wide and fifteen feet long. Though it was barely big enough for the three desks and few file cabinets it held, there were now seven people crammed into Room 101: Antron and his parents, two detectives, a camera operator, and Elizabeth Lederer. (The prosecutors had moved everybody to this stationhouse at about midnight because the cops at the Twentieth Precinct could not agree which room in that building was the designated "youth room.")

The Manhattan district attorney's office had begun taping the statements of suspects about ten years earlier. Videos were essentially no more than a logical technological improvement on the old system of having a stenographer record a prosecutor's initial Q and A session with a suspect. But there was no comparison when it came to emotional impact. No matter how incriminating or compelling a defendant's story, there was always the danger a jury would tune out while listening to a witness read it aloud in monotone in a stuffy courtroom. Videotape, however, packed all the immediacy, and attendant credibility, that were lacking in a mere transcript. Videotape was a lot tougher for a defense lawyer to impeach with accusations that it was forced, contrived or even doctored. And video made jurors feel right at home; as though they were in their own living rooms watching television.

In selecting the order in which to tape interviews with the suspects, Lederer had to consider their ages, how long they'd been waiting and the substance of the written statements they'd already given the police. The last consideration was paramount. She wanted first to get through the kids who incriminated themselves the most, leaving them as little time as possible to change their stories, to decide they didn't want to talk anymore, or for their parents to demand a lawyer. Since one of the detectives who'd taken McCray's written confession had told her that he admitted penetrating the rape victim with his penis, Lederer decided she'd talk to him first.

She began by asking the McCrays to state their names and their relationships to the boy. The camera swiveled to provide a shot of Linda McCray, looking small, tired and sad, and her angry husband. They were squeezed together behind a desk a few feet from Antron, Bobby's stepson and Linda's only child. Both parents were silent as the teenager waived his rights.

"You have the right to remain silent and the right to refuse to answer any questions," said Lederer. "Do you understand?"

"Yes," said the boy.

"Anything you say can be used against you in court. Do you understand?"

"Yes."

"You have the right to consult a lawyer now, before any questioning,

and to have a lawyer present during any questioning. Do you understand?"

"Yes."

"If you have no lawyer, or cannot afford a lawyer, a lawyer will be
provided for you now, free of charge, before any questioning. Do you
understand?"

"Yes."

"Now that I've advised you of your rights, are you willing to speak
to me and tell me the truth about what happened in Central Park on
the night of April 19, 1989?"

"Yes," said McCray.

Lederer considered video sessions fact-finding missions. Over the
years she had learned that confrontation did not often produce cooperation, and she developed a Q and A style that was indicative of her
personality: direct but respectful, tough but courteous, her emotions,
even in a rape case, sublimated to the professional task. She always tried
to keep in mind what a tape would look like, maybe a year later, to a
judge and jury. With juveniles she was careful not to be overbearing,
thinking pressure was likely to make a kid clam up or trigger a protective response in parents that could bring the whole thing to a halt. The
McCrays, after all, had the right to end the interview at any time.

Gathering information was not the prosecutor's only purpose.
McCray and most of the others had already implicated themselves to
one degree or another in the crimes of Wednesday night, so Lederer
wanted to use the tapes to preclude possible defenses. When McCray,
in response to Lederer's questions, said he wasn't drunk when he went
out with his friends that night, had not smoked crack or used any other
drugs, he wasn't exonerating himself of additional charges; he was
eliminating the potential defense that he hadn't been responsible for
his actions because his judgment was impaired. Likewise, when
McCray and each of her other subjects told Lederer on camera that
they'd been fed recently and were feeling fine, they were making it
more difficult for their future lawyers to argue that their statements had
been coerced.

Lederer also knew that the nature of the crimes—a large group of
perpetrators assaulting multiple victims and committing a gang-rape—
was likely to lead to indictments under the acting-in-concert theory,
which held that those who aided, abetted or encouraged the worst
actors were equally responsible, though their roles might seem relatively
minor. So when McCray, in his childlike voice, matter-of-factly de-

scribed holding the female jogger's left arm down until it was his turn to "get on top of her," Lederer asked: "When you got on top of her somebody else took her arm, right?" And when he finished his description of his "turn," the prosecutor asked: "What were the other people saying while you did that?"

McCray's interview took about half an hour. When he was done he had implicated himself, his friend Clarence Thomas, Steve Lopez, Raymond Santana, Kevin Richardson and somebody named Tony in the assault of the woman. His list of those who "got on top of her" included himself, Thomas, Richardson, a Puerto Rican in a black hooded sweatshirt whom he didn't know, and "a tall, skinny black kid." Lederer would come to believe that the tall black kid was Yusef Salaam, who stood six-three, but McCray did not know his name. McCray had come to the park with the crew from the Taft Houses and Salaam was one of the boys from Schomburg Plaza. In McCray's story, the tall kid was vicious, hitting the woman twice with an iron pipe, the second strike being a parting shot as the gang was leaving the scene. Fairstein had told Lederer that Salaam had admitted as much. McCray also said he picked up the pipe when the tall kid dropped it at the reservoir and used it himself to beat a male jogger.

Lederer thought the session with McCray had gone well but she was disappointed that he denied penetrating the woman. "Did you have your pants down?" she'd asked.

"No," said McCray.

"Did you have your fly open?"

"Yeah," he said, "but my penis wasn't in her."

"What happened?" asked Lederer.

"I just like, my penis wasn't in her. I didn't do nothin' to her," he insisted.

"When you got on top of her," Lederer continued, "you got on top of her so you could have sex with her, right?"

"Not really," said McCray. "I was just doin' it so everybody. . . . So . . . I didn't do anything."

"You said you were doing it so everybody, what?" asked Lederer.

"Everybody would just like, would know I did it."

He was looking for an out, but Lederer did not want to let it go yet. "When you got on top of her you had your penis out of your pants?"

"Yes."

"And it was between her legs?" she asked.

"No."

"It was against her?"

"Yeah."

"Did you rub against her?"

"Yeah."

"Did you have an erection?"

"No."

Lederer didn't press it any further. Under the law, he had admitted sex abuse and, if she could later establish that any of the boys had penetrated the victim, he was an accomplice to rape, also.

———

Raymond Santana and his father sat down in the tiny green room to make a videotape at 2:20 A.M. Friday. Santana, a small, wiry fourteen-year-old with thick curly hair, had little in common with his friend McCray. While McCray seemed meek and embarrassed during his interview with Lederer, Santana was defiant and resentful. His parents were separated and Raymond shuttled between two East Harlem apartments, his father's and his grandmother's. He was a surly kid.

Despite his reticence, Santana would occasionally launch into detailed descriptions of events, such as his account of the assault of John Loughlin, the jogger whom McCray had admitted beating with a pipe at the reservoir. Lederer knew that Loughlin, a schoolteacher, was currently in St. Luke's Hospital. Santana told her how Jermain Robinson, whom other boys had described simply as "the kid with gold caps on his front teeth," had been particularly fierce, even after the others had tired of pounding Loughlin.

"So everybody stopped. Everybody walked away," Santana recalled. "And Jermain was like, 'Nah, nah, nah. He ripped my coat! He ripped my coat!' So Jermain didn't want to stop. Kept beatin' the man; kept beatin' the man. So everybody pulled him away. Everybody said, 'Stop. Get off, man!' So we was walkin' off . . ."

"Why were you pulling him away?" Lederer interrupted.

"Because he was tryin' to murder the man! He didn't want to stop. Kept hittin' the man."

"So you took Jermain, the group took Jermain away?" asked Lederer.

"Yeah. We took him away. And as soon as we took him away, you know, he ran back and hit the man a couple of more times."

"Did anybody else run back with him and hit him?"

"No," said Santana. "Just him. Kept hittin' the man."

Like McCray, Santana didn't know the name of the "tall skinny black kid" but he agreed the kid had been dressed in white denim. The kid had hit Loughlin in the head with a brick, said Santana. Unlike McCray, however, Santana did not place Yusef Salaam at the rape scene. There were only four people there, according to Santana: himself, McCray, Richardson and Lopez. And Richardson was the only one he had seen "having sex" with the victim.

"Were you watching?" asked Lederer.

"No," Santana replied with a smirk. "I was grabbin' the lady's tits." (Being ignorant of the acting-in-concert theory, Santana thought this exonerated him of the rape. A detective would later testify that, on the previous evening, Santana had said to him: "I had nothing to do with the rape. All I did was feel the woman's tits. I had nothing to do with the rape.")

To solidify a rape charge Lederer had to prove penetration by at least one boy. If a defendant didn't confess to that she might be able to prove it through the victim's testimony or scientific evidence. But it was certainly worth trying to get Santana to corroborate any future evidence she might gather.

"Did he penetrate her?" she asked, referring to Richardson. "Did he put his penis inside of her?"

"Um hmm," he confirmed.

"Did he say that he had?"

"Excuse me?" said the boy.

"Did he say that he had?"

"No, he didn't *say* it," Santana scoffed.

"But you could tell?"

"Yeah."

"How could you tell?"

Perhaps Santana's fragile sense of machismo was offended by discussing such details with a woman. He treated her questions as though they were stupid. "Because he was havin' sex with her!" he said. "That's what you're supposed to do when you havin' sex!"

Lederer persisted. "Well, when he was doing that, was he moving up and down?"

"Yeah," Santana replied and, rather than wait for her to ask again how he could tell, added: " 'Cause I seen it."

"And so you could see that he was moving," said Lederer, "thrusting up and down . . . thrusting into her?"

"Yeah," said Santana. "That's how I knew he was havin' sex with her."

In the written statement detectives had shown Lederer, Santana had described Lopez playing a particularly brutal role. She wanted to get that on tape, too.

"You said that he was kneeling on her arms?" she said of Lopez.

"Yeah," said Santana, "on her arms."

"And what was he doing with his hands?"

"He was coverin' her mouth, but every time she. . . . He was smackin' her, he was sayin', 'Shut up, bitch!' Just smackin' her."

"How many times did he smack her?" asked Lederer.

"I think twice or three times."

"And did she keep screaming?"

"Um hmm. And he just kept smackin'."

"Did somebody stuff something in her mouth?"

"No," said Santana. "He picked up the brick and he hit her with the brick, twice."

"Where did he hit her with the brick?"

"Around the face."

"After he hit her in the head with the brick, did she stop screaming?" asked the prosecutor.

"Yeah," said the boy. " 'Cause she was like, shocked."

Lederer began her interview with Steve Lopez at 3:30 A.M. in a manner that could almost be described as deferential. She knew it wouldn't be an easy session. Nearly every other suspect had described Lopez as a vicious leader of the gang. When he had been interrogated earlier by detectives, however, the boy, a confident fifteen-year-old, had stead-fastly denied ever seeing a female jogger in the park. Lederer also knew that Lopez's father, a mail carrier who now sat in Room 101 with his wife to witness the taping, had abruptly halted the earlier interview when the cops kept pressing his son for information about the rape. She proceeded with caution.

Lederer quickly realized Lopez was smarter and more mature than the other boys she'd interviewed. He didn't stammer, was clearer in his description of the chaotic march through the park, and didn't seem the least bit scared or nervous. Being from Schomburg Plaza, Lopez knew the "tall skinny kid" was named Yusef. He told Lederer that his neighbor had been carrying a kitchen knife with which he tried to cut a passing jogger at the reservoir. He also provided a graphic description of Salaam's role in the assault on the schoolteacher, Loughlin.

"How many times did Yusef hit him with the pipe?" asked Lederer.

"Well, he was, he was goin' to work!" said Lopez, lifting his hand over his head and swinging his arm down repeatedly. "He was like, pow, pow, pow!"

Lopez maintained that he was nothing but a spectator, watching the series of assaults from "the background" or from a hiding place in the bushes "15 or 20 feet away." He only went into the park to bother people, he said, to call them names and "throw little rocks at them." After the beating of Loughlin, he said, he left the park with his friend Orlando. He never saw a woman.

Lederer ran through the list of suspects—he had acknowledged knowing all of them—who placed Lopez at the rape scene. "These are not people that have any kind of argument with you?" she asked.

"Nah."

"Okay. Every single person says that you were with them when this woman was raped," she said, as Lopez sat up straight and stared coldly, calmly into her eyes. "Why is everybody saying you were there?"

"I don't know," said the boy.

"They have no reason to make it up, right?"

"I don't know why they did it," he repeated, " 'cause I wasn't there. . . . I didn't even see no lady. So, right there, they lyin'."

"I'll tell ya," said Lederer casually, "if these guys are all saying you were there, and you're saying you weren't there, it doesn't look so good for you."

"I know it doesn't," said Lopez coolly.

She continued to thrust and he continued to parry. "It just seems a little funny," said Lederer, "that all of a sudden, just before this thing happens, you leave. And people who have no beef with you say that you were there. Now, I want to give you a chance to say exactly what happened . . ."

"I told you exactly what happened," he interrupted, his voice controlled but full of indignation. "Told you everything to my knowledge."

"You don't have any reason that you can tell me why your friends . . . would say that you were there?"

"They probably just gettin' out," Lopez responded. "They probably just sayin' that 'cause they don't want no more . . . they don't want to have nothin' more to do with this, man."

He wasn't budging, but Lederer didn't want to give it up yet. "I don't want you to misunderstand," she said. "I'm not saying that each of these guys says, 'Oh, the only guy who did this was Steve

Lopez.' . . . Everybody's saying, we were all there, this is what I did, this is what Steve did, this is what Kevin did. . . . It's not like they're putting all the blame on you. Everybody's giving a detailed story about what each of you did. I just want to give you a chance to tell us, if you were there, what you did and what you didn't do, so we can get it all straightened out."

"Yeah," he replied, "but I'm tellin' you, I wasn't there."

Lederer was frustrated. There was no place else to go. She couldn't force the boy to incriminate himself. But maybe she could get him to impeach his own credibility. When he'd been arrested at about 10:30 P.M. Wednesday on Central Park West, before the body of the woman had even been found, Lopez told the cops he was coming from the movies. Now Lederer asked him on camera whether that had been a lie. Yes, he said.

"You thought you would get in trouble if you admitted you were in the park?" she continued.

"Yeah."

"So you lied?"

"Uh hmmm," he acknowledged with the slightest nod.

"I have no further questions," said the prosecutor.

Like Lopez, fourteen-year-old Kevin Richardson, sitting opposite Lederer with a scratch on his left cheek, tried to portray himself as a spectator; but he was less successful.

In Richardson's story, McCray and Santana were ringleaders, while he merely tagged along like a puppy dog, even urging them to stop beating up one victim or another. His account was devoid of emotion. While Santana and Lopez were clearly not upset about the level of violence, they were at least animated in their descriptions of the destruction. Richardson was completely deadpan. In a low voice and a dull manner, he told Lederer about McCray beating Loughlin with the pipe.

"He kept on hittin' him and hittin' him and blood was, like, comin' out."

"Where was he hitting him, in the head?" asked Lederer.

"Yeah," said Richardson, "and it was like, bustin'."

"Hmmm?" Lederer apparently misunderstood.

"Like, his forehead, it was like, it was bustin'," Richardson explained. "And like, blood was comin' out." Then, he said, the man fell to the ground and the other boys "start hittin' him, kickin' him and stuff, punchin' him."

"What did you do?" asked Lederer.

"I was just standing there," he replied.

That was Richardson's stock answer. Like Lopez, he had witnessed a lot of mayhem but was never a participant. Until they came upon "the lady." That was when his detachment broke down.

At the rape scene, again, he was nonplussed by the violence. He told Lederer how Mike Briscoe, one of the Taft crew, quieted the screaming victim. "It's like, she tried to get up, and he hit her. And she tried to get up again, and he hit her. He did it two more times."

"And then she stopped trying to get up?" asked Lederer.

"Yeah," he said. "And then she was like, kind of like, knocked out."

While she was unconscious, said Richardson, the woman was raped by McCray, Santana and Lopez. He then listed several others who fondled her breasts. Richardson insisted he did none of those things, but his distant manner was chilling in itself and he was digging himself into a pretty deep hole. At the rape scene Richardson took action for the first time, according to his narrative.

"Didn't you tell the police earlier today that you had tried to grab her?" asked Lederer. "And that was when you got scratched?"

"No," he said, "not like . . . like feelin' her . . . feelin' her up."

"Okay," said Lederer, "not like that."

"Tryin' to stop it," Richardson explained.

Lederer was confused. "But you tried . . ."

"Well, grabbed, like, grabbed her arms or somethin'," he offered.

"You tried to grab her arm?"

"Tryin' to stop it," he repeated.

"Well, you grabbed *her* arm when you wanted to stop it?"

"Yes," he said, apparently thinking that was a satisfactory explanation.

At 4:35 A.M. Lederer was nearing the end of another disappointing interrogation when she asked Richardson flat out, "Did you have intercourse with her?"

"No."

Perhaps he'd bend if she confronted him with the possibility that irrefutable scientific evidence might later expose him as a liar. "If we do a DNA test. . . . Do you know what DNA is? The chromosome test?" she asked.

"Oh," said Richardson, "the sperm test?"

"Yeah. If we test what is found in her and we test you, are we gonna get a match?"

"No."

"Are you sure?"

"Yes."

"Alright," she said, "because we're gonna do a test . . . and if it's gonna come out to be a match, it would be better if you were gonna tell us that now."

"No," he replied. "I didn't do nothin'."

"You're sure?"

"Yes."

"You know that other people say that you did?" she asked.

"Well I know I didn't," he insisted.

―――――――

At 6:30 A.M. on Friday Lederer was smoking a cigarette on the front stoop of the Twenty-fourth Precinct. She'd gone without sleep for about twenty-four hours, the past ten of which had been spent in stationhouses, and she'd been making videos nonstop since 1:00 A.M. Linda Fairstein and Arthur "Tim" Clements, the young prosecutor out of Yale Law School who'd been summoned from home in the middle of the night to assist Lederer, had finally convinced her to take a break.

Lederer hadn't been inclined to stop working. New York law mandates that a suspect charged with a felony must be released if he is not indicted within five days of arrest. Since a Sunday would fall within that period, Lederer would get an extra day, but the number of suspects was growing hourly. Detectives were cross-referencing the names mentioned in each kid's statement and trying to find and interview as many as thirty teenagers. Every time the cops came back from Schomburg Plaza or the Taft neighborhood with another kid, it reduced the prosecutor's chances of getting such a big case through the grand jury under the deadline. She could indict more defendants later, but Lederer didn't want to put a rapist—or potential killer—back on the street because she hadn't gotten her case together quickly enough.

Still, she recognized her own fatigue and was glad to get out of Room 101 and into the fresh air for a few minutes. She filled in Clements on the interviews he'd missed and thought about what she might have done differently. Several highly incriminating statements were on tape, but Lederer was distracted by disappointments. Most frustrating was the session with Lopez, whose case already had her seriously worried.

But there were other problems, too; if the kids were telling the truth in their accusations against one another, then each had succeeded in minimizing his own role.

Over the years, Lederer, thirty-six, had learned that the only way to prepare a case was to learn everything that anybody involved might know. During a year-long hiatus from the district attorney's office back in 1985–86 she had also learned just how strongly her identity was tied up with criminal trials. Lederer spent that year at Kramer, Levin, Nessen, Kamin and Frankel, a large corporate law firm, doing what most associates in private practice do with the bulk of their time: researching law in the firm library and writing briefs in a comfortable office. The job didn't suit Lederer, who thrived on the stress of being on trial, at the center of that small but very public stage in front of a judge and jury. She knew of no greater challenge.

Lederer also learned during that dry year of paper warfare that she found little reward in a fat paycheck. In addition to missing the intense excitement of a trial, she found it hard to do without the clearcut moral satisfaction she derived from putting the bad guys in jail. "In criminal work there is a right and wrong, a sense of justice," she explained to Jeffrey Kanige in *Manhattan Lawyer.* "I hadn't realized what that meant to me." So she left the mercenary world of civil litigators (and a 1986 salary of about $100,000) to return to the city's grimy criminal courtrooms (where she was paid $68,500 in 1989).

Lederer's reputation for thorough trial preparation was unsurpassed in the DA's office. Now, as she and Clements mulled their next move, she suggested that this might be a good time to take a look at the rape scene.

When Lederer and Clements got to the park the sun hadn't yet risen high enough to illuminate the heavily wooded ravine below the roadway where the rape had taken place, so they came back at about 8:30 A.M. with Fairstein, who'd been there earlier with detectives and a couple of suspects. The three lawyers were stunned by the amount of blood soaking the leaves and ground cover. Nearly thirty-six hours had passed since the victim's skull was crushed here and most of the blood would have soaked into the muddy ground by this time. If this much blood were still visible, she must have lost a staggering amount.

The crime scene was crowded. Detectives from the NYPD's Crime Scene Unit were taking photographs and gathering evidence—the victim's jogging clothes, leaves, rocks, a brick, a canceled check, two whiskey bottles, anything they might later be able to link to a suspect through blood tests or fingerprints. John Hartigan and another homicide detective were walking around with Kevin Richardson. A local television station had a news crew there with a van equipped to transmit video from the scene.

Lederer, who lived not far from the park on the Upper West Side, knew the 102nd Street Crossdrive well. It was closed to all but official vehicles and, like hundreds of other avid joggers and cyclists, Lederer had often run through this shortcut that linked the East Drive and the West Drive. As she walked around the area, from the ravine where the rape took place up to the spot on the crossdrive where the victim had been snatched, Lederer was struck by how different the scene would have been on Wednesday night; how isolated the victim was, down in that hollow, out of sight and earshot of the nearby cops who were searching for the kids who had menaced several bikers. She remembered asking Richardson if they had done anything to stop the victim's screaming for help. "Well, not really," he replied, "because there wasn't really nobody around."

Back at the precinct Lederer talked to the cops about gathering more potential evidence. Could somebody go out there with a metal scanner and look for the woman's keys? Where were the weapons? Could one of the kids have taken the pipe home? Did they need a search warrant? Had they confiscated the clothing each of the suspects had been wearing that night? Could they get a helicopter up to take aerial photos of the entire area the gang had covered? For that matter, had they searched the park to make sure there wasn't another victim out there lying unconscious—or dead?

Better informed about the scene of the crime, Lederer and Clements spent the rest of Friday interviewing more suspects. Jermain Robinson, Jomo Smith and Michael Briscoe were brought in that day, and Clarence Thomas and Lamont McCall were still waiting for their turns in front of the video camera. Of all the suspects, however, it was Kharey Wise who would give the prosecutors the most candid, most horrifying account of the gang's rampage. And it was Kharey Wise who would also present the greatest challenge to Lederer's considerable skills.

CHAPTER 3

A TANGLED WEB

KHAREY WISE SAT DOWN WITH THE PROSECUTORS AND THEIR VIDEO camera on Friday at 12:30 P.M. He began the interview the same way six other black and Latino teenagers had before him: he waived his rights to remain silent and to have an attorney present during questioning. The other boys who had made videos that morning, ranging in age from thirteen to fifteen, had all been accompanied by parents when they waived their *Miranda* rights. But Wise, at age sixteen, was an adult under New York law and was therefore on his own.

As Wise mumbled along in broken syntax, his legs perpetually bouncing in unison, Lederer quickly realized that his version of the now familiar story would be the least coherent. Before going into the park, he said, he'd been with his girlfriend, Lisa, whose last name he didn't know. He ran down a list of the friends he'd been with, including his best friends Yusef and Eddie, and while he told Lederer their Schomburg Plaza apartment numbers, he didn't know their last names, either. He described "the bum" they had mugged as weighing three hundred pounds, while nobody else had remarked on his size at all. He contradicted himself repeatedly. "Was he moving?" Lederer asked when

Wise described the condition in which the boys left the bum. "Yes. And he wasn't moving," said Wise, "so they thought he was dead."

Lederer tried to keep Wise focused on the rape, showing him photos she had just received from the police, photos none of the other suspects had seen: the woman's white pullover jersey, now dyed deep red with blood; her legs scratched, cut and bruised; her head, resting unconscious on a hospital pillow, the left side of her skull crushed and still bleeding through stitches twelve hours after the assault. Wise, clearly shaken by the photos, identified each one. He had been agitated from the start; now he was crying slightly, shaking his head, terrified by what he was suddenly seeing in the cold light of day.

Wise insisted he had not participated in the rape. He was running from the police, he said, running through the woods with his friend Al Morris, when he heard a suspicious noise. "See, I knew it wasn't no rabbit," Wise told Lederer, " 'cause a rabbit don't make noise when you're comin' toward trees and stuff. But I heard how they were gigglin' and I heard her . . . I heard 'Help!' " Then he and Al saw Lopez, Richardson and Santana holding a woman on the ground, said Wise. They hid behind a tree to watch.

Despite the rambling, confused nature of his story, Wise was giving Lederer details she had been lacking up to that point. "I heard Steve's voice," said Wise. "He say, 'Yo, we will rape this woman. That's what we'll do, rape her.' And she was still screaming. And Kevin, I think he put somethin' in her mouth. They gag her so she can't yell or nothin'. They put their hand across her mouth."

Wise's story was changing fast. In a written statement he had given to detectives earlier, Wise had accused Lopez and Richardson of raping the woman; now he was adding Santana to the list. He had also told the cops that Antron McCray fondled the woman's legs, but in this interview he hadn't even placed McCray at the scene. As Wise continued the narrative, his friend Al seemed to suddenly disappear, to be replaced by Eddie as Wise's companion behind the tree.

Lederer felt she was whittling away at a complex series of lies, slowly exposing the truth, but she was losing patience. When Wise described the brutal rape as "the accident" Lederer upbraided him. "An accident is when somebody slips and falls down, alright?" she demanded. "What you saw. . . . You saw people drag her down there?"

"Yes," said Wise.

"You saw people beating her up?"

"Yes."

"You saw her so beaten up," Lederer continued, "that she looks the way she does in these pictures. You call that an accident?"

Wise, chagrined, had no reply.

He had told Lederer that Lopez slapped the woman twice and Richardson punched her. After showing Wise the photo of the woman's crushed skull, Lederer asked if he had seen anybody hit her with a stone, brick or other heavy object. Wise said no and took off on another confused tangent about having seen his friends in police custody on the news. Lederer finally steered him back to the head injuries, the result of blows that had landed with enough force to put the woman into a coma from which she would not emerge for two full weeks.

"Kharey, you saw that picture," said the prosecutor. "I'm asking you . . ."

"I understand, I understand," Wise anxiously interjected.

". . . how did she get the injuries?" Lederer continued, pressing but not shouting. "I mean, you get a punch. . . . You've seen a fighter. You get a punch, you get a bruise."

"Yeah," Wise interrupted again. "I understand."

"You don't get, you don't get bleeding. . . . You don't get a fractured skull from it," insisted Lederer.

"Yeah," said Wise, "the more it look like it's, look like, look like a rock, a rock wound."

That was it. "Did you see anybody hit her with a . . . with anything but their hands?" asked Lederer. "I'm telling you, Kharey, I don't want you to think you have to say that, but I want to know what you saw that explains how she got so badly hurt."

Wise surrendered. "I did see Kevin pick up his, a hand rock, a small hand rock and hit her across the face with it."

"Are you just saying that because I asked you?" said Lederer.

"No," Wise insisted. "No."

"Then why didn't you say it before?" she asked.

"Because I was remembering."

With that, Lederer ended the interview. The work she had put into this interrogation had paid off, but the relentless style she had brought to it would haunt the case.

———

While Lederer was taping that interview with Wise, Detective John Hartigan was at Schomburg Plaza talking to Eddie de la Paz, who had been picked up the previous evening with Wise and Salaam but had since been released. Hartigan, a detective for twenty years, had taken two written statements from Wise before turning him over to the DA.

Wise was still talking to the prosecutor when Hartigan got back to the stationhouse. The detective stepped into the interview room and silently passed a note to Lederer, who then told Wise, on camera, that Eddie denied having been in the park with him. Wise slumped in the chair, dropped his chin to his chest, then looked up, his face seemingly torn between dejection and anger. He stumbled through an explanation: "This is what, this what Eddie told me before all this happened. Because he was there, I said, 'Bein' that you was here, you ain't do nothin'. I want, need you for evidence, man.' I said, 'I ain't doin' no time for nothin' I didn't do. I mean, you seen what was goin' on.' He said, he said, 'I, I might get in trouble.' I said, 'You not gonna get in trouble. All you got to do is tell 'em what you seen. That's about it. Don't make me look like a liar.' So he say, 'I don't know, man, I don't know. You know how it is with the police when they come and interview me.' "

Despite Lederer's obvious skepticism, Wise stuck to the story. After the rapists left the scene, he said, Eddie "tippy-toed" over to the woman to get a closer look at her injuries. He and Eddie then left the park and went straight home, said Wise, thinking the woman was going · to die.

When Lederer was finished with Wise, Hartigan took him through the bustling detective squad room, crowded with cops, teenagers and their relatives, to a corner room that contained a holding cell. Wise stood outside the empty cell in the narrow space between it and the wall, his back against the bars. Hartigan was about six inches taller than Wise's five feet five inches, with a square jaw, slightly cleft chin and a head of thick, silver-gray hair. The detective was fifty-one years old, had been promoted to second grade eighteen months earlier, and was three months from retirement. A father of six, Hartigan knew how to deal with kids and his fellow detectives admired his knack for gaining the confidence of people who had information he wanted. Hartigan told Wise that he knew Wise had lied to him about his involvement and that, furthermore, Eddie wasn't backing him up.

"You don't understand," said Wise. "He's my blood. He's supposed to swear by anything I said."

"Kharey," said Hartigan, "this girl is in critical condition. She's likely to die. It's almost two days later. Everybody is out there talking about it and thinking about it. Do you think that Eddie is going to put himself into a position where he's going to be involved in a homicide?"

Wise slid his back down the bars and sat on the floor. Hartigan told him to get up and they went to the back of the room, where there was barely enough space for both of them to sit on the floor, the boy, in his red-and-white-striped sweatshirt, with his back to the bars and the detective, in jacket and tie, with his back against the wall.

"Kharey," said Hartigan, "put yourself in the position of other people. If this case is going to go to trial, there will be jurors listening to this story. Make believe you are one of them and you are listening to this, your story. . . . These are people just like yourself; they come from the street, they come from the street just like you and I do; they're working people. If you heard that story; if you heard a person come in and tell three different stories and you heard other people telling that you are implicated in that crime, would you believe what you are saying?"

"No," said Wise.

Lederer did not welcome the news that Wise wanted to sit down in front of the camera a second time. Considering their previous encounter, she was skeptical when Hartigan said, "He wants to tell the truth." But she agreed to suspend standard procedure and give him another chance.

After announcing that he was now prepared to tell "the whole truth, nothin' but the truth," Wise launched into a litany of self-incriminating changes in his story. He was clearly still nervous, but he spoke more slowly than he had during the first taping. Wise told Lederer he had kicked the bum in the side twice and had kicked one of the male joggers at the reservoir once in the stomach. "Then," he said without pause, "comin' toward the rape, we came down from the, from the park, from the, from the field, from the reservoir to the field, that's when we came toward the rape." When Lederer asked who "we" was, Wise repeated the names of those he'd placed at the rape scene earlier and also included, for the first time, his friend Yusef.

"We ran in the back of her," said Wise, "and she looked back at Raymond, and she started runnin' a little fast." Something in his voice seemed authentic to Lederer. She could almost see the woman running in the eerie light of the park's antiquated lampposts. "Steve came up toward the front and grabbed her from the front," Wise continued.

"Then, in from, from the front, like, from the beginning right there, that's when they start a little rape. Then they brought her all the way down."

Wise continued to insist he did not rape the woman, that he just "played with her legs," demonstrating for Lederer by reaching out his right hand and sliding it back and forth in the air. "I didn't want to just sit right there, look at what was going on," he explained. "If you with them, you have to show a little effort around them, too. So, I had to get into it, too." He was steadfast in his assertion that only Lopez, Santana and Richardson "fucked" the jogger. He and Yusef "just played with her."

As he described the vicious beating the woman was taking, Wise provided a glimpse of the fierce struggle she had put up. "She couldn't even take a hit. Steve hit her one time: Boom! She closed her eyes for quite a while. That's when he ripped her pants. And she open, she just open her eyes, she's got . . . just got into it. Her ego or her body just took over her. She started goin' wild. . . . My friend Yusef say, 'Kharey, go for her legs,' because she kickin' wild, she kickin' wild! . . . She kicked Kevin in his chest. Kevin went wild on her and punch her in her face! Half of them punchin' her stomach; half of them punchin' her leg."

When the violence finally ended, said Wise, he felt bad. "I could imagine anyone rapin' a woman. If I have to rape a woman, I'm gonna rape her. But I can't beat her up. Can't look at it that way. Look at all that blood squirtin' and all this? Uh-uh!"

As he had in the first video, Wise acknowledged thinking the woman was going to die. "But you thought that if she was dead, she wouldn't be able to identify anybody?" asked Lederer.

"Steve was gonna kill her," said Wise. "They was gonna kill her so she won't identify us. And Yusef was saying, 'Don't kill her, man, don't kill her. Bad enough you rapin' her! Don't kill her, man.'"

Lederer, who had been prosecuting heinous murders and rapes for nearly ten years, would later tell a judge this account was the most "chilling" she'd heard from the Central Park suspects. And she would go to trial eighteen months later thinking the case against Wise was among her strongest. But she had to ask one more question before turning off the camera. "Did anyone make you change your story?"

"No," said Wise without hesitation. "Uh-uh. I thought about it. I thought about all the lies I said. And all the . . . all the detectives came in my face, arguing with me, cursing at me, hittin' on me. I thought about it. . . . All I had to do was tell the truth, I probably would have been home. But no. Then I told a lie. I gotta face up to what I gotta live up to now."

It was the kind of answer that left a defense lawyer a lot of room to maneuver.

CHAPTER 4.

THE BEGINNINGS
OF STRATEGY

SUNDAY, APRIL 23, WAS A BRIGHT SPRING DAY AND THE LARGE WINDOWS of the surgical intensive care unit on the ninth floor of Metropolitan Hospital afforded a stirring view. It was about 10:00 A.M. and the sun was high over the shimmering East River. But the brilliant light highlighted the contrast between the beauty of the day and the hideous evidence in front of Lederer of what had happened Wednesday night in Central Park.

By this time Lederer had learned that Paula Harris,* twenty-eight, was an honors graduate of Wellesley and Yale, and a rising star at Salomon Brothers investment bank. Lederer had met friends and relatives of the victim who had been keeping a twenty-four-hour watch at the Harlem hospital, in rotating shifts, since Harris had been identified by a coworker on Thursday morning. Feeling somewhat helpless, she assured the family—a retired Westinghouse executive, his wife and two sons, both lawyers, from an affluent Pittsburgh suburb—that she was available to assist with anything they needed. What Lederer needed,

*Paula Harris is a pseudonym. No other names have been changed.

49

and received, was the family's permission to have Paula's injuries photographed before any significant healing took place.

Only eight hours earlier Lederer had recounted for an arraignment judge the horrendous stories told by the suspects. Better than anyone, she knew how Paula Harris came to be in her present condition. Lederer also knew her doctors believed that if the patient lived she would never be more than a vegetable. And, of course, Lederer had examined the grisly photos of the woman's crushed skull and heavily lacerated legs. Yet none of that prepared the prosecutor for the few minutes she would spend in this room.

Paula Harris, who had studied ballet as a girl, was of medium height and slender, about five feet five inches tall, weighing approximately one hundred pounds. Her regimen of jogging and bike riding in Central Park had kept her in fine condition but now, with her head broken and her body covered with dozens of ugly cuts and bruises, she seemed small and quite frail. She had lost nearly 80 percent of her blood, she had suffered severe brain damage, her windpipe had nearly been crushed and she was in a deep coma. A respirator tube had been stuffed down her throat and a catheter protruded from her swollen vulva. Her short, straight blonde hair had been shaved away from the three large cracks above the left side of her forehead. Her left eye was swollen shut and the flesh around it had turned a sickening deep purple. The eye injury was called a blowout fracture; every one of the bones supporting the socket had been broken.

More upsetting than the injuries themselves was the sight of Harris thrashing around on the bed. As she watched Harris writhe, pulling against the restraints that fastened her arms and legs to the bed, Lederer was shaken. She found it hard to believe the doctors who said these movements were unconscious muscle reflexes, that they did not represent psychological torment. Lederer couldn't avoid the obvious conclusion: Harris was in the throes of a terrifying nightmare. It seemed to her that Harris was reliving the desperate struggle that she had put up in the woods, punching, kicking and scratching at those who had done this to her. Lederer noticed the bruises on Harris's knuckles and palms, testimony to the ferocity of the defense she had mustered. Here she was, thought Lederer, more than three days later, still fighting back.

As she stood there, overwhelmed with sorrow, one question kept running through Lederer's mind: *How could anyone do this to another human being?*

Lederer had been shocked on Friday night at the Twenty-fourth Precinct after the video sessions were over and Tim Clements, Fairstein and she were discussing how to proceed with the investigation and get ready for arraignments. Those suspects who had been formally charged by then were locked in the holding cell adjacent to the detective squad room. The group included Wise, Richardson, Lopez, Salaam, McCray, Santana and Clarence Thomas and they were making a commotion so boisterous that it distracted the detectives. Lederer and her colleagues listened as the teenagers joked, compared the details of the stories they'd told Lederer, and entertained themselves with the hip-hop hit "Wild Thing," a few providing the beat with sound effects while others rapped the lyrics that celebrate sexual conquest. A female detective walking past the cell was greeted with whistles, catcalls and remarks such as "nice legs" and "nice ass." Finally, Detective Robert Nugent told them to sit down and shut up. Lopez answered with a macho challenge, surrendering only when Nugent said: Sit down or I'll come in there and sit you down.

Lederer was deeply offended. Even if they had committed their crimes while caught up in a momentary gang frenzy, she thought they might naturally be remorseful. And if remorse was beyond their capacity at that moment, she thought they might at least be afraid. To Lederer, the fact that these kids were totally unmoved by what they'd done, compounded by the fact that they seemed not the least bit scared for their own sakes, was truly frightening.

As Fairstein had judged, one of Lederer's strengths was the empathy and understanding she brought to a case. Not least among the factors that motivated Lederer was the sense she got from rape victims that they trusted her to help ease the humiliation, degradation and fear that had suddenly enveloped their lives. Lederer accepted that responsibility willingly. She knew herself well enough to understand that her effectiveness as a prosecutor would diminish if she ever lost her ability to respond emotionally. Yet she also had learned to control those human reactions, keeping them separate from her professional judgment. But at this time, in this place, Lederer was exhausted. In the past three days she had slept for perhaps ten hours. Now, at Harris's bedside, she wept.

The next morning, refreshed after a night's sleep, Lederer sat down with a half-dozen colleagues in Trial Bureau 40 to formulate a strategy with which she and Clements, who would act as her co-counsel for the duration, could prosecute this complex case. Such brainstorming sessions were called homicide meetings because they were held whenever an assistant district attorney in the bureau picked up a homicide case. In the criminal justice system murder is in a class by itself. The crime is treated differently from all others; the higher stakes make it special. A prosecutor taking a murder charge to trial faces more intense pressure—from the judge, the media, his bosses and colleagues—and often a more complex defense than in most other cases. In the old days there had been a separate homicide bureau in the Manhattan DA's office. Now, however, this specialized experience was integrated into the larger Trial Division, and a prosecutor with a murder case relied on the homicide meetings as a means to dip into that cumulative pool of wisdom.

Even if Central Park did not become a murder case, the complexity resulting from multiple defendants, most juveniles, and multiple victims, one mortally injured, raised it to that level of difficulty. The reaction of an outraged, frightened public, fed by competitive press attention, put sustained political pressure on Robert Morgenthau's office.

On that same Monday, a grand jury of twenty-three Manhattan residents was convened to hear evidence against the Central Park defendants. They returned indictments on Wednesday, Thursday and Friday. Because New York grand juries are the exclusive domain of prosecutors—no judge presides and defense attorneys are barred—they can usually be relied on to approve whatever charges the district attorney seeks. Therefore a prosecutor must decide which charges to offer the jury as applicable.

The key questions Lederer's team had kicked around in the homicide meetings that week concerned the limitations presented by the juvenile status of the defendants. Of the nine suspects in custody only two were adults under New York law; Briscoe at seventeen and Wise at sixteen. The others—McCray, Santana, Salaam, Richardson, Lopez, Thomas and Robinson—were all under sixteen years old and were therefore juveniles. Juveniles are prosecuted in Family Court, where proceedings are often closed to the public and sentences are lighter, unless they are indicted for certain violent acts specifically designated as crimes for which they can be prosecuted in Supreme Court (the misnamed felony trial court, which is *not* the state's highest court). Such crimes are called designated felonies.

State law also provides that the maximum sentence a Supreme Court judge can impose on a juvenile is three and one-third to ten years (except in cases of murder, arson or kidnapping). While the prosecutors were frustrated that the maximum could not be increased under any circumstances, they could at least get an increase in the minimum—up to five years—if the juveniles were convicted of more than one designated felony and a judge ordered consecutive sentences. They decided, therefore, to seek indictment on as many designated felonies as possible. As a result, the grand jury was presented with charges including the attempted murder of Paula Harris, assault with intent to cause serious injury to Harris, rape, sodomy, and two types of robbery, both stemming from the disappearance of John Loughlin's radio headset.

The prosecutors next had to decide whether to seek indictment on nondesignated felonies. Here they faced a standard risk: Lesser charges provide a trial jury with opportunities for compromise. If, for example, the trial jurors are split between acquittal and conviction on a rape count (a designated felony), they might compromise with conviction on a sex abuse count (nondesignated). Moreover, if convicted only of nondesignated felonies, the juveniles would be sentenced in the more lenient Family Court.

On the other hand, some of the lesser charges gave the prosecutors opportunities to expand their case. For example, Lederer and Clements wanted to use the testimony of several bicyclists and joggers who had been harassed by the gang but had escaped. Since no felonies had been committed against those people, however, and they had not witnessed the assaults of Harris or Loughlin, their testimony might be ruled inadmissible at trial. But if the prosecutors included a riot charge in the indictment, they could argue that the assaults had grown out of the riot, so the testimony of people who witnessed riotous activity in the park that night would be relevant. This strategy would allow Lederer and Clements to put as many as six additional, sympathetic victims on the witness stand. Furthermore, those witnesses could provide specific corroboration of essential points on the suspects' videotapes. All of the kids, for example, talked about an unsuccessful attempt to dismount a couple on a tandem bike. With the riot charge included, the prosecutors could put that couple on the stand to tell, from their innocent perspective, a harrowing story that bolstered the self-incriminating statements of the defendants. Ultimately, the prosecutors decided to seek indictment on as many felonies as they thought they could prove.

When they weren't in homicide meetings or the grand jury room, Lederer and Clements were busy with the continuing investigation, working until about eleven o'clock every night that first week. Detectives from the homicide and Central Park squads were still riding the elevators of Schomburg Plaza and knocking on doors around the Taft Houses, trying to interview each of the thirty-three kids whose names had been mentioned by one suspect or another. With the media playing the sensational story for all it was worth and word quickly spreading that most of the kids who had been arrested were locked up without bail, the cops were finding more and more of those doors locked and more and more of the parents they encountered unwilling to permit their sons to be questioned.

Meanwhile, the prosecutors had to prepare witnesses for the grand jury—the joggers who'd been attacked at the reservoir, the bikers who'd gotten away, the doctors who'd been treating Paula Harris and the cops who'd interrogated the suspects. They also had paralegals glued to VCRs, dissecting the videos so they could construct charts cross-referencing what the nine suspects said about one another and about accomplices who hadn't been arrested. They had a stenographer watching the tapes, too, trying to produce instant transcripts.

It was a week full of frustrations, such as the futile search for David Good. The prosecutors had seen an interview with Good, a young engineer, in *The New York Times*. He had been quoted as saying he had been running around the reservoir Wednesday night when he was accosted by a group of about twelve teenagers. As he ran by them, one threw a branch, which hit him in the leg. Good kept running and eventually came upon a cop. He reported the incident but the officer did not take his name or address. The investigators knew nothing about this potential witness except what they read in the *Times*. They would later learn that the reason they couldn't find Good in time for the grand jury presentation was that he'd left town on his honeymoon.

The grand jury approved the indictment Lederer and Clements wanted, but the prosecutors were not entirely satisfied. They had so far found no victims or independent witnesses who could identify the assailants; it was too soon to tell what physical evidence might develop; and Paula Harris was still in a coma. For these reasons, the case rested on the self-incriminating statements of the defendants. As a result, some suspects walked away and others were indicted for less serious crimes than they might have been.

The good news for the prosecutors was the indictment of six teenagers—Lopez, Wise, Richardson, McCray, Salaam and Santana—on thirteen felonies: attempted murder, rape, sodomy, sexual abuse, two assault counts related to Harris, three robbery counts, two assault counts related to Loughlin, one assault count related to jogger David Lewis, and riot.

Jermain Robinson, whom no defendant had named as present at the rape scene, was charged with the assaults of Loughlin and Lewis, as well as robbery and riot.

Briscoe, alleged by Richardson to have beaten Paula Harris unconscious, insisted on videotape that he had never seen a female jogger. Without any evidence to corroborate Richardson's accusation, he was indicted solely for the assault of Lewis and riot.

Clarence Thomas, who according to McCray's statement had raped Harris, was released after a week in detention. His case was never presented to the grand jury. Thomas had admitted only going into the park with the gang and said he and McCray had gone home after witnessing the assault of Loughlin from a distance. The charges against Thomas, unlawful assembly and assault, were adjudicated in Family Court.

Then there was Lamont McCall, a thirteen-year-old who had been picked up with four other suspects Wednesday night on Central Park West. McCall, whose nickname among the Taft crowd was "Man," had told detectives he witnessed the assault of the "bum" and then left the park. McCall's case was also left to Family Court.

The media were an annoying distraction to Lederer. The confidence for which she was well known on Centre Street, downtown Manhattan's short avenue of courthouses, did not extend to her dealings with the press. Photographs of Lederer accented the natural bags under her dark brown eyes, rather than the striking brightness they projected. She took seriously the litigator's cliché, more often employed as a dodge: "I'm not going to try this case in the newspapers." As a prosecutor she held all the cards, at least in the early stages of a case, and saw no reason to show any of them to her adversaries prematurely.

In this case, dealing with the media might become a full-time job. Following longstanding tradition, the vast majority of media were preserving the rape victim's anonymity by withholding her name. Paula Harris became known, immediately and internationally, simply as the Central Park Jogger. Little else about her life, however, was left uncovered. While Lederer resolutely refused to discuss the woman at all, others with knowledge of her—from loving friends and admiring teachers to defense lawyers with a different agenda—were willing to share information. The portrait that initially emerged seemed to have been drawn by a fairy godmother. The Jogger had graduated at the top of her class from the best schools in the country, was considered a whiz kid even among the talented crop of Ivy Leaguers at Salomon Brothers, was pretty, popular, fit and optimistic. And, as if to assure the public that this daughter of privilege was not without conscience, it was reported that she did volunteer work helping the less fortunate and worried about the ethics of the hostile corporate takeovers she was helping to arrange on Wall Street. (Only later was there a leak designed to dull the luster of the Jogger's media halo: Hospital records acknowledged an earlier diagnosis of anorexia nervosa.)

With such a heroine as the victim, the media had a gripping story from the start. But this was more than a great news story. It was that rare criminal saga that got better with every new lead the reporters chased, until it took on mythic proportions. It was about sex and violence, haves and have-nots, blacks and whites, the depravity of a lost generation and the decay of a great city. It became a story so big that public people couldn't resist the temptation to grab a piece. Mayor Edward Koch and Governor Mario Cuomo felt the need to comment; Cardinal John O'Connor rushed not only to the Jogger's bedside but to the cells of Rikers Island and to Spofford Juvenile Center to visit the defendants, too; and Donald Trump spent eighty thousand dollars on newspaper ads calling for reinstatement of the death penalty. Everybody in the case became famous, including the doctors who gave the press corps daily briefings on the Jogger's condition.

As the early days went by, the role of race in the crime and its aftermath began to take on more prominence in the coverage. In a city in which race relations had been recently strained by racist killings of blacks in Howard Beach, Queens, and Bensonhurst, Brooklyn, the issue was debated from nearly every perspective. Morgenthau's office was quick to publicly reject race as a motive for the assaults or as a factor in the prosecution of the black and Latino suspects. At the other extreme were black radicals such as attorney Alton Maddox, who suggested there was no Central Park Jogger, she was a straw person created by the government as an excuse to put more young, African-American males in prison. "What are we going to do, accept some white person's word that she's over there . . . at Metropolitan Hospital?" asked Maddox during a radio interview. "This whole thing could be an outright hoax!"

Before long, the nature of the media coverage itself became a hotly debated issue and a think tank affiliated with the American Jewish Committee undertook a statistical analysis of the reporting. The panel studied the coverage for the fifteen days beginning April 20 in five newspapers—*The New York Times,* the *Daily News, New York Post, Newsday* and Harlem's weekly *Amsterdam News*—and on six television stations. Among its findings were the following points:

The outlets studied carried 406 news items about the case in those two weeks, amounting to 3,415 column inches of print coverage and 4.25 hours of television.

Race was cited as a possible explanation for the crimes 54 times, more than double any other factor. But its relevance was denied in 80 percent of the items in which it was mentioned.

The crime was most often presented as a random act, a product of the subculture of "wild youth."

There were only 6 references to the assault of the Jogger as a crime against women.

The suspects were described in what the study called "emotional negative language" 390 times, including 185 instances of animal imagery such as wolfpack or herd.

The study came to a sensible, high-minded conclusion that was hopelessly naive in the context of pack journalism: "In place of emotional coverage that denied the relevance of race," the panelists wrote, "a calmer approach that probed more deeply into race relations might have better served the twin goals of good journalism and good citizenship."

Lederer, whose career was committed to prosecuting sex offenders, was troubled by the increasing role race was playing in the public debate. But she couldn't keep the issue out of the courtroom. That became clear on Friday, April 28, when Supreme Court Justice Carol Berkman held a bail hearing for Michael Briscoe at the deteriorating, art-deco Criminal Courts building at 100 Centre Street.

Joe Mack, an activist lawyer who wore his hair in long dreadlocks, had been retained for the Briscoe family by the United Africa Movement. The UAM was a civil rights organization controlled by Maddox, the Reverend Al Sharpton and attorney C. Vernon Mason, the trio that had, for a while, skillfully exploited Tawana Brawley, the black teenager whose explosive allegation of rape by a group of white men was later exposed as a fraud. Maddox joined Mack at the defense table for Briscoe's bail hearing and persisted in addressing the court after

Berkman said she'd listen only to Mack, the attorney of record. The judge finally ordered Maddox to step back into the audience and take a seat.

"Out of the well," said Berkman. "Out of the well," referring to the area inside the railing where the court's business is conducted.

"This is an outrage," shouted Maddox. "This is racism."

Several court officers, their standard-issue .38 caliber pistols tucked into their holsters, approached Maddox to escort him to a seat in the audience. Sharpton and about a dozen supporters immediately jumped from their seats. "Don't lay a hand on him!" they cried. "Don't touch him!"

As the screaming continued and Maddox refused to move, Berkman walked off the bench and into the safety of an adjacent hallway, where a dozen court officers were standing by with riot gear. Lederer and Clements quickly followed the judge. "We didn't know if there was going to be a riot in the courtroom," Clements later recalled. "That was the first of several frightening experiences in this case."

———————

In any sensational story the first impressions created by a media blitz become etched into the public consciousness, despite any number of inaccuracies that may later be revealed. In the early days of the Central Park case, for example, the *Times* reported that Schomburg Plaza, where four of the defendants lived, was a "doorman building." The doorman turned out to be a security guard ensconced in a glass cubicle in the lobby. The dominant image in the media's early profile of the defendants was one of good kids from middle-class families, a circumstance that supposedly made their crime all the more horrifying, as though minority boys from less secure families were expected to rape and murder white people.

The first holes in the fledgling myth about the stable lives of the suspects became apparent at their May 10 arraignment, as Lederer tried to convince Judge Berkman that the boys should be held for trial without bail. It was true that among the defendants only Briscoe had a criminal record (he was on probation for a mugging at the time of the Central Park wilding). But most of the other boys had histories that few New Yorkers would consider consistent with middle-class upbringing. For example, only two of the defendants, McCray and Lopez, lived in homes in which both parents were regularly present.

However, there was so much to report after the arraignment that the media paid scant attention to Lederer's disclosures, the most revealing of which concerned Kharey Wise. The sixteen-year-old lived in Schomburg Plaza with his mother, three brothers and sometimes his father, a truck driver who, at the time of Kharey's arraignment, was wanted on two warrants for skipping court appearances in the Bronx. One of Wise's brothers, Lederer told the judge, had two felony narcotics convictions on his record. The boy's mother, Delores, was concerned that Kharey's older brothers might be using drugs in the apartment while she was at work, according to records of the Bureau of Child Welfare. Mrs. Wise had directed Kharey to find out if her suspicions were correct, the records stated. She was also concerned about Kharey's truancy and his possession of unexplained sums of money.

In the fall of 1985 Mrs. Wise and Kharey attended a "crisis intervention session" with a social worker. Reading from the social worker's report, Lederer told Judge Berkman: "Mrs. Wise was very upset in the office. She threatened to hit Kharey. Expressed fear that she would seriously hurt him. And twice in the office slapped him. She talked about having Kharey put away." As a result of that session, said Lederer, Wise was placed in a group foster home in the Bronx, where he lived for the better part of a year.

"Your honor," said Lederer, concluding her argument against bail for Wise, "the evidence against this defendant is perhaps among the strongest of the defendants charged."

Nobody in the courtroom was more aware than Berkman that it would have been highly unusual for an arraignment judge to refuse to set bail in any case other than a homicide. Lederer, however, made a game argument against the odds. In response to a defense lawyer's noting that Paula Harris had come out of her coma a week earlier, Lederer told the judge: "If this victim levels off and maintains at the level of recovery that she has now achieved, she will be in an institution for the remainder of her life."

Lederer had briefly described for Berkman the nature of each suspect's confession. This left her little to say when it came to Lopez, so she told Berkman what others had said about his role. "There is a witness," said Lederer, "not charged and not named in any of the indictments, who was present at that time, who saw Steve Lopez between the legs of the female jogger as she was in the woods being raped." The identity of that witness was not revealed.

Given the strength of the state's case, said Berkman, bail would be set for Lopez and Wise at $250,000 bond or $50,000 cash. As to the others charged with the crimes against Paula Harris, bail for McCray and Salaam was also a $250,000 bond but they could get out by posting $25,000 cash. For reasons known only to himself, Raymond Santana's lawyer, Peter Rivera, made no bail application.

Berkman set no bail for Kevin Richardson because his lawyer, Howard Diller, requested that she order a psychiatric evaluation of the boy to determine whether he was mentally competent. "This boy," Diller told the judge, "this young boy who is 14 years old, is not mentally what you and I would call 100 percent. . . . Yesterday I had interviewed him in the presence of a social worker, and it was clear the boy did not even know that he was visited by Cardinal O'Connor just two days earlier."

Richardson was evaluated by two court-appointed psychiatrists five days later and was certified as "fit to proceed." The standard for determining whether a defendant is fit to go to trial is simple: Does he understand the nature of the charges against him and the nature of the proceedings? The brief reports with which psychiatrists relay their conclusions to the court include some pertinent dialogue between the doctor and subject. A sampling from Dr. Emilia Salanga's interview with Richardson follows:

Q: What is the charge against you?
A: Assault, attempted murder and rape.
Q: What plea have you entered?
A: Not guilty.
Q: What is the name of your attorney?
A: Howard Diller.
Q: What is the function of a defense attorney?
A: Tell the judge not guilty, try to get me out.
Q: What is the function of a district attorney?
A: Go against me, to say that I'm guilty.
Q: What is the function of a judge?
A: Decides how long I am to be in jail or to release me.
Q: What is the function of a jury?
A: They decide if I'm guilty or not.
Q: What are the consequences of being found guilty?
A: They'll give me years upstate.

Mickey Joseph, forty-four, knew a week after the crime spree when he accepted court appointment as attorney for Antron McCray, without having seen his client's videotape, that he was taking on a multitude of problems. At the May 10 arraignment he saw things go from bad to worse when Judge Berkman announced that she had been ordered to bypass the standard procedure by which trial judges were randomly selected and instead assign the case directly to Justice Thomas Galligan.

Joseph's colleagues at the defense table were as stunned as he was. The normal course of events at arraignment was to spin a small, wooden drum, called a wheel, containing the names of six trial judges and send the case to the jurist whose name was pulled out by the clerk. That system served several purposes, not the least of which was to avoid the appearance of judge shopping by prosecutors or bias on the part of court officials. This departure from the system, nearly four years after it had been instituted, was itself enough to make the defense lawyers suspicious. The additional fact that Judge Galligan had a widespread reputation as staunchly pro-prosecution increased their fears.

Joseph angrily registered an objection. "For the administrative judge to secretively . . . determine that this case will be treated differently seems to be a denial of due process rights. . . . My client should have a right to know why he is being singled out and sent to a specific judge." Joseph asked Berkman to ignore her orders and spin the wheel. The other defense lawyers present all joined in his application. Lederer was silent.

Berkman offered no explanation, other than to say, "I have my instructions." All inquiries on the matter, she told a courtroom packed with journalists, should be addressed to the Office of Court Administration, the state agency that runs the courts. Berkman then put on the record the names of the judges who were in the wheel she had been ordered to bypass: Howard Bell, John Bradley, Richard Carruthers, Bernard Fried, Roger Hayes and Edwin Torres.

The decision to publicly highlight the fact that the powerful men who run the court system had singled out the Central Park case for special treatment was not out of character for Berkman, a feisty former public defender who'd been appointed to the bench ten years earlier by Mayor Ed Koch. She was tough, smart and active in the politically powerful Association of the Bar of the City of New York. As a frequent critic of the bureaucracy of the state's sprawling court system, Berkman was a constant annoyance to its top administrators.

When administrative judge Peter McQuillan had told her to assign the case to Galligan, Berkman had resisted. Since the courts had been reorganized in 1986 under the Individual Assignment System, she had been one of three felony arraignment judges in Manhattan. The job of these so-called "up-front" judges was to dispose of as many cases as possible in the early stages; in other words, to facilitate and approve plea bargains. In Manhattan alone in 1989 there were 17,225 defendants indicted on felony charges and marched into arraignment courtrooms. Approximately 10 percent of those cases were dismissed and another 80 percent were resolved by plea bargains, with the defendant most often pleading guilty to something less than the top count to avoid the risk of being convicted at trial on the higher charge. Approximately 25 percent of those plea bargains were settled by the arraignment judges. When the prosecutor and defense counsel could not make a deal, the case would be assigned to another judge for trial. (Only 1,078 trials were actually begun in Manhattan in 1989.)

Since Berkman was responsible for roughly one-third of the district attorney's cases, on a typical day her calendar might carry the names of nearly one hundred defendants. McQuillan's order to send the Central Park case to Judge Galligan was the first time Berkman had ever been told to skip the wheel. And she didn't like it for two reasons. First, she believed in the basic fairness of random assignment. If court administrators wanted to override that system she thought they should publicly disclose their reasons. (Her position on this matter was unrelated to Galligan, whom she admired personally and whom she considered a good judge.)

Second, Berkman believed the decision was wrongheaded in this case. The episode in which Maddox and Sharpton had disrupted her courtroom barely ten days ago was very much on her mind. Now, she told McQuillan, she had a courtroom crowded with defense supporters who believed the courts were racist, who believed that the judges who ran those courts would ensure that these black and Latino boys would never get a fair trial. How was Berkman supposed to explain a decision to abandon a standard procedure that had been instituted to prevent people in her position from doing precisely what McQuillan was ordering her to do: steer a case to a specific judge?

But Berkman had no authority to override the order. The decision to send the case to Galligan had been sanctioned by Matthew Crosson, the chief administrator of state courts, during a conference call with McQuillan and deputy chief administrative judge Milton Williams.

The defense lawyers refused to let the matter rest. When they got into Galligan's courtroom on May 17, several made oral motions for the judge to remove himself and send the case back to Berkman for random assignment. When Galligan refused, Maddox went so far as to allege that Robert Morgenthau, arguably the single most powerful man in the state criminal justice system, had specifically asked court administrators to give the case to Galligan to ensure convictions. Galligan later described Maddox's allegation as "fantasy" and spokesmen for the DA and the Office of Court Administration vehemently denied the charge.

Mickey Joseph and Jesse Berman, who was representing Steve Lopez, later submitted written motions to remove Galligan. Joseph repeated his argument that the arbitrary nature of the selection was unfair and improper. Berman, a more radical lawyer whose clients had included Black Panthers and Black Liberation Army members, leaned more toward the conspiracy theory, demanding that the record be clarified "on whether the district attorney's office had any input into the specific selection of Judge Galligan." Added Berman: "What has transpired thus far in this case, in terms of the way in which Judge Galligan, a white man, was hand-picked to handle this highly-publicized case involving Black defendants and white victims, has unfortunately set back the appearance of justice in this city by at least three years."

In their own papers, the prosecutors opposed the motions to remove Galligan, who refused for the second, but not yet final time, to give up the case.

The battle over Galligan's selection brought to light a growing trend in the Office of Court Administration to steer high-profile criminal cases to a handful of trusted judges. The system's top administrators— Crosson, Williams and McQuillan—could justify the practice under a procedural rule that empowered them to bypass the random assignment system "as a matter of administrative discretion." But they could not or would not be entirely open about their motives. This reticence not only angered many judges but gave defense lawyers the opportunity to argue, and some citizens reason to believe, that when it came to such cases the fix was in.

There were always cases that could not be left to random assignment, such as the felony indictment against powerful state Senator Manfred Ohrenstein for alleged misuse of public funds or the perjury trial of personal injury litigator Theodore Friedman, whose wife was a Supreme Court judge in Manhattan. For obvious reasons, many judges would be unable to try such cases because of conflicts of interest. But

Central Park was specially assigned for a public policy reason: it was a trial that was seen by administrators as one that would showcase, for good or ill, the quality of the courts. Crosson and Williams knew well enough what could happen if such a case landed in the hands of a judge who could be intimidated or bullied by a skilled defense lawyer or the media.

Galligan was one judge the bosses didn't have to worry about. Most defense lawyers and prosecutors described Galligan, a bachelor, as a nice guy whose considerable temper was easily inflamed by attorneys who came into his courtroom unprepared. He had a reputation for fairness, despite sharing a tendency of his brethren to see themselves as performing a role similar to that of the prosecutor, that is, helping to relieve society of the growing criminal menace, a disposition that leads many defense attorneys to describe judges as "pro-prosecution." The trait for which Galligan was best known was his propensity for heavy sentencing. "Father Time" was one of his nicknames, and the courthouse security guards referred to Rikers Island, the East River complex of city jails, as "Galligan's Island."

During the Central Park trials, supporters of the defendants liked to casually remark that Galligan had "bought his judgeship." This was a reference to a 1976 front-page story in *The New York Times* about an investigation by special prosecutor Maurice Nadjari to determine whether Patrick Cunningham, who controlled the Bronx Democratic party machine at the time, accepted a bribe from a judge for his seat on the Criminal Court bench. The judge was identified by two anonymous sources, reported Marcia Chambers, as Thomas Galligan, who had supposedly made a $5,000 to $10,000 payment in exchange for his nomination. Since Criminal Court judges were appointed by the Democratic mayor, Cunningham's support virtually guaranteed a seat. Investigators believed the practice was common and described the Bronx as a "marketplace" where judgeships were bought and sold. But Nadjari's successor, John Keenan (now a federal judge in New York), says he fully investigated the allegation against Galligan and determined that it was "absolutely untrue." Galligan, who refused to comment on the allegation, was never charged and his career remained otherwise free of scandal.

The defense supporters were later provided with what they saw as more evidence of a political conspiracy, however, when Governor Mario Cuomo elevated Galligan to the Court of Claims. Although Galligan would continue to preside over criminal cases in Manhattan, the promotion freed him, at age sixty-five, from having to worry about appointment when his term expired at the end of 1994. The designation also carried a salary increase to $95,000 from $86,000.

The pro-prosecution label stuck to Galligan so firmly as to become part of the conventional wisdom. Jesse Berman liked to tell reporters, "Only Galligan's friends would describe him as fair." It was a good line but it wasn't accurate. The truth was, defense lawyers were usually representing guilty people, and Galligan didn't seem to like guilty people any more than he liked lousy lawyers.

CHAPTER 5

THE DA MAKES A DEAL

AFTER TWENTY YEARS WITH THE LEGAL AID SOCIETY, NEW YORK'S PUB-
lic defender agency, Elliot Cook knew a losing case when he saw one.
Jermain Robinson's case was a loser.

Cook's client, a fifteen-year-old who lived with an aunt near the Taft
Houses project, was charged with robbery, the assaults of joggers John
Loughlin and David Lewis and riot. While Loughlin's radio headset
might have been of minimal value, its disappearance led to the armed
robbery charge (the weapon being the 14-inch iron pipe the boys had
passed around during the rampage), and Robinson therefore faced a
sentence of three and one-third to ten years. As he evaluated the case
against his client, Cook weighed the considerable risks of going to trial
and began to discuss with his co-counsel, Natasha Lapiner, what kind
of deal they might make with Lederer.

Robinson had admitted to detectives limited involvement in the
reservoir assaults and the beating of the so-called bum, who had since
been identified as Antonio Diaz, a drug addict in his fifties who had
survived with minor cuts and bruises. While those statements were
probably enough to send Cook's client to jail, they did not approach
Santana's vivid description of Robinson being pulled away from Lough-

lin by his cohorts, only to run back moments later and resume pummel-
ing his victim. Unless Santana copped a plea and agreed to testify
against the others, his allegation could not be used against Robinson,
but Cook couldn't afford to count out that possibility. Besides, who
knew whether Lederer would come up with other, equally damaging
witnesses?

At least the prosecutors did not have the kid on videotape. When
Robinson, whose parents were divorced, was interrogated on Friday
afternoon, April 21, he was accompanied by his mother, Linda White,
a New York City corrections officer who lived in the Bronx. As she sat
and listened to her son describe the terror in the park and his own role
in it, White became so horrified that she slapped him in the face, right
in front of the two detectives who were taking his statement. But later,
when Robinson's father arrived at the Twenty-fourth Precinct, he
refused to let the prosecutors interview the boy on camera.

There was, however, another oral statement Cook had to worry
about. At 3:30 A.M. on Saturday, April 22, two detectives were driving
Robinson from the Twenty-fourth Precinct down to the central booking office in lower Manhattan. On the way, according to the cops,
Robinson said: "You know, this whole thing got out of hand . . . We
were going to the park to bug out. You know, just assaulting people.
We was going to get some whites, whiteys. Just beat them, but not that
bad." That remark, coupled with the admission in his written statement that the boys called some cyclists "fucking white people," was
bound to convince more than a few jurors that Robinson was a racist.

Then there was the identification problem. Robinson was the only
defendant identified by any of the joggers or bicyclists who'd been
accosted in the park. Loughlin, a former Marine and National Guard
training officer, had been wearing camouflage fatigues on the night of
April 19. As he jogged around the northeast corner of the reservoir,
Loughlin saw a group apparently beating someone on the ground in the
shadows below the jogging path. Loughlin stopped. Just before he was
smacked over the head, a tall black kid asked, "What are you lookin'
at? What are you, one of those vigilantes?"

Yusef Salaam was the tallest of the boys whom the prosecutors
believed were at the reservoir. DA Tim Clements arranged a lineup
with Salaam as the target on April 24, just a couple of days after
Loughlin had been released from the hospital. Clements, who had not
seen Loughlin until that day, was shocked when the forty-one-year-old
schoolteacher showed up at his office. Loughlin, who stood six-four and

was built like a football player, had the two worst black eyes Clements had ever seen. The circular bruises were so large and their purple-black color so deep that to call them shiners would do them no justice. In fact, they were not the result of punches to the eyes at all, but evidence of internal bleeding caused by severe blows to the head, producing concussion.

Loughlin did not recognize Salaam. He picked a stand-in out of the lineup, later saying he was 80 percent sure that was the kid who spoke to him. The teenager, however, was an innocent student from a school near the DA's office. Several weeks later, while watching a television newscast, Loughlin saw footage of Robinson taken on the night of his arrest. He called the DA and said he recognized Jermain Robinson. At a lineup on May 24, more than a month after the crime, Loughlin asked if he could hear Robinson's voice. When he did, he fingered Robinson, with what he would describe as 95 percent certainty.

The delay, the possible influence of the television newscast, and the mistake by Loughlin in the first lineup all gave Cook grounds to challenge the reliability of the identification. He knew, however, that these deficiencies did not add up to sufficient reason for Galligan to suppress the identification.

———

Cook's hopes further dimmed when, as pretrial hearings to determine the admissibility of the suspects' videotaped and written statements approached, he attended a meeting of the defense lawyers. Seven of the eight attorneys met on September 21 at Jesse Berman's low-rent office two blocks from the courthouse. Only Alton Maddox, who was tied up on another case, was missing. The purpose of the meeting was not so much to plot a common strategy, which would have been difficult given that the defendants blamed one another for the worst of what happened, but to find a way to avoid conflicts.

"We want to eliminate the element of surprise among ourselves," said Colin Moore, a civil rights activist who was representing Kharey Wise free of charge.

"I'd like to know whether people are fighting each other or if they are going to get in each other's way," said Robert Burns, the attorney for Salaam.

When Cook arrived he found that he was not entirely welcome. Knowing that Cook had been meeting with Lederer to discuss a plea bargain, some of the other lawyers resented his presence. What are you doing here if you're talking to the DA? somebody asked. Cook made no apology for exploring a plea and scoffed at the suggestion that he was a spy for Lederer. The meeting proceeded.

These guys have no clue, Cook thought as he listened to the discussion. It quickly became clear that only Jesse Berman, Mickey Joseph and himself—representing Lopez, McCray and Robinson, respectively—understood what they were up against. Several of the others didn't even know what sentences their clients were facing. Howard Diller, who had been hired by Kevin Richardson's family on a five-thousand-dollar retainer, seemed more concerned with courting the press than anything else. Burns seemed out of his league. Moore and Peter Rivera, a former Bronx prosecutor with political aspirations who represented Santana, did not impress Cook either.

As Cook and Lapiner left Berman's office, Diller was ushering in some reporters. On the short walk back to Legal Aid, an amazed Cook said to his co-counsel, "Man, oh man. This is a disaster. We're going to get dragged down with these guys if we don't get severed." The next day Cook, Lapiner and the prosecutors met with Judge Galligan to get his preliminary approval of the terms of Robinson's plea bargain.

Severance was something all the defense lawyers were seeking. Nobody wanted a jury to see his client as part of a group, sitting at a crowded defense table with a bunch of other guys, most of whom had revealed on videotape the details of a gang-rape. Galligan, however, had said he wouldn't make a decision on whether to try the boys separately until after the pretrial hearings. Since Robinson was not charged with any of the crimes related to the attack on Paula Harris, Cook thought his chances of getting a separate trial were better than most. This gave him one more bargaining chip in his negotiations with the prosecutors.

A deal with Robinson appealed to Lederer and Clements, who were working together for the first time since Clements had joined the DA's office four years earlier. For one thing, they had no evidence that he was involved in the rape and beating of Harris. None of the other defendants placed Robinson at the scene of the rape, and while detectives had interviewed about a half-dozen kids to whom Robinson had bragged about beating up Loughlin or "the bum," they found nobody who had heard him talk about attacking a woman. This gave the prosecutors the possibility of gaining an accomplice-witness—a player who could candidly tell the jury about the gang's intentions—without facing criticism for making a deal with a rapist. In a similar vein, while Robinson was a major force in instigating and carrying out the brutal beating of Loughlin, the prosecutors had no reason to believe he personally used a weapon in that assault. Depending on whom you believed, Salaam or McCray, or both, had hit Loughlin with the pipe while somebody else beat him with a tree limb. So the prosecutors could negotiate with Cook without feeling they were shaking hands with the devil.

Another benefit to the plea bargain would be Legal Aid's agreement to withdraw a suit in the Court of Appeals, the state's highest court, challenging the district attorney's right to force Robinson to provide a blood sample for DNA testing. At Lederer's request, Judge Galligan had ordered all of the defendants to provide blood samples to determine whether semen that had been found in the victim's cervix and rectum and on her clothing could be genetically identified as coming from any of the suspects. The Legal Aid Society appealed Galligan's order on the grounds that the prosecutor had no probable cause to believe Robinson was involved in the rape.

But Lederer and Clements didn't want to let Robinson plead to a minor charge if later tests might determine that he had been involved in the rape. The plea bargain they eventually struck with Cook therefore included two key provisions related to the blood: First, Robinson must voluntarily provide a sample, and if tests on that blood linked him to the semen recovered from the victim, the whole deal was off; second, Legal Aid must withdraw the suit in the Court of Appeals.

Among Cook's colleagues at Legal Aid there were those who did not want to see him make the deal. The appellate bureau wanted to press the Court of Appeals case. And some in the agency's upper management were hesitant to set a precedent by voluntarily providing a sample of a client's blood. There were also those at Legal Aid who didn't want to deal with Morgenthau's office for political reasons, who saw a racist element in the prosecution of this case. The debate proceeded to the inevitable conclusion that the agency's priority had to be what was in the best interests of the client. Cook, who had a reputation as one of Legal Aid's best trial lawyers, was convinced he could not win the case in court. Reluctantly, the bosses agreed to drop the appeal and provide the blood sample.

Before agreeing to give up the blood, the defense lawyers wanted to be sure their client was telling the truth. It would be an unmitigated disaster, for Cook and Lapiner personally and for the Legal Aid Society, if they agreed to provide a blood sample that led to their client's conviction on a rape charge he would otherwise not have faced. So they quizzed Robinson for more than four hours, then had him take a polygraph test. Next, Cook had an intense conversation with Robinson's mother and her boyfriend, also a corrections officer, explaining that this was probably the most important decision the boy would ever make. "If he was present at that rape," Cook told them, "he should not give up his blood. If he was not there, then he's got nothing to worry about." When Linda White came back to Cook after a weekend of discussions with her son, who was free on seventy-five-hundred-dollars' bail, she told him she was satisfied that Jermain was telling the truth. Finally, Cook asked three senior Legal Aid lawyers to grill Robinson again. That team spent more than two hours cross-examining the teenager, who did not waiver.

Robinson may have thought he'd been through some hostile questioning during those sessions with the defense team, but he hadn't met Elizabeth Lederer yet. "She hated him," Natasha Lapiner would later say. "She hated all of the defendants, because the city hated them."

Lederer demanded complete honesty and full cooperation from Robinson. Admitting his own role in the attacks was not enough. He had to agree to help the prosecutors make their cases against the defendants already indicted and, if he could, against others they hadn't yet arrested. Plus, he had to agree to testify at as many trials as the prosecutors saw fit. If this cooperation, this decision to rat out his friends, put the teenager at risk in his East Harlem neighborhood, so be it. In exchange Cook would get what he wanted: Robinson would be sentenced to one year in jail on the robbery charge and receive youthful offender status, meaning he would officially have no criminal record. In other words, he would be able to tell future employers that he had never been convicted of a crime.

Lederer and Clements knew any defense lawyer cross-examining Robinson on behalf of his own client would have plenty of ammunition to attack his credibility. The only protection against that was to have him admit on the witness stand, under *their* questioning, his own role in the crimes. If he held back, if he lied, a jury might sense it and discount everything he said against the other defendants. So the prosecutors questioned him relentlessly on his actions, his motives, anything a defense lawyer might use to discredit him. Lederer and

Clements debriefed Robinson as many as five times, the meetings often stretching over several hours. The prosecutors never took notes, for if they did they would have to turn them over to all of the defense lawyers before calling Robinson to testify. Cook was impressed with Lederer's ability to keep straight in her mind the multitude of facts and allegations involving so many defendants and victims. She knows her case cold, he thought.

Robinson was always accompanied at those meetings by his mother as well as his lawyers. Sometimes the prosecutors had one or two detectives with them, the resulting crowd filling Lederer's dreary office. Her status as senior trial counsel entitled Lederer to more space than most assistant district attorneys in Manhattan but the perk did not extend to furnishings or decoration. Her big space was dull in the style typical to municipal offices in New York, with bad lighting, a high ceiling, one large window, several metal file cabinets that did not match and an old-fashioned, heavy wooden desk and chairs. Personal touches were few: a collection of toy police cars atop a bookcase and a single large vase with a Japanese-style arrangement of dry flowers.

The walls, painted long ago in a nondescript institutional shade, were dominated by eight charts, one for each defendant. These were drawn with magic markers on sheets of paper that were at least two feet square. The charts were done as grids, with a list of codefendants down the left side and a series of crimes arranged across the top. They were cross-referenced so that one could, for example, choose "Kharey Wise" in the left column of any defendant's chart and "assault of bum" from the top and find the square at which they intersected. There would be writing in that square detailing the allegation against Wise concerning the beating of the bum; in red if the allegation came from a videotape and in black if it came from a written statement. Each defendant had named so many others, and their stories were so riddled with conflicting information, that these charts were the only way for the prosecutors to keep track of who said what about whom.

As Lederer listened to Robinson's chilling account of his night in the park, she could see a jury spellbound by the detailed narrative. Sure, she had five other defendants on videotape telling parts of what was essentially the same story, but they were reluctant, confused, sometimes without credibility and always minimizing their own roles. In Robinson, she would have a live witness who willingly told the tale from start to finish, except, of course, for the rape. The boy added details that made the story even more frightening. For example, he said there had been an older guy with the gang, a known drug dealer who was carrying a gun. The dealer left the park, said Robinson, at the first sighting of a police car, before Diaz was attacked.

Under interrogation by the prosecutors, Robinson admitted more than he had divulged to the police back in April. At one session, to encourage full disclosure, Clements played a portion of a videotaped statement by Jomo Smith, a cousin of Robinson's who had come to the park with his brother Ramsey and the Taft boys. Smith described in detail Robinson's vicious beating of Loughlin, saying it was he who pulled Robinson away, asking, What are you trying to prove? That you're a big man?

When he turned off the VCR, Clements said to Robinson: And that's your cousin. The message was clear: You're not the only one talking; everybody's ratting out everybody else.

Eventually Robinson admitted his leading role in the assaults of Loughlin and Diaz and revealed details that could also help the prosecutors nail Steve Lopez on the assault and robbery charges. Lopez claimed to have watched the Loughlin assault from a distance, but Robinson said he was in the thick of it, that he injured his leg when the tree limb with which someone was beating Loughlin broke and smacked Lopez in the shin. This was damning corroboration for the moment on Lopez's own videotape when he pulled up his pants leg to show Lederer a bruised shin, claiming he had slipped and fallen while running out of the park. Additionally, Robinson could testify to admissions other defendants had made to him in conversations after the rampage.

Robinson gave the prosecutors a wealth of information that helped them put together a cohesive, credible version of what happened in Central Park on April 19. One afternoon they all piled into a van and drove uptown to the park, where Robinson took them on a three-hour tour, recreating the route the gang had taken that night. Here was where they attacked Antonio Diaz and stole his bag of food and beer; here was where they tried to dismount the couple on the tandem bike; here were the ballfields where Salaam showed him the pipe; this was the hole in the fence they crawled through on their way up to the reservoir; these were the trees that shielded them as they waited in ambush for joggers; and this was where they left John Loughlin, lying unconscious, his head drenched in blood.

There was only one significant problem with Robinson's story. When the police arrived at his aunt's apartment to take him into

custody Robinson himself told a detective, "Jermain's not here." But
the cops soon found out who he was, Robinson claimed, and the
detective to whom he had lied threw him to the floor. The prosecutors
expected lawyers for the other defendants to claim detectives had
coerced incriminating statements from their clients. What a field day
they could have with this testimony of police brutality from a prosecution witness!

Lederer didn't consider the flaw fatal but she wanted it eliminated.
One day she had the detective in question, who denied Robinson's
allegation, come to her office for a meeting with the youth. Lederer
didn't believe Robinson, but if she expected him to back down when
confronted again by the detective she was mistaken. Robinson stood
his ground, essentially calling the cop a liar to his face. The prosecutors
would just have to live with Robinson's allegation.

Robinson did not testify to the grand jury but the information he gave
the prosecutors helped them get indictments of two more youths from
the Taft crew, Antonio Montalvo, eighteen, and Orlando Escobar,
sixteen, on charges of robbery, assault and riot. Montalvo was accused
of kicking Diaz in the head and stealing his food. Escobar was alleged
to have participated in the attack on Loughlin. The prosecutors could
not connect either suspect to the rape.

If he had kept his mouth shut, Tony Montalvo might have escaped,
but he liked to tell stories about himself and be the center of attention.
Back on Saturday, April 22, Montalvo told a reporter from *Newsday*
that he had declined an invitation from his friends to join the wilding
spree in Central Park. But he had been out with the boys a week earlier,
Montalvo assured the reporter, when they beat up a man at a housing
project on 106th Street.

Four days after the *Newsday* article appeared Montalvo changed his
story when questioned by detectives Bert Arroyo and John Hartigan.
The cops took him to the park, where Montalvo showed them the
boulder he sat on as he ate the chicken he'd taken from Diaz. He was
questioned by detectives again in May, June and September.

Finally, on October 3, two days before Robinson pled guilty to
robbery in Galligan's courtroom, Montalvo talked himself into trouble
during a rambling interview with Lederer. Montalvo seemed to love the
video camera. He bragged about several previous episodes of wilding,
which means, he explained, "to go out and beat people up, and keep

on going." Montalvo revealed himself on the video as a woefully unso-
cialized eighteen-year-old. He spent a long time squirming uncomfortably, with his hands in his lap under the table, until Lederer asked if
he had to go to the bathroom. Yes, he said, and they took a break. One
detective later testified that he recited Montalvo's rights aloud because
it was apparent that the boy was having trouble reading the simple
language from the printed card he'd been given.

Montalvo eventually admitted enough to convict himself of the Diaz
assault but he denied having been at the rape scene. Lederer pressed.
Antron McCray had told her a "Tony" had been there and McCray's
list of those who had intercourse with the victim included a Puerto
Rican wearing a black "hoody." Montalvo admitted he had been wearing a black hooded sweatshirt that night but insisted he never saw a
woman jogger. He did, however, corroborate Santana's statement that,
after leaving the park, McCray had offered the pipe to "Tony." Montalvo told Lederer he refused to take the pipe because he didn't want
to get his fingerprints on it. Why not, asked Lederer, if you didn't know
they'd used it to beat the female jogger? "Because I knew they used
it for something," said Montalvo.

The prosecutors knew that Santana had recruited boys for the Central
Park rampage at the junior high school he attended with McCray,
Escobar and Montalvo. Now Tony was explaining to Lederer that there
was really nothing irregular about the events of April 19. In fact, he
said, he and his pals frequently went wilding and they only ended up
in Central Park by happenstance. When "the posse" gathered at the
Taft Houses that night to decide where to go, said Montalvo, somebody
asked, "Why don't we just beat people up right here?" Others wanted
to go to a street carnival at 101st Street, where some of them, including
Santana, had been wilding before. They decided, however, to go to the
park and they ran into the Schomburg crew on their way.

Lederer had already heard about the violence at the street carnival.
On April 14, five days before the Central Park attacks, a man who ran
a concession had been severely beaten with his own baseball bat when
he tried to run off a group of kids intent on stealing teddy bears from
his stand. The victim, Eddie Rivera, suffered a broken arm and a stab
wound in his side.

The carnival assault came to the attention of the Central Park
investigators at about midnight on April 23, when Detective Hartigan

interrogated Terrance "T-Bone" Campbell at the Twenty-fourth Precinct. At least three of the Central Park defendants had said Campbell, fifteen, was with them in the park. Campbell refused to incriminate himself in the park attacks, however, and might have stayed out of trouble entirely had he not protested a little too much, telling Hartigan he had only gone wilding twice. The first time, he said, was a couple of months earlier, and the last time was the previous Friday night at a street carnival.

As a result of that admission, Campbell was convicted six months later of assault and riot for his role in the carnival violence.

CHAPTER 6

DRESS REHEARSAL

THEY COULDN'T AFFORD TO SAY SO PUBLICLY BUT MOST OF THE DEFENSE lawyers believed from the start that the kids who had incriminated themselves were finished if a jury got to see the videotapes. As Detective Hartigan told Kharey Wise, the jurors, drawn from a pool of registered voters in Manhattan, would be people who "come from the street just like you and I do; they're working people." If any of the defense attorneys were somehow still in doubt about how these working people might react to the tapes, they got a wake-up call in late September when *Newsday*'s courthouse reporter, Timothy Clifford, obtained a set of the videos.

Previously, only Kevin Richardson's tape had been available to the daily press, although Michael Stone had access to the others for a comprehensive article he published in August in *New York* magazine. Richardson's tape had been released by the fifteen-year-old's lawyer, Howard Diller, to coincide with the May 10 arraignment. Diller's intention had been to debunk the myth that all of the defendants had confessed to taking part in the wilding. His client's statement, insisted Diller, was not a confession, since Richardson admitted nothing more than witnessing the crimes. The video, Diller maintained, proved his point.

The videotape on which Richardson calmly described the rape had been a hot story for a day or two, but it disappeared as the media pursued Paula Harris's remarkable recovery. On May 15 it was disclosed that she had taken her first unsteady steps; two days later surgeons rebuilt the crushed socket of her left eye and on June 7 she was well enough to leave Metropolitan Hospital and begin rehabilitation at Gaylord Hospital in suburban Connecticut.

By autumn attention was turning to the pretrial hearings and *Newsday* played Clifford's scoop for all it was worth. The paper printed transcripts of the most sensational segments of the tapes on September 25, accompanied by photos of the defendants taken off a television monitor. Others scrambled to get copies of the videos and in the next few days local television newscasts were running clips in prime time. There was Wise saying, "This is my first rape." There was Raymond Santana saying, "Every time she was talking he was smacking her, saying, 'Shut up, bitch.' " There was Antron McCray saying, "We all took turns getting on top of her."

While it is common for the defense to complain that such extraordinary publicity pollutes the jury pool, in this case that danger seemed real. But the jury selection process was some time off. For the time being the only viable option the defense lawyers had was to convince the court to throw out the tapes on the grounds that they had been obtained in violation of the defendants' constitutional rights. They gathered in Judge Galligan's large, windowless courtroom on October 10 for hearings that would consume the next eight weeks.

At the outset Alton Maddox, whose fame rested in large part on his skillful manipulation of the media during the Tawana Brawley hoax, asked Galligan to exclude the press from the hearings. Jesse Berman, Colin Moore and Robert Burns also sought restrictions.

Berman was particularly concerned. His client, Steve Lopez, admitted next to nothing, though several of the others had described Lopez as the most vicious of Harris's attackers. Berman was not eager to have the public adopt that image. Even if Galligan eventually refused to suppress the tapes, Berman argued, the allegations against Lopez by his codefendants would not be admissible at his trial. Berman was right, but protecting his client's public image was not Galligan's problem.

The release of the tapes, the most recent in a long line of leaks from the defense camp, led Lederer to consider this request to close the courtroom ironic, and she said as much to the judge. She was, however, seeking a gag order of her own, asking Galligan to prohibit lawyers on both sides from disseminating any further evidence to the press.

While the release of the videos did nothing to hurt the state's case, Lederer's cause had been damaged less than a week earlier when the media ran excerpts from Paula Harris's medical records. Those records revealed that back in June, though she still could not remember the night she was attacked, Harris had told Dr. Mary Ann Cohen at Metropolitan Hospital that she was willing to try to help the prosecutors. "I don't know what happened," said Harris, "and maybe I will never know. But I know I was attacked and I will just have to accept it and deal with it."

The public airing of those records, which Lederer had been required to turn over to the defense lawyers, would haunt the prosecutor because Harris's family was angry about such a blatant invasion of privacy. As a result, Lederer later found it more difficult to get their cooperation on some matters. Worse, when the DA sought more medical records, this time from Gaylord Hospital, authorities there were reluctant to help because of the earlier breach of confidentiality. The defense lawyers who leaked the Metropolitan records, protected by the press corps' promises of anonymity, had succeeded in making Lederer's life more difficult.

Galligan refused to close his courtroom but he did issue a gag order. As the hearings got under way, one more bit of crucial information was leaked to the press, this time by persons variously described as "prosecution sources," "law enforcement sources" and "court sources." The results of the DNA tests that might have linked the defendants to the crimes, said these sources, were "inconclusive."

That story underlined the importance of the hearings: Without the videotapes, Lederer would not be able to make a case at all. A judge theoretically does not let public sentiment—or even the consequences of his own rulings—affect his decisions. But the pressure was squarely on Galligan. If he suppressed the tapes, he'd effectively be setting the suspects free.

To varying degrees, the defense lawyers argued that the videotapes were the products of coercion. They had little choice. A written statement can be edited, embellished, even entirely faked by corrupt cops, but a videotape is unarguably genuine. The lawyers couldn't very well deny that their clients said the things the camera had captured them saying. And how could you argue that the suspect wasn't given his *Miranda* rights when the prosecutor was there reading them to him on the TV screen?

A successful coercion defense must convince a judge or jury that the incriminating statement was not voluntary. Under New York law an involuntary statement—whether true or false—may not be used against the person who made it. The law defines a statement as involuntary if it was obtained in any of the following three ways: by the use or threatened use of physical force, or by undue pressure that impaired the defendant's ability to make a choice about whether to give the statement; by any promise or statement of fact that created a substantial risk that the defendant might falsely incriminate himself; by violating his constitutional rights.

Nobody's coercion defense was as complete as the one Colin Moore mounted on behalf of Kharey Wise. In seeking to suppress Wise's two written statements and two videos, Moore claimed that all three criteria that would render the statements involuntary applied to his client's case. First, he alleged that the sixteen-year-old—an adult who was legally interrogated without a parent or guardian present—had been beaten at the stationhouse and was terrified by police with threats of incarceration. Second, he claimed his client's interrogators had created a risk of false incrimination by promising that Wise would be allowed to go home if he confessed. Last, Moore claimed Wise was not intellectually capable of understanding the *Miranda* rights he had waived.

Moore's defense had potential. It was not inconceivable, for example, that a cop might slap around an uncooperative suspect who was, according to several other defendants, involved in a rape. It was only four years earlier, after all, that three white New York City policemen had been convicted of using stun guns to get confessions out of drug suspects, all of whom were minority group members. Second, Wise's statements were so full of contradictions and revisions that it was possible he had fabricated portions of them in the expectation that he'd be rewarded with his freedom. And his speech was so poor, his vocabulary so limited, that perhaps he was unable to grasp the significance of waiving his rights.

Moore bolstered the last possibility by putting his client's mother, Delores Wise, on the stand. "He's in a special ed class and his mentality is, like, ten years old really, you know?" she said. "I mean . . . you can talk but he don't understand."

The coercion defense became something of a Catch-22 for Moore. On the upside, Wise was questioned without a guardian present. The other defense counsel might have a hard time convincing the judge that the cops applied undue pressure—let alone physical abuse—to a teenager whose parents were in the same room. But Moore's client was on his own and in police custody for seventeen hours before finishing his last statement. If a cop was inclined to hit a suspect, or if Lederer thought she could push one suspect harder than the others, wasn't that suspect more likely to be an adult than a juvenile?

The downside to Moore's defense was that it ultimately depended on the personal credibility of Kharey Wise. Who else could provide the evidence of coercion?

When Wise took the stand he put his lawyer's strategy to the test. Detective Robert Nugent, he said, slapped him four times, resulting in his having problems hearing in one ear for weeks. Nugent also screamed at him for hours, said Wise, calling him, among other things, a "scumbag." Wise denied having said most of the things contained in his two written statements, testifying that he was virtually incapable of reading anything other than his own signature. He had actually witnessed none of the crimes he claimed to have witnessed, he maintained, and anything he said to Lederer on videotape had been dictated to him by detectives. In short, Wise testified that he had been thoroughly framed.

The problem Wise now posed for Moore—regardless of whether his story was true—was that his answers sometimes undercut his own case. Moore's position was that Detective Hartigan's speech to Wise about potentially going on trial for murder, with a story no jury would believe, constituted psychological duress that led to false incrimination. But when Moore asked about his conversation with Hartigan, the teenager said he didn't even remember that crucial part. Similarly, Moore argued that Hartigan had improperly overborne his client's will when he told Wise that his friend Eddie was not supporting his contention that they had been together in the park. Wise, however, testified that, rather than having been shaken by this news, his response to Hartigan was: "I never told you that." Hardly indicative of a broken will.

Wise's hostile attitude toward Lederer during her cross-examination also did little to help his credibility with Galligan. Wise refused at one point to answer. "Ma'am," he said, "I don't want to answer any of your questions. Your questions are what got me here."

When he did respond, his answers rarely helped his case. He accused

Lederer, for example, of watching Nugent "beat me up." The prosecutor later pointed out to Galligan that several of the videotapes she'd made with other defendants proved she was at another precinct at the time Wise claimed to have been slapped.

Nor was the defendant alone in damaging his own case. Moore put into evidence a letter he wrote to authorities at the Rikers Island jail demanding a medical examination of Wise because he had suffered "contusions and abrasions . . . and temporary loss of hearing" as a result of "continuous and brutal police interrogation." The examination resulted in a finding that Wise had no such injuries.

In an exhaustive, 390-page brief submitted to Galligan after the hearing, Lederer and her co-counsel, Clements, turned the tapes around on Wise, urging that they be used as a window into his soul. "The videotape of Kharey's statements clearly provides the best evidence of his physical and mental condition," the prosecutors wrote, "and it reveals that Kharey was clearly not overborne but was speaking voluntarily." Thus, the state's strongest argument for the admissibility of the tapes was to be found in the tapes themselves.

Jesse Berman had little to fear from his client's videotape. If he failed to get the statement suppressed, he intended to urge jurors to believe everything Steve Lopez said on the tape. The fifteen-year-old had frustrated Lederer by refusing to incriminate himself. He had admitted going into the park "to bother people" and said he had witnessed the assaults at the reservoir from a distance. But Lopez did not admit participating in any crimes and vehemently denied seeing a female jogger.

Berman was not, however, home free. At arraignment, Lederer had referred to a mystery witness who would testify that he had seen Lopez raping Paula Harris. Berman was also worried about what Jermain Robinson knew of Lopez's activities in the park and whether Lederer would make deals with any other suspects—whether already indicted or still under investigation—who could hurt his client.

A leftist lawyer who had represented violent radicals for decades, Berman often focused on the political dimensions of his cases. In the Central Park prosecution he saw large elements of class conflict, no small amount of racism and an unbridled lust for revenge on the part of the Establishment. In his effort to have the evidence against Lopez suppressed, Berman put the government on trial, claiming the conduct of the police and prosecutors was riddled with illegalities. Berman maintained that the police had no probable cause to arrest Lopez in the first place; that his right to counsel had been violated; and that the investigators had ignored the protections afforded juveniles by the state Family Court Act.

Lopez had been picked up with Santana on Central Park West after ten o'clock on the night of the crime. He was held at the Central Park Precinct for about twenty hours before detectives got around to questioning him; twenty-nine hours had passed by the time he gave a videotaped statement at the Twenty-fourth Precinct. Berman was arguing that the law required the police to either release Lopez into his parents' custody or have him arraigned in Family Court and held in a juvenile detention center. (In a similar vein, Mickey Joseph was arguing that McCray should have been arraigned, at the latest, after signing his written statement, rather than being held for at least six more hours until Lederer was ready to videotape his self-incriminations.) The passage of so much time without regular meals or a bed to sleep in was coercive, said Berman; it had overborne Lopez's will and made it impossible for him to make a statement that was truly voluntary.

But the prosecutors argued in their brief that the Family Court Act was on their side. The statute, they pointed out, requires release or arraignment "with all reasonable speed . . . unless the officer determines it is necessary to question the child." In that case, the juvenile may be questioned in a room that has been designated by the court as suitable for that purpose, and Lopez was questioned in such rooms. In fact, the prosecutors argued, one reason for the delay in questioning the defendants was that there is only one juvenile room at each precinct and there were at least a dozen boys to be questioned during the period in question. The investigation could have proceeded much faster, said the prosecutors, if they and the police had not so scrupulously followed the Family Court Act.

To support his *Miranda* claim that Lopez's right to counsel had been violated, Berman put Lopez's father, Edelmiro Lopez, on the stand. The mail carrier testified that he had asked Detective Bert Arroyo about an hour into the questioning of his son: "Should I have legal advice here before I go any further?" Arroyo did not respond, said Lopez, so he repeated the question and again got no response. The interview had continued.

Arroyo testified that when he told Lopez at the start of their session that his son had a right to have a lawyer present, the father said, "Does that mean I have to have a lawyer?" Arroyo replied that it was the father's choice and then he read that right a second time. Lopez, the detective testified, chose not to invoke the right.

Later in the interview, according to Edelmiro Lopez, Detective Hartigan aggressively pressed Steve Lopez about his alleged involvement in the rape. At that point, the father said, he grew angry and told the policemen: "My son will not provide any more answers." But Arroyo and Lopez Sr. differed about when this had been said. Arroyo testified that the remark was made after the teenager signed his written statement. But Edelmiro Lopez said it preceded the signing, giving Berman grounds to argue that the remark invalidated the written statement and rendered all subsequent questioning improper, including the video that was made in the father's presence. Since his client's right to counsel and right to remain silent had both been violated, argued Berman, neither the written nor the taped statement could be used as evidence.

Going into the pretrial hearings, Berman was also confident about a probable cause claim. It is well-settled law that police may not arrest a suspect unless they have good reason to believe he has been involved in a crime. Among the dozens of officers scouring the northern part of Central Park on the night of April 19 in search of a roving group of black and Latino teenagers were three officers who believed the suspects might have left the park. On Central Park West near 100th Street they saw a group of fifteen to twenty kids who fit the description walking north on the west side of the street, opposite the park. When the cops pulled up, the group scattered, except for Lopez and Santana. The two Puerto Rican boys claimed they were not with the others and, in fact, had been afraid the gang was about to attack them when the cops appeared. They claimed to have been on their way home from dates.

If Lopez and Santana were telling the truth the state's grounds for arrest were, at best, shaky, and thus jeopardized the admissibility of the boys' later incriminating statements. Lederer put the arresting officers on the stand at the hearing. Eric Reynolds and Robert Powers claimed they had seen Lopez and Santana with the group of teens who fled; they were not walking together separate from the group. Because of this, the prosecutors maintained, the cops knew the boys were lying, and their lie strengthened the officers' already reasonable suspicion.

Powers's testimony also strengthened the state's probable cause position regarding several other defendants. As Reynolds held Lopez and Santana on Central Park West, Powers and Ivelisse Flores had chased some of the others into the park and caught Kevin Richardson and Clarence Thomas. Powers testified that he was in a police car with the suspects when Thomas, crying, said: "I know who did the murder . . . it was Antron McCray." Added Richardson: "Yeah, that's who did it." The boys had thus given the police reason to suspect they were present at the assault of John Loughlin (Paula Harris had not yet been found).

Under Lederer's questioning, Powers's testimony had not done any comparable damage to Lopez. But on cross-examination, Berman inexplicably asked Powers a wholly unnecessary question: Did any of the other suspects implicate Lopez before his arrest was processed?

Yes, said Powers, one of the other kids, seeing Lopez and Santana in the back of a cruiser in handcuffs, said, "Those guys were with us."

Berman was stunned and immediately tried to weaken the statement. "How did you know they meant in the park and not on Central Park West?"

The answer was devastating to Berman's case: "Because," said Powers, "they said it: 'They were with us in the park.'"

Berman, who had received no prior notice of this statement, complained to the judge. Under the New York Court of Appeals's landmark *Rosario* decision, the prosecution is required to give the defense any written or recorded statements previously made by a witness that relate to the subject of his testimony. The rule covers a police officer's notes or the notes a prosecutor makes during an interview with a witness.

The reason for the lack of notice, Lederer explained to Galligan, was that the prosecutors had never heard the statement before. When Powers blurted it out on the witness stand, they were as shocked as Berman.

The defense lawyer scrambled for some way to have the testimony stricken. If Lederer did not know about the statement, he argued, she should have known. He cited a provision of the Criminal Procedure Law that requires the prosecutor to make a diligent effort to ascertain the existence of material to which the defense is entitled. That Lederer did not know about this statement, Berman claimed, demonstrated that she did not make a good faith effort to find out whether Powers had any information other than that which he had already provided.

But Lederer's counterargument was convincing. If she knew of the statement, which could be of great help to her probable cause argument, why would she not have brought it out during her own questioning of Powers? As to the procedural question, she said, "Because Mr. Berman in his vigorous cross-examination brings to mind something . . . which did not come out in questions put to [the witness] in preparation for a hearing, does not indicate that there was not due diligence by the prosecution."

Berman sought other grounds. First, he said Powers was not credible, implying that the officer had fabricated the statement when he realized there might be a probable cause problem. Second, Berman said the fact that Powers had not come up with the incriminating statement until this moment put the defense at an unfair disadvantage.

"I don't think the Court has to resolve whether Miss Lederer was not duly diligent," Berman told Galligan. "The Court can say this is so unlikely I'm not going to consider it. I think the best way to do it is to say, because of the surprise and late notice . . . the Court is going to strike that evidence as not reliable."

Lederer asked for a chance to respond to Berman's motion in writing and Galligan agreed to reserve decision until after the hearing. It was clear, however, that Berman had outsmarted himself by asking one question too many.

The cops had made a mistake when they questioned Yusef Salaam without notifying a parent first, and Bobby Burns meant to exploit that error. With the possible exception of Lopez, the state's weakest case was against Salaam. The prosecutors failed to get a videotaped interview with Burns's client, nor did they have a written statement. The case rested almost entirely on Salaam's oral statements to Detective McKenna. If those statements were ruled admissible a jury would hear McKenna testify that Salaam admitted hitting the female jogger twice with a pipe and fondling her breasts, as well as hitting John Loughlin three times in the head with his fist.

Burns's strategy was to deny Salaam ever said such things to McKenna. It would be a classic case of the cop's word against the suspect's. In such situations juries more often than not give the benefit of the doubt to the police officer. But the cops had given Burns the means to argue that his client's statements were illegally obtained and therefore must be suppressed.

Both New York state's Family Court Act and Criminal Procedure Law require that police immediately notify a parent or guardian when they arrest a person under age sixteen without a warrant. The Criminal Procedure Law also states that they must tell the parent or guardian where the juvenile is being detained. The Family Court Act further dictates that a juvenile in custody cannot be questioned unless he and a parent or guardian, if present, have been advised of the juvenile's *Miranda* rights.

The key phrase in that last sentence is *if present.* In the Central Park case, the defense team argued that the law should be interpreted to mean that a juvenile cannot be interrogated without a parent or guardian present. (In fact, several detectives would testify at trial that they believed that was the law.) What else was the point of the notification requirement? The reason for the requirement that a guardian be notified was to give the adult the opportunity to be present and, subsequently, to invoke or waive the child's *Miranda* rights. Certainly, the defense believed, the intent of the law was not merely to require the cops to call a parent and say, "We've got your kid down here," after which they could hang up the phone and conduct an interrogation!

The prosecutors argued that a requirement to notify is nothing more than a requirement to notify. In fact, the Family Court Act speaks of the need to make "every reasonable effort to give notice." It does not say those efforts must succeed before an investigation can continue. The law's inclusion of the phrase *if present* regarding reading of the *Miranda* rights to a guardian confirmed that position, according to this interpretation. The defense, Lederer and Clements believed, was trying to expand the law, the letter of which was clear: *If present* means *if present,* nothing more.

The debate over the proper interpretation of the law would continue well beyond the pretrial hearings. In Salaam's case however, the prosecutors were in trouble. They had to acknowledge that the boy was only fifteen, that the police interrogated him without first notifying his mother, who was not home when they picked him up at Schomburg Plaza, and that they denied his mother access to him during the interview. Lederer's argument in defense of that conduct was based on two points: First, she said Salaam was not under arrest when he made his first incriminating statements and therefore notice to a guardian was not required. Second, and more important, the prosecutors maintained that Salaam himself led the cops to believe that he was sixteen; he said so to one detective, they claimed, and he showed McKenna a transit pass with a date of birth that would have made him sixteen.

Burns's strategy, again, was denial. To get the statements suppressed he had to convince the judge that the cops were lying. He marched a host of witnesses to the stand to support his contention that the cops knew all along that Salaam was only fifteen and that they purposely isolated the boy from his family so they'd have an opportunity to trick him into a confession.

Based on the confrontations between Linda Fairstein and Salaam's mother and his Big Brother, David Nocenti, the prosecutors expected that Burns would have them testify at the pretrial hearing. Lederer was not prepared, however, for the testimony of Salaam's aunt, Marilyn Hatcher, and her fiancé, Vincent Jones. They were an intelligent, credible couple, Jones a postal service worker and Hatcher an employee of St. Luke's Hospital. On the night of Salaam's arrest, Hatcher and Jones arrived at the precinct before the boy's mother or Nocenti. They testified that they had a conversation with Detective John Taglioni in which they told him Salaam was only fifteen. Taglioni's response, according to Jones, was, "Well, we'll have to wait for the mother."

The defendant's sister, Aisha, testified that when Taglioni and other detectives came to their apartment to pick up her brother she heard him tell the cops he was fifteen. Sharonne Salaam testified that she told Fairstein immediately upon meeting her that her son was only fifteen and that she would not grant the police permission to question him. "Miss Fairstein said that she didn't need my permission to speak with him," testified Ms. Salaam, because the boy was holding what Fairstein referred to as "phony ID." And finally, in another move that surprised the prosecutors, Burns put Yusef Salaam on the stand to say he told the cops who picked him up that he was only fifteen.

Burns had laid a good foundation but he could not prevent Lederer from exposing cracks in the credibility of his witnesses. When Lederer called Taglioni to rebut the testimony of Hatcher and Jones the detective denied having had such a conversation with anyone and said he never met the couple. To counter Aisha's testimony, Taglioni said that Salaam told him at the apartment house that he was sixteen. Regarding Fairstein's supposed description of Salaam's transit pass as "phony ID," the prosecutors stated in their post-hearing brief: "Even if the police were going to question Yusef illegally, they would certainly not announce this fact to his mother as they were doing it."

Most damaging to Salaam's defense was the testimony of Nocenti, the civil lawyer who was a federal prosecutor. While jurors are often told not to lend added credibility to the testimony of law enforcement professionals simply because of their occupation, it is not implausible that a judge would consider it unlikely for a federal prosecutor to commit perjury. Under cross-examination by Lederer, Nocenti testified that at no time during his many hours at the police precinct, in none of his many discussions with Salaam's relatives about the boy's rights, did he tell anybody that Yusef was fifteen, nor was he ever asked his "little brother's" age, nor did he ever hear anybody even discuss the question. This strongly contradicted the testimony of Salaam's other witnesses, who claimed the issue was discussed almost constantly with policemen and Fairstein, including Hatcher's assertion that she brought it up because she knew the law treated fifteen-year-olds differently from sixteen-year-olds.

Finally, taking advantage of the opportunity to cross-examine the defendant, Lederer succeeded in getting Salaam to admit that Detective McKenna examined the transit pass with the false date of birth. Next, she coaxed Salaam to undercut his own case even further, asking whether he had ever previously used the transit pass to misrepresent his age.

Seeing the question coming, Burns rose to object before Lederer had finished speaking, a common breach of decorum in most courtrooms but one that irritated Galligan.

"Excuse me one second," said the judge to Lederer. Then to Burns he asked: "Are you standing for a reason?"

Replied Burns: "I'm getting ready to object at the conclusion of her question. I didn't want to interrupt her."

"How can you object if you don't know what the question is?" asked Galligan.

"Because it is starting out bad, Judge," said Burns.

It would finish badly, too. When Lederer was permitted to continue she asked: "Have you ever passed yourself off as 16 years old or older?"

"To girls, yes," answered Salaam.

As the pretrial hearings drew to a close on November 28, the prosecution gave the defense an FBI report detailing the results of DNA testing of the evidence. A few days later a banner headline in the *Amsterdam News*, the city's leading black newspaper, screamed: "Semen On Park Victim Traced To Her Boyfriend." The accompanying article by J. Zamgba Browne immediately fueled a conspiracy theory that would relentlessly dog the Central Park case.

Browne's story explained that DNA tests had failed to link any of the suspects to the rape of Paula Harris. The new technology, which could identify so-called genetic fingerprints in bodily fluids, had been applied to blood samples taken from Harris's boyfriend, the defendants and three suspects who had not been indicted. The DNA patterns in those samples had been compared at the FBI laboratory in Quantico, Virginia, to semen found in the victim's cervix and rectum and to a semen stain on the black tights she'd been wearing on the night of the crime. The DNA pattern of the semen on the tights matched the boyfriend; the other two semen samples could not be matched to anybody whose blood had been tested because the DNA reading was too weak.

The *Amsterdam News* story centered on an interview with Colin Moore, who maintained that the DNA evidence "strongly indicates that the victim and her boyfriend were involved in rough sex in the park that resulted in bloodshed." Moore speculated that the defendants may have accidentally happened upon the couple, wrote Browne, and "now find themselves being blamed for the alleged rape-assault." Thus began the infamous "The Boyfriend Did It" theory of the case, which took hold among a small but vocal group of blacks who were inclined to believe the defendants were being railroaded by a corrupt, racist criminal justice system.

The Boyfriend Theory was rejected out of hand by most New Yorkers because four of the six defendants charged with rape had admitted, on videotape, participating in that crime. But a great many African-American and Latino citizens were automatically suspicious of confessions obtained by police from minority teenagers. That distrust of the police was widespread and based on a long history of undisputed oppression and police brutality. Now the results of the DNA tests revealed that there was no conclusive physical evidence against the suspects. Add the facts that the victim could not remember the crime and that none of the other joggers or cyclists could identify the defendants awaiting trial. The cumulative effect of these holes in the state's case was to render the tapes suspect in the minds of many.

Complicating these matters, Lopez admitted nothing on his tape, Wise's story changed dramatically from one tape to the next and Salaam never made a video. It seemed possible, not only to the supporters of the suspects but to a few lawyers and journalists as well, that this might be that rare type of multidefendant case in which an innocent person could get run over by a steamrolling prosecution and a jury reacting emotionally to an atrocious crime. The group of trial spectators who would later be referred to by themselves and the press corps as "The Supporters" began to grow, sustained in part by the skeptical reporting of the black media, sometimes as biased in favor of the defense as the white media were in favor of the prosecution.

Back in April the *Amsterdam News* had been one of the first news organizations to report Harris's name. Since then the vast majority of media had continued to withhold her identity, with occasional exceptions among black newspapers and radio stations. To justify that decision black editors pointed to two factors: The defendants had a constitutional right to publicly confront their accuser, and the white media had unfairly abandoned another traditional policy when they publicized the names and photos of the juvenile suspects, even before they were indicted.

The identity of Harris's boyfriend, however, was conspicuous by its absence from the *Amsterdam News*'s DNA story of December 2. The reason was simple: Judge Galligan had held an unorthodox, private meeting with the prosecutors and agreed to delete the boyfriend's name from the FBI report before giving it to the defense team. Galligan also agreed to let the DA withhold the names of three suspects who had not been indicted on the rape charge but whose blood had been examined by the FBI: Clarence Thomas, Lamont McCall and Tony Montalvo. The judge then ordered the stenographic record of that meeting sealed.

Galligan's action was an extraordinary accommodation of the prosecutor's wishes. Jesse Berman was outraged. "It is obvious to me that those are people that the district attorney is thinking of using as potential witnesses in this case," said Berman. "And they decided to get blood from their three potential witnesses, send it down, to make sure their witnesses' blood didn't match any of the exhibits. . . . They got a judge to agree to let them redact the names. . . . We have a right to know who they did the tests on. . . . They can't take the names out . . . merely because they don't want us to know who their witnesses are!"

But Galligan said they could. Thus the name of Paula Harris's boyfriend was protected for a little while longer.

A week after the pretrial hearings Alton Maddox and Reverend Sharpton organized a community fund drive to raise bail for the defendants who were still in jail: Wise, Lopez, Santana and McCray.

Salaam's family had posted his $25,000 bail one month after the crime. Maddox had made a belated motion to reduce Michael Briscoe's bail in September, at which time the youth's grandmother put up the $5,000 that freed him after five months on Rikers Island. And a Catholic priest, Father Louis Gigante, had posted the $25,000 bail that freed Richardson two months after his arrest. Gigante, whose brother Carmine was the reputed boss of the Genovese crime family of La Cosa Nostra, said he took pity on the Richardsons when he read that they couldn't raise bail.

The McCrays had raised about $19,000 and on December 8 the community fund provided the $6,000 they still needed to bail out Antron. The organizers of the fund also offered to provide the $12,000 that Wise's family needed to make Kharey's bail, which Judge Galligan had reduced to $25,000 from $50,000. But the defendant's mother, Delores Wise, was a born-again Christian who had theological differences with Sharpton. For that reason she refused to accept the money, and her son would remain jailed on Rikers Island throughout his trial.

The balance in the bail fund was then offered to the Lopez family, which was now able to put up the $50,000 that got Steve out of Spofford Juvenile Center in the Bronx on December 21.

Peter Rivera finally made a bail application for his client, Raymond Santana, on December 9, asking Galligan to cut the teenager's bail from $25,000 to $10,000. The judge refused. Months later Rivera would tell Galligan that Santana could post $18,000, but the judge again refused to give him a discount.

———

On February 23, 1990, Judge Galligan ruled on the issues that had been argued in the pretrial hearings. His 116-page decision stated that all of the written and videotaped statements of the defendants were admissible at trial, and that the police had probable cause for all of the arrests. In upholding the arrests of Lopez and Santana, Galligan twice cited the response Officer Powers had given to Berman's unnecessary question. State law did not permit the defense to appeal the ruling before trial.

The judge also ruled that no defendant's *Miranda* rights had been violated. In the Lopez case, as in most matters at issue during the hearings, Galligan found the testimony of the police detectives more credible than that of the defense witnesses. Detective Arroyo, he ruled, had given the proper response to Edelmiro Lopez's question about whether he should get a lawyer for his son when he said, in effect: The choice is yours. The U.S. Supreme Court's decision in *Miranda* v. *Arizona*, noted Galligan, guarantees that "if a suspect indicates in any manner and at any stage of the process that he wished to consult with an attorney . . . there can be no questioning." But Galligan cited New York case law to support his finding that "a defendant's expression of such a desire must be unequivocal and explicit." Lopez's question did not meet that test, wrote Galligan.

On the related question of whether the elder Lopez rendered the videotape invalid because he had said several hours earlier, "My son will not provide any more answers," Galligan ruled that he did not. Relying on a slew of U.S. Supreme Court and New York cases, the judge quoted one that stated that such a finding "would transform the *Miranda* safeguards into wholly irrational obstacles to legitimate police investigative activity."

That left the allegation that the prosecution had violated the Family Court Act by holding the juveniles for such an extended period without taking them to court or to a detention center. The judge decided that "the Family Court Act provisions are not applicable to the prosecution of juvenile offenders in Supreme Court." But even if that law were applicable, added Galligan, it had not been violated. Because of what Galligan called "the special circumstances of this case"—an apparent reference to the number of suspects and the fact that the investigation grew as each teenager implicated others—the judge found that the questioning was completed "as expeditiously as possible."

As for Salaam's claims, the judge wrote: "Clearly, there is no dispute that the police made no effort to notify Salaam's mother." But Galligan also accepted the prosecution's positon that Salaam told the cops he was sixteen. Thus he rejected the central point—not to mention the credibility—of the testimony of Marilyn Hatcher, Vincent Jones, Sharonne Salaam and Yusef's sister, Aisha. "I find that the reliance by the police on his misrepresentation was reasonable," the judge concluded.

The question in Salaam's case then became: Even if the failure of police to notify his mother was the boy's fault, doesn't the law still require that his oral statement to Detective McKenna be suppressed? No, said Galligan. State courts had issued many conflicting rulings on the question and, as the prosecutors pointed out in their brief, New York's highest court, the Court of Appeals, had not resolved the issue. Galligan, citing some of the same cases on which the district attorney relied, ruled that suppression was not mandated by the existing case law. "Defendant should not derive a benefit from his deliberate falsification," wrote the judge.

Moore's coercion defense fell when Galligan decided that he did not believe the testimony of Kharey Wise. Addressing the argument that Wise's statements should be suppressed because he made them in response to a promise that he could go home if he did so, the judge wrote: "The only basis in the record for this proposition is defendant's own testimony, which I find incredible."

Likewise, Galligan rejected the contention that Wise had been slapped around, noting that the videotapes revealed no bruises on his face. As the prosecutor had hoped, the judge also cited the videotapes in the cases of other defendants as evidence that the teenagers were not speaking under duress. Somehow, the defense lawyers would have to convince a jury of something that was not apparent to the judge or anybody else who watched the tapes.

Perhaps the strongest point in the state's counterargument to the coercion defense was the testimony of Linda Fairstein and two detectives about the suspects' raucous behavior in the holding cell at the Twenty-fourth Precinct after all the videos had been completed. That episode, which so appalled Lederer, also repulsed Galligan, who cited it in response to the arguments of Moore and Berman. Regarding Lopez, Galligan wrote: "His allegation that he was reduced to passivity and subordination is entirely inconsistent with his loud and vulgar behavior when in the pens amongst his co-defendants." Again, the defense counsel were left to wonder why a jury would see it any differently.

———

Michael "Boogie Blind" Briscoe got into trouble again five months after leaving Rikers Island on bail. On March 4, 1990, Briscoe was arrested for selling a small amount of angel dust to an undercover cop.

His lawyer, Maddox, was getting into some hot water himself at about the same time. In the spring of 1990 the state attorney disciplinary panel in Brooklyn indefinitely suspended Maddox's license to practice law because he refused to cooperate with its probe of his conduct during the Tawana Brawley hoax.

Briscoe was thus left without a lawyer in the Central Park case. His attorney on the drug charge, Joseph Klempner, had been trying to work out a plea bargain and now sought to get a package deal from the DA to cover the Central Park charges as well.

Lederer and Clements were willing to deal with Klempner. Briscoe admitted being at the reservoir but denied having seen a female jogger. Because he was only charged with riot and the assault of David Lewis, he faced a maximum prison term of two and one-third to seven years. (Jermain Robinson, by contrast, had faced a possible term of three and one-third to ten years.) A real problem Briscoe posed for the prosecutors was that he had a strong argument for severance from the other six defendants, all of whom faced thirteen identical charges. The prosecutors wanted to avoid putting their witnesses—particularly Harris and the other victims—through any more trials than absolutely necessary. Briscoe was their lowest priority.

The DA and Klempner struck a bargain under which Briscoe pled guilty to the assault of Lewis and the drug sale in exchange for a sentence of one year in jail. Briscoe would not be required to testify. He would also get credit for the five months he had spent in jail awaiting bail and, if he earned the customary one-third reduction for good behavior, Briscoe would only have to serve three more months. He walked away from the Central Park case nearly unscathed, leaving people to wonder why Maddox hadn't been able to accomplish in the previous year what Klempner had done for the kid in a matter of weeks.

Defense motions for separate trials were based on a defendant's right under the Sixth Amendment to confront the witnesses against him. As a practical matter, that means a right to cross-examine those witnesses in front of a jury. When the witness is a codefendant, however, cross-examination may be impossible because, under the Fifth Amendment, a defendant cannot be forced to testify. Therefore, the defense argued, any defendants who implicated each other could not be tried together.

In its landmark 1968 ruling in *Bruton* v. *United States,* the Supreme Court held that the use at trial of a defendant's out-of-court statement that incriminates his codefendant is a violation of the latter's Sixth Amendment right, even when the court instructs the jury only to consider the statement against the person who made it. However, as DA Clements pointed out in the brief filed after the hearing, the Supreme Court left open the possibility that a defendant's statement could be edited to remove elements that were prejudicial to his codefendants. Citing three cases to support his position, Clements wrote: "New York courts have permitted joint trials when a *Bruton* problem can be remedied by redaction without prejudice to either the defendant or the co-defendant."

That was fine in theory but none of the defense lawyers thought it would work in the Central Park case. Most of them believed their clients would suffer from guilt by association just by sitting at the same table with a guy who described a gang-rape on videotape. How much could it help that the client's name had been removed from the other kid's tape?

Galligan, however, was willing to let the prosecutors try to edit the tapes in a way that would satisfy the *Bruton* ruling. He gave them three weeks to show him how it could be done.

The prosecutors had already begun to pore over the transcripts of the videos, looking for combinations of defendants that would require as little editing as possible. It was no small task. When Briscoe was still in the case, there were no fewer than 5,040 possible combinations of the seven defendants. Clements eventually drew up a series of charts, structured in the manner of a football betting pool, to tally how many times each defendant referred to the others on tape or in his written statements.

In their brief the prosecutors had held up the pairing of Santana and Salaam as an example of how editing could avoid a Sixth Amendment conflict. Since they did not know each other, Santana never mentioned Salaam's name, describing him on several occasions only as a tall black kid with a flattop haircut. Each instance of that description could be removed, wrote Clements, by eliminating only 250 words from a tape which ran to thirty-nine pages when transcribed. In each of Santana's written statements, such a redaction would require the elimination of only one sentence. "Clearly, in the case of these two defendants the *Bruton* problem can be remedied and they can be tried together without prejudice to either defendant," Clements concluded.

Clements also quoted the U.S. Supreme Court's ruling in *Richardson* v. *Marsh* to provide further justification for joint trials: "It would impair both the efficiency and the fairness of the criminal justice system to require, in all these cases of joint crimes where incriminating statements exist, that prosecutors bring separate proceedings, presenting the same evidence again and again, requiring victims and witnesses to repeat the inconvenience (and sometimes trauma) of testifying, and randomly favoring the last-tried defendants who have the advantage of knowing the prosecution's case beforehand."

But there was more than logistics at work in the state's groupings of the defendants. Even if they could find a way to justify trying the six remaining suspects together, that was not in the prosecution's interest. By the time all of the necessary editing was done, the videos would have lost much of their power to shock. Strategically, Lederer and Clements knew their strongest cases were against McCray, Richardson and Santana, whose videos were highly incriminating (as opposed to Lopez's) and unambiguous (as opposed to Wise's). It made sense to spread the weaker cases out, pairing them with stronger cases whenever possible.

In selecting the defendants they wanted to try first, the prosecutors followed Clements's formula, putting Salaam, against whom they had no video, with Santana and McCray. In addition to the benefit of being able to show a jury two horrifying tapes with very little editing, this combination put the silent Salaam into especially bad company. A by-product of the *Bruton* rule in this case was that the jury would not be told that neither Santana nor McCray ever placed Salaam at the rape scene by name.

Furthermore, by leaving out Richardson the prosecutors would have the luxury of symbolically trying him *in absentia.* Both McCray and Santana said on tape that Richardson had raped the victim, and Detective McKenna would testify that Salaam told him the same thing. If the jury believed that, Lederer could argue that the trio on trial were all guilty of rape as accomplices to Richardson. She had a built-in advantage in that Richardson would not have a lawyer in the courtroom to fight back.

Everybody was back in court on March 16 to hear Galligan approve, over defense objections, Lederer's request to try McCray, Salaam and Santana first as a group. Lopez, Wise and Richardson would be dealt with later. The judge set a trial date for the first trio of April 16, three days shy of the first anniversary of the Central Park wilding.

In the meantime, Paula Harris continued her remarkable recovery, having been released from Gaylord Hospital during the pretrial hearings. She was back at Salomon Brothers now, with a promotion to vice-president, and had moved into an apartment in swank Battery Park City.

None of this was lost on Delores Wise, who leaped to her feet at the end of the court proceedings shouting, "Where is she? Where is she? Ain't nobody raped her!" Out on the sidewalk she yelled at the press corps: "Her man raped her! She's back jogging, she's back working. . . . My boy spent a whole year in jail! For what? Give me my damn son back home!"

ACTING IN CONCERT

Part Two

CHAPTER 7

THE PEOPLE V. McCRAY, SALAAM AND SANTANA

——

BY LATE APRIL, LEDERER HAD BEEN BACK TO THE RAPE SCENE MANY times since the morning of the video sessions at the nearby Twenty-fourth Precinct. Each excursion had been for a specific reason. This time, barely a week after the first anniversary of the crime, the prosecutor was thinking of the opening statement she would deliver in a few weeks. She wanted to tell the jury exactly what this place had looked like, to victim and defendants, on the night of April 19, 1989, not what it was like on the visits she'd made last summer, when the woods below the crossdrive were thick, or in the fall, when the trees, going bare, provided even less cover than they had in the spring.

Tim Clements and a detective were down in the ravine, examining the scene of the rape, as Lederer wandered around on the crossdrive. The crossdrive runs downhill from east to west, winding around a ridge near the East Drive and settling onto a plateau before it crosses a stream and merges with the West Drive. The baseball fields from which the gang launched the assaults border the crossdrive near that spot where it flattens out. From the north edge of the ballfields there is a clear view of the illuminated roadway.

Lederer was looking for answers to some questions raised at the pretrial hearings that could not be left open at the upcoming trial. After knocking out Harris on the roadway and carrying her to a spot shielded by a large tree, why would the suspects drag her another 225 feet over difficult terrain down into the ravine? If they were struggling with her in the ravine for as long as twenty minutes, with Harris screaming for part of that time, why hadn't anyone heard the racket? If, as the pretrial testimony had established, cops were cruising that part of the park looking for kids who had chased the bikers, and firemen were dousing a brush fire no more than one hundred yards away, how could the suspects have avoided discovery?

As Lederer stood at the spot where Harris was grabbed, seventeen feet west of lamppost number 206, she looked into the woods at the rocky place behind the tree where, as Kharey Wise had told her, "They started a little rape." She was struck by how much the setting seemed like a theater. She was on a stage, under a spotlight, looking into the darkness of an audience. Likewise, when she looked back at the roadway from the woods, Lederer understood that the attackers would have felt exposed. The lamplight illuminated these front rows as well as the stage, making the distance between them seem much less than the seventy-five feet detectives had measured. Of course, she thought, the assailants had to move farther from the lights.

Down in the cool ravine it is hard to believe you are in Manhattan at all. The muddy place near the stream where Paula Harris had been found is well below the roadway, and the hillside in between is thick with trees, bushes and fallen branches. The West Drive seems far away and it's feasible that police officers might not hear a scream over the sound of their car's engine. Certainly from the crossdrive you couldn't *see* anybody down there. It's also darker in the ravine; even the moon shining through the overhanging limbs of oaks and maples seems farther away. Cops in cars and on scooters, forbidden by park regulations from driving off the paved paths, couldn't know what was happening down in the coolness of that hollow. And in the Central Park Precinct there were no foot patrols except at the zoo and Bethesda Fountain.

When showtime finally arrived in the Central Park case with jury selection on June 13, 1990, Lederer believed she had prepared as well as any lawyer could. She had never lost a rape case, though in more than two dozen felony trials she had been defeated three or four times.

The start of the trial had been delayed for seven weeks when Judge

Galligan reluctantly agreed to Lederer's request for another DNA test. A police department chemist, double-checking all of the prosecution's exhibits on the eve of trial, had discovered a semen stain on one of Paula Harris's socks. The stain had been missed the first time around, the chemist later explained; it was now visible because bacteria had turned it yellow. Galligan publicly remonstrated before postponing the trial. "It seems to me almost negligence on the part of the police or whoever is in charge of the lab," he complained. "A year later they are finding *this?*"

Given the disappointing results of the first series of DNA tests, the prosecutors had high hopes for this last chance to link the defendants scientifically with the rape. They were sorely disappointed. The FBI reported that, unlike the semen in the victim's cervix and rectum, the DNA pattern in the semen on the sock *was* strong enough to identify. But it did not match any of the suspects. Worse in one respect was that, unlike the semen on the tights, it didn't match the victim's boyfriend, either.

The press corps duly noted the inescapable conclusion that at least one guilty party had slipped through the hands of the police and prosecutors. There was little room for dispute on that point. Linda Fairstein thought it probable that the semen on the sock belonged to someone who had raped Harris. (The probability was later bolstered by the testimony of a DNA expert that the semen on the sock was "similar" to the unidentifiable semen in the victim's cervix.)

Lederer knew enough about what had happened that night to have already suspected that some of the culprits escaped. She was not convinced, however, that this semen belonged to somebody who had penetrated the victim. It could have come from a kid who masturbated at the scene and wiped himself off on the sock. Even so, she was disturbed by this irrefutable evidence that her net hadn't caught everybody.

The defense lawyers immediately seized upon this finding to mount a new assault on the state's case. Clearly, they said, the *real* rapist got away. These kids were scapegoats, forced by the cops to confess to a crime they didn't commit. This thesis, like the Boyfriend Theory, was embraced by the diverse group of trial spectators known as the Supporters. This contingent was by no means limited to the angry gadflies who came to the courthouse daily whenever a trial with a racial element was in progress. The Supporters also included sincere friends and neighbors of the defendants and their parents; people who thought the boys might have assaulted the male joggers but could not believe they'd rape and viciously beat a woman.

Harlem itself was split by the case. Tenants of Schomburg Plaza and the surrounding neighborhood—including some of the most staunch Supporters—were appalled by the violence. Less than a week after the crime they had organized a prayer vigil at Metropolitan Hospital to show support for the Jogger. But Harlemites also resented what they perceived as the media's trashing of the whole community and the placing of blame on an entire generation of black youth. This deep distrust of the criminal justice system, reflected constantly in the black media, surfaced in the courtroom as early as jury selection.

The case had received so much publicity that Galligan had to convene a pool of approximately three hundred potential jurors, from which the lawyers would select twelve panelists and four alternates. The first three days of the process were spent eliminating nearly two hundred people by means of a long questionnaire designed to root out prejudice, as well as those who'd already formed strong opinions about the case. The document included questions such as: Did you attend an integrated school? Do you believe persons are racially discriminated against in this country? Do you have any close personal friends who are persons of another race? Have you, or any of your family members or close friends, ever been involved in any type of organization which educates the public or counsels individuals with respect to rape, sexual harassment or sexual assault? If selected as a juror, will you feel pressured to return a verdict which reflects the views of your community, family or friends? If you are familiar with the allegations in this case, has it affected your use or enjoyment of Central Park?

The questioning of individual jurors proceeded without incident for a few days. Mickey Joseph asked jurors: "Can you accept the possibility that a person may say 'I'm guilty' and not be guilty?" Lederer sought assurances that jurors would not decide the case on the basis of racial issues. Bobby Burns got into an argument with Galligan about the propriety of his suggestion that the Central Park case got more publicity than the killings in Howard Beach or Bensonhurst because the Jogger was white.

The orderly process was disrupted on June 20 when one of the Supporters was arrested for jury tampering. Paul Antonio Williams, twenty-five, was caught passing out fliers to potential jurors who were sitting in the courtroom awaiting their turn to be questioned. The fliers claimed, among other things, that Galligan was biased against the defendants. (Williams later pled guilty to disorderly conduct and received a conditional discharge.)

After only eight days of jury selection, Galligan seated a panel of ten men and two women on Friday, June 22. The jury consisted of four whites, four African-Americans, three Latinos and one Asian.

With openings slated for Monday morning, Lederer turned her attention to other matters. She had never had to prove a rape solely with circumstantial evidence, yet that was the prospect she was facing. The DNA testing had only made things worse, opening rather than closing avenues of reasonable doubt. And the victim was not even able to remember the crime, let alone describe it convincingly for a jury. The defense might argue that the unidentified semen in Harris's body could have come from a partner with whom she had consented to have sex. And why not? The only way to refute such an argument was to put the victim on the witness stand, a prospect with which the Harris family was less than pleased.

———

"You will see as you watch that videotape and as you listen to the evidence how McCray coldly and calmly in an almost matter-of-fact way—in the presence of both of his parents—described how Paula Harris was struck with a pipe. About how her clothes were removed; and how, one after the other, several young men took turns getting on top of her while others held her down. And she was forced to submit to repeated sexual intercourse, as each person took his turn upon her."

With those few sentences Lederer gave the jury the state's case in a nutshell. The defendants, she promised, would bury themselves with their own words. The specific actions of each defendant were not as important as that they were all acting together—"in concert" as the law put it—with a shared intent to commit rape and murder.

Lederer's steady, monotonous voice was not loud but it had a sharp edge that carried it through the big, hot courtroom on the afternoon of June 25. Dressed in a dark, stylish suit, the short, thin prosecutor walked back and forth in front of the jury box, making eye contact with each panelist in turn, occasionally glancing at a pad of notes on the shelf attached to the railing.

Of the twelve rows of seats in the courtroom five were reserved for the media and even that was not enough to contain the expanded press corps. The New York regulars were joined by suburban reporters and others from such papers as the *Pittsburgh Gazette* (Harris's hometown paper), the *Chicago Tribune* and the *Los Angeles Times.* During the course of the trial reporters would visit from England, France, West Germany and Australia. Other observers on hand for opening statements included Lederer's proud father and Lisa Sliwa of the Guardian Angels. The Supporters filled several rows behind the defense table where Antron McCray, Yusef Salaam and Raymond Santana listened to the DA's remarks with their lawyers at their sides.

Mickey Joseph was working by court appointment because McCray's father and mother, who worked in a parking garage and a day-care center, respectively, didn't make enough money to hire a lawyer. The state would pay Joseph $25 per hour for preparation and $40 per hour for court appearances, a piddling sum in New York, where top-flight lawyers billed about $300 per hour. (Joseph would ultimately collect $28,972 for his representation of McCray, which consumed the equivalent of twenty-one weeks of eight-hour days and forced him to neglect the bulk of his criminal and divorce practice for months at a time.)

Bobby Burns, sixty, had been brought into the case by Salaam's mother, whose divorce he had handled four years earlier. Because Sharonne Salaam, who was raising three teenagers, did not earn enough money as a freelance fashion designer and part-time teacher at Parson's School of Design to pay his fees, Burns applied for court appointment. As a result he would collect the same minimal wages as Joseph. He was the only black lawyer in the courtroom.

Peter Rivera, a former prosecutor who ran losing campaigns for City Council in 1977 and for Bronx district attorney in 1988, had been in private practice for the past dozen years, keeping his political profile up with the presidency of the Puerto Rican Bar Association. He was hired by Santana's father, who believed his son's original court-appointed lawyer looked down on him because he was Latino. The elder Santana had withdrawn his life savings, between $10,000 and $12,000, to retain Rivera. Although the attorney denied any intention to run for office again, he was inexorably drawn to television cameras throughout the trial.

During her fifty-five-minute speech Lederer carefully described how her case would be proved, explaining that none of the joggers, cyclists or police who would testify could identify McCray, Santana or Salaam as the perpetrators of the crimes. But, she promised, the testimony of her witnesses, particularly the people who had been attacked in Central Park, would confirm many of the details recounted by the defendants themselves. While she acknowledged that the DNA evidence would not clinch her case, Lederer promised that photographs of the injuries inflicted on Harris, John Loughlin and David Lewis would show that the assaults occurred just as they were described by the defendants.

In a twist to the normal course of a criminal trial, Lederer was preparing the jury for a case that would be proved in reverse: rather than having the victims identify the defendants, the youths on trial would, in effect, identify their victims. "You will learn," she said, "by looking at the statements and watching the videos that these defendants corroborate the accounts given by the victims, because they themselves describe who they attacked and describe what they did to those people."

Next the prosecutor took the jurors chronologically through the events of April 19, 1989. After leaving Antonio Diaz, the man they called "the bum," unconscious, the boys kept walking through the park "still looking for another victim."

Lederer then surprised most of the press corps with the contention that the wilding spree ended not with the rape but with the assaults of Loughlin and Lewis at the reservoir. (In fact, not all of the defendants agreed with Lederer's timetable, which served to emphasize the viciousness of the marauders.) Even the horrors inflicted on Harris did not satisfy them, she said. "When they finished with Paula Harris, they left Paula Harris to die," she stated flatly, "stripped and naked in the dark and empty woods." The gang kept going, continued Lederer, "still looking for another victim."

She recapped what each defendant said about the reservoir assaults, concluding with McCray's description of somebody hitting Loughlin over the head with a branch again and again, until it broke. "As they had left Antonio Diaz and as they had left Paula Harris," said Lederer, "they left John Loughlin, lying unconscious in a pool of blood."

Kevin Richardson, who was awaiting a later trial, loomed large in Lederer's opening at this one. Confident that the judge's ultimate instructions to the jury would clearly explain the shared guilt of all accomplices, Lederer mentioned Richardson's name sixteen times. "Each of these three defendants described how Kevin Richardson raped Paula Harris that night," she said. Furthermore, she added, hair was found on Richardson's clothing that "matched and was consistent with" the victim's head and pubic hair.

"If you use your common sense," Lederer concluded, ". . . you will find that these defendants are guilty of the savage attempted murder, rape, sodomy, sexual abuse and assault of Paula Harris."

It was a strong opening, delivered without visible emotion. Lederer did, however, know how to stretch a point without breaking it. For example, she took a notorious comment by Salaam out of context and thus multiplied its already damning impact. "Yusef Salaam told the police that someone struck her with a brick," Lederer told the jury. "And after he described to the detective what he and the others had done to Paula Harris, he told Detective McKenna that it was fun."

In fact, Salaam did not specifically tell McKenna the assault on Harris was fun. As the detective would later testify, after Salaam finished relating the events of that night, McKenna asked him how he could have become involved in such a thing. "He said it was something to do; it was fun," McKenna said.

Lederer was leading the jury and to many it seemed as though she were on a crusade.

Before the defense attorneys had a chance to address the jury, Joseph and Burns suffered a significant defeat in the privacy of Galligan's chambers. Both had requested permission to call expert witnesses to testify that their teenage clients were susceptible to psychological coercion, thus indicating that their self-incriminating statements were neither voluntary nor truthful. This strategy was one of the few open to the defense lawyers, since it provided a feasible explanation of why somebody would confess to a crime he hadn't committed.

McCray, now sixteen, had been examined by Naftali G. Berrill, a clinical psychologist in Brooklyn who was experienced in testifying for both prosecutors and defense lawyers. Berrill wrote in his report that McCray had an IQ of 87, which he considered "in the borderline to average range of intellectual functioning."* The series of tests Berrill gave McCray also demonstrated that the ninth-grader was far behind in basic academic skills: he read at a fourth-grade level, spelled at a third-grade level and did arithmetic at a seventh-grade level.

*Psychologists note that an IQ does not indicate a subject's intelligence so much as it reflects his performance on tests, measured against the examiner's expectations for someone in that age group. A so-called average IQ is anywhere from 90 to 100 points, with some experts considering the range as wide as 85 to 110 points.

When he is yelled at, McCray told the psychologist, he "stutters" and "doesn't answer back." Berrill reported that the teenager lacked self-confidence and "tends to rely on his parents a great deal for emotional support and sustenance." That finding would support Joseph's contention that McCray had succumbed to his father's urgings that he cooperate with the police and incriminate himself in the rape.

"It is conceivable, if not likely," Berrill wrote, "that the interaction between Antron's personal vulnerabilities (cognitive and emotional) and the novel, anxiety-provoking situation that existed at the police station during his two days or so of questioning would have produced the requisite conditions for Antron's making inaccurate or markedly distorted statements about his involvement in the Central Park incident.

"Thus," the psychologist concluded, "definite questions about the validity of his statements to the police and district attorney must be considered when reviewing both the written and videotaped material." As is the way with expert testimony, Berrill's report had said what the lawyer who hired him hoped it would. Had it not done so, Joseph would not have offered it as evidence.

Tim Clements, in a brief filed during jury selection and again during the opening-day conference in Galligan's chambers, attacked Berrill's report on three main grounds: The DA had not received sufficient warning of such testimony; the expert's conclusions were not stated with the required "reasonable degree of scientific certainty"; and the jury was capable of deciding whether the confessions were voluntary without the expert's help.

On the question of timeliness Joseph had a strong counterargument. As court-appointed counsel, he was entitled to state funds to hire experts and investigators, but each expenditure had to be approved by the trial judge. Joseph reminded Galligan that he had refused to authorize the expert's fees on at least two occasions in the previous year. The judge finally approved his third or fourth application a month before trial, the attorney noted.

In ruling that the testimony was inadmissible, Galligan denied he was considering timeliness a factor but he apparently accepted Clements's other arguments. The judge described Berrill's conclusion as "equivocal" and "speculative" and said the psychologist's report "does not relate to any mental disease, defect or condition which renders the defendant incapable of understanding or waiving his constitutional rights or incapable of making a voluntary statement." (If the judge had admitted the evidence the trial would have been delayed so the prosecution could have its own experts examine the defendant.)

Having already lost what would have formed the cornerstone of his defense, Joseph made a short opening statement in which the word "rape" was not uttered and the content of his client's video was not mentioned. Joseph was smarter and better versed in the law than Burns or Rivera. At bench conferences throughout the long trial he would take the lead in battles with the prosecutors, trying to protect the interests of Santana and Salaam as well as his own client. Partly this was because the fate of his client was tied to that of the other defendants as a consequence of the joint trial; partly it was because he felt an ethical obligation to assist his co-counsel when possible.

But Joseph was by no means an imposing presence in the courtroom. At five feet three inches, Joseph was no taller than Lederer and his high voice did not naturally command respect. After promising the jury that no physical evidence would link his client to the crime, Joseph turned to the incriminating statements. "I suggest to you, when you hear the evidence relating to these statements, you will see that it's not as clean as the prosecution would want you to believe." He went on to describe a group of detectives under intense pressure to solve the case quickly "no matter what it meant to the rights of individuals." Joseph gave the jury a scenario in which McCray's parents were manipulated and tricked by the police with threats and false promises until Antron's father finally told his son, "Just tell them what they want to hear. That's the only way you're coming home. You have got to cooperate."

As had Lederer, Joseph asked the jurors to apply their common sense to the evidence. "I'm not going to tell you that a police officer will come in here and say . . . I admit I pushed this kid too far. [But] if you analyze the testimony . . . that's what you are going to find."

In making his case for Salaam, Burns had also applied for permission to enter psychiatric evidence, but Galligan rejected the bid on the same grounds with which he had thwarted Joseph.

Salaam was sixteen when he was examined by Ramona Whaley, a psychologist with a family practice in Harlem, who reported that his IQ was an above-average 110. Whaley's report described a young man with a domineering mother and low self-esteem, a teenager who "has not been allowed to grow and develop to a real mature level." Whaley diagnosed Salaam as suffering from "identity disorder," which she attributed partially to his single-parent home. "The absence of parental authority adds to his sex role confusion," wrote Whaley. "However, Yusef has a strong sense of right and wrong and has learned to follow the rules projected by his mother in order to live in the family setting."

The psychologist also found in Salaam a "social immaturity," which led him to "willfully listen and give in to authority figures, i.e., his mother, school authorities and law enforcement persons." Ultimately, Whaley concluded, "Yusef's psychological problems . . . could probably affect his ability to make a voluntary statement."

Galligan's refusal to permit Whaley's testimony was yet another significant ruling that Burns found extremely frustrating. As a tactical defeat, however, it was secondary to the judge's acquiescence to the DA's request to try Salaam with McCray and Santana. Like the other defense lawyers, Burns wanted his client to be tried alone and he considered the judge's denial of severance blatantly unfair.

When Lederer, during her opening statement, quoted McCray using the pronoun "we" several times as he described the beating of Loughlin, Burns had risen to object. Both prosecutors and the three defense attorneys crowded onto the little platform in front of Galligan's bench, so the jurors could not hear. The court stenographer took up a position behind the bench to record the sidebar conference.

This subverts the purpose of editing the tapes, Burns had told the judge. By emphasizing the fact that McCray repeatedly says "we" the district attorney is in effect implicating Salaam and Santana, he argued.

Galligan disagreed. "I said [before trial] that I was permitting these defendants to be tried together," said the judge. "To the extent there are allegedly thirty-odd people involved in the park . . . there is nothing about 'we' that would identify any person other than [his being] one of 33 people."

Responded Burns: "Other than the fact that there is three of the 'we' on trial before this jury."

Galligan's denial of severance would undoubtedly become an appellate issue if Salaam were convicted but Burns could not afford to hold his complaint. If he failed to make a record of his objection now, any subsequent appeal would lack credibility. Burns's bitterness over his client's predicament would grow as the trial proceeded but for now he, like Joseph, was forced to plow ahead, despite the grating conviction that he wasn't being permitted to mount a complete defense.

In his disjointed opening statement Burns described a police conspiracy against his client, encouraged by vindictive media. He briefly alluded to the race issue, noting that the police investigation of what the black and Latino boys had been up to in the park intensified sharply after the white Jogger was found. Top police brass and the district attorney were quickly called in, said Burns, and the investigation's "command center" was moved out of the Central Park Precinct. "All of the police officers who worked on this case worked together," said Burns, as though the jury should see something sinister in that fact.

Wrapping up, the inarticulate Burns told the panel, "That, in short, and in brief, is the defense case as it relates to the defense in this case."

Peter Rivera had made no attempt to present psychiatric evidence of Santana's susceptibility to coercion. A former police officer and federal drug agent, Rivera had decided to rely on the argument that his client's *Miranda* rights had been violated by overzealous cops.

Rivera was better on his feet than Joseph or Burns and his fifteen-minute opening was simple and clear. A Puerto Rican, as were Santana and two of the jurors, Rivera suggested that his client was arrested only because he was a Latino walking with a group of other minority kids in the vicinity of Central Park on April 19. Santana, fourteen years old at the time, had been held for fifteen hours before his interrogation began, Rivera noted, and did not eat or sleep until he'd been in custody for twenty-two hours. His videotaped interview with Lederer began twenty-eight hours after his arrest. Santana's grandmother, who spoke very little English, and his father were cruelly manipulated until the police had the incriminating statements they needed from young Raymond, charged Rivera.

"The first concept I want you to keep in mind is the awesome power of the police department and the district attorney," Rivera told the jurors. That power was used, he said, to squeeze an incriminating statement from Santana and would now be employed again to try to convince the jury that the statement was voluntary. But, Rivera promised, the jurors would conclude that the statement was coerced "because much of the language that appears in that statement came from the lips and the mouths of the police officers."

There was more to Rivera's defense than this unadorned outline of corruption, but he chose to save his most sensational allegations.

CHAPTER 8

A PARADE OF
VICTIMS

THE JURY SPENT MOST OF THE NEXT THREE DAYS, June 26–28, LISTENING
to seven joggers and cyclists called by the prosecution to describe the
events of April 19, 1989. Mickey Joseph tried to keep this parade of
innocent, clean-cut witnesses off the stand on the grounds that, with
the exceptions of Loughlin and Lewis, they would be testifying to
crimes with which the defendants were not charged.

But the DA's decision to put the riot count in the indictment paid
off. Lederer argued at the bench that the testimony of these witnesses
was necessary to prove first-degree riot, which state law defines as
"tumultuous and violent conduct" engaged in by ten or more persons,
causing "public alarm" and resulting in physical injury to someone
other than the participants.

The prosecution's other ground for the relevance of the testimony
was that it would confirm the accuracy of the statements made by the
defendants, all of whom described the events with remarkable
similarity to the testimony of the state's witnesses. "Essentially what
we have is a reverse identification, by the defendants, of the victims,"
Lederer told Judge Galligan.

As they marched one after another to the stand and told their harrowing stories, these witnesses seemed to personify the significance of the case to middle-class New Yorkers. They had survived a common urban nightmare—the threat of random violence—and their experiences confirmed the notion that such fear was rational. They also reinforced the belief, held for decades by most New Yorkers, that the city's parks were unsafe at night, that they were the dark territory of dope addicts and thieves.

The witnesses also dramatized the racial and class aspects of the Central Park case, which, though only gingerly touched on in the courtroom so far, dominated the hallway discussions among reporters, spectators and the Supporters, some of whom had taken to describing the trial as a "legal lynching." It would be two weeks before the jury would see Antonio Diaz, the only victim who was not a gainfully employed white person.

William Glaberson deftly captured the symbolism several weeks later in *The New York Times*. "Their presence in the courtroom seemed to announce what it was about this case that gripped people from the start," he wrote. "They were handsome and pretty and educated and white. And if they believed they owned the world, they had reason to." He went on to describe the witnesses as "part of the wave of young professionals who took over New York in the 1980s. Some among them had seemed convinced that if you worked hard enough and exercised long enough, you could do anything; even go into the park at night."

The witnesses were called in a sequence corresponding to Lederer's chronology. She began with James Lansing, twenty-seven, a salesman for Merrill Lynch who lived in the same East Side apartment building as Paula Harris. Lansing testified that Harris left the building that night at about 8:55, telling him she was going to the park to jog.

Next up was Michael Vigna, a clean-shaven thirty-one-year-old with close-cropped hair who, in April 1989, was a college student and part-time bicycle messenger who rode competitively in his spare time. Vigna testified that he was making the first of three six-mile laps around the park on his custom-made Italian racing bike at about 9:05 P.M. when he was harassed by "a gang of youths."

As she would over the next six weeks with each witness who had been in the park, Lederer asked Vigna to approach the colorful, four-by-six-foot map propped on an easel beside the witness stand and indicate to the jury where he had encountered the gang. With the long wooden pointer handed him by a court officer, Vigna indicated a spot on the East Drive slightly north of the 102nd Street Crossdrive.

Vigna said he was pedaling at about twenty-five miles per hour when he first saw the kids on the grass on the side of the road, "jumping about, joking with each other." As Vigna got closer the kids spread out across the roadway, forcing him to the extreme left side of the drive.

"When I was passing by," said Vigna, "one of the youths struck his arm out in the direction of my face and just barely missed my head. And I could in fact hear the sound of his fist, the force of his blow, just nearly nicking the side of my head."

He escaped and kept riding. Twenty minutes later, as Vigna approached the same spot on his second lap, he saw a police car and stopped to tell the officer what had happened. "When you spoke with that officer was there anybody else in that police car?" asked Lederer.

"Yes there was," he replied. "An older Hispanic man in the back seat whose face was bloodied."

Police Officer Ray Alvarez, who had just picked up Antonio Diaz, had not asked Vigna for his name, address or phone number. This oversight was typical of the actions of many of the uniformed officers who worked the case, a sloppiness that had later complicated the prosecution's search for witnesses.

Vigna had been initially turned away the following night when he stopped at the Twenty-fourth Precinct to report the incident again. He was taking his usual route home from the park after another workout on the night of Thursday, April 20, when Vigna noticed a crowd of reporters and television cameras outside the Twenty-fourth Precinct on 100th Street. Having by then heard about the attacks in the park the previous night, he went inside and asked the desk officer if he should file a report. The officer asked Vigna whether he would be able to identify any of the kids who had harassed him. When Vigna said no she lost interest and sent him on his way without having taken his name.

Outside, however, Vigna decided to ask a news photographer about the brush fire he'd seen the night before on the West Drive, just north of the 102nd Street Crossdrive. When some reporters thus learned that he had been in the park on the fateful night, Vigna recalled, "it was like bees on honey. Media types attacked me. Only then did two plainclothes detectives come over."

The next witness, Gerald Malone, a strapping young man in a chic European suit, exuded confidence as he walked the few steps to the witness stand from a private courtroom entrance beside the jury box. He stood about six-two and weighed perhaps two hundred pounds, his straight brown hair stylishly cut away from his clean-shaven face but hanging well below his collar in the back. At age thirty-five, Malone had been in the advertising business for ten years and was a semiprofessional bicycle racer. (Less than two months after testifying in this trial he would win an important international race in the Soviet Union, modestly commenting later that he'd "had a good day.")

Malone had been on the front seat of a tandem racer with his fiancée, Patricia Dean, on the back seat when they saw the group of thirty to forty kids on the righthand side of the East Drive. Malone was drifting the bike to the left when the kids began to spread out across the road, some pulling the hoods of sweatshirts over their heads to conceal their faces. In an instant the boys started yelling and dropped into crouching stances, as if to spring into attack. Suddenly Malone felt a burst of power from his fiancée and responded in kind, boosting the bike's speed from twenty-eight miles per hour up to perhaps thirty-five. Still, he doubted they would escape.

"My first thought was: there was absolutely no way I was *not* going to go down," Malone explained to the jury. If those kids were going to force him and Dean off the bike, Malone decided, he was not going to make it easy. "What I did was, as we were sprinting as hard as we could, up to the last minute I didn't commit myself to which way I was going. I acted like I was going to go to the outside. And within about maybe ten feet of them I veered and tried to hit the first guy in the very front. I was going to use him as my mattress."

Like a karate fighter about to deliver a powerful blow, Malone let out a screech of his own as the bike bore down on the group. "I just yelled," he said. "I'm just throwing everything out, going as hard as I can."

At the last second the kid Malone had chosen as a target jumped out of the way and the bike slipped through the gap, with three or four teens running alongside, grabbing at Dean's shoulders and legs.

How, Lederer asked him, did you choose the one you tried to run over?

"He seemed to be the one that was basically calling the shots or leading everybody," said Malone. "He seemed to be the energy."

"Did you notice anything about that particular person?"

"He was particularly taller than anyone else."

The jurors had no way of knowing whether six-foot-three-inch Yusef Salaam was the tallest of the thirty-three boys in the park that night. But they could plainly see that he towered over Raymond Santana on his left and Antron McCray on his right.

Malone stopped at a police call box on the West Drive: "I told them that we were just attacked by a group of thirty to forty black kids, 13 to 19 years old; that I thought they were a threat to somebody else in the park and if they didn't break them up they were going to hurt somebody." Only minutes later, according to the prosecution's chronology, Paula Harris was attacked.

Although the cop who answered the phone at the Central Park Precinct at least asked for Malone's name and phone number, he didn't *seem* to consider what happened very serious. So, when the couple came across a police officer on a scooter they stopped and told her of the encounter also. Ivelisse Flores, a smallish woman who had only been a police officer for four years, threw her coffee cup to the ground and took off in the direction of the attack. If she runs into that gang by herself, thought Malone, she could be in real trouble.

Joseph's purpose in his cross-examinations of Vigna and Malone was to establish two facts: first, that the group of kids in the park was very large, and second, that neither witness could identify McCray. To the consternation of many Supporters, Joseph did not dispute any of the events to which the two men testified, nor did he try to belittle their fears. He did, however, want the jury to understand that neither witness could specifically link McCray to what had happened. No more than five teens combined had made physical contact with the cyclists. The fact that small subgroups of kids had attacked these people did not necessarily mean Joseph's client was one of the assailants, even if he did admit to being part of the larger gang.

Peter Rivera was trying to convey much the same thing on Santana's behalf but, perhaps because he had taken so few cases to trial over the previous decade, he botched the job and the whole defense team paid the price. Neither Joseph nor Rivera employed the time-honored tactic of simply having his client stand and asking the witness if he recognized the defendant. In such a situation, Vigna and Malone would each have said no.

Joseph asked the witnesses whether they could identify anybody in the gang and both said they could not. Rivera went a step further, a step that took him off the edge of a steep cliff. Rivera showed Malone five Polaroid snapshots taken at the Central Park Precinct of the kids who were arrested on the night of April 19: Santana, Kevin Richardson, Steve Lopez, Clarence Thomas and Lamont McCall. In response to Rivera's questions, Malone acknowledged that he had been shown the photos late that night, after police had called him at home and asked him to come back to the park to make a report. "You were not able to identify anybody?" asked Rivera. "No," said Malone.

As Rivera was taking the snapshots back, Malone noticed a large, round, white logo on Richardson's blue windbreaker. He had a flashback to that night in the park; he could see the kid wearing that windbreaker, with a larger jacket pulled up over his head, crouching about ten feet behind the big kid at whom Malone had aimed his bike. When court was dismissed that day Malone told Lederer that he had recognized the logo in the photo.

At the bench the next morning Lederer asked the judge for permission to recall Malone and have him testify that the kid in the snapshot had been one of his would-be assailants. Joseph scrambled for evidentiary reasons with which to prevent this testimony, while Rivera and Burns, who represented Salaam, voiced suspicion about this lucky break for the prosecution. "I did not show [the photos] to him," Lederer pointed out. "Mr. Rivera did."

Complaining that the prosecutors were "trying to make a connection" between the three defendants now on trial and Richardson, who would be tried later, Joseph argued that the defense had not been given the Polaroids until a few days before and was therefore at an unfair disadvantage. But Lederer told the judge all of the defense lawyers had been notified "probably a year ago" and only Jesse Berman, representing Lopez, had taken the trouble to visit her office to look at the snapshots.

Burns demanded to know why Malone had not noticed the logo at the precinct on April 19, particularly if, as Lederer now revealed, he had told detectives that night that one kid was wearing a windbreaker with a logo that stood out. Lederer's explanation was that Malone had been focusing on the faces the first time he saw the photos, not the clothing.

Galligan allowed Malone's testimony and he also permitted Lederer to tell the jury that the kid wearing the logo was Richardson. The prosecution then put the photo into evidence so that eventually the jurors would see it themselves.

Rivera asserted that Lederer knew all along that if Malone were shown the photo he would identify the logo. "I think D. A. Lederer tried to sandbag me with this witness on this matter," he told Galligan angrily, "and I would ask that this testimony be stricken." Rivera did not offer an explanation for why, if Lederer had known Malone could identify Richardson, she had not shown him the snapshot herself. The judge refused Rivera's request.

The defense had to live with Rivera's blunder, which bolstered the prosecution's contention that the trio on trial was at least guilty by association with Richardson. The damage was compounded when Lederer's next witness, Patricia Dean, took the stand.

As she and Malone sped through the gang on the tandem bike, Dean testified, three boys to her right and one to her left were grabbing and tugging her, trying to knock her to the ground. Lederer showed Dean the photo of Richardson, which she did not remember having seen before. "Do you recognize anything worn by the individual in that photograph?"

"I recognize the type of logo . . ." Dean answered. "I don't know if this is the logo but this is exactly what I recall it looking like."

What was the person wearing that logo doing to you? asked Lederer.

"He was the thinner one, who was pushing my shoulder and pushing at my thigh."

The next witness, David Lewis, testified that when he walked into the Central Park stationhouse shortly after 9:30 on that Wednesday night, the cop at the desk said, "Here comes another one." Lewis told the officer he had just been jumped by a bunch of kids at the reservoir. The cop, who knew there were already plenty of patrolmen out looking for the gang, was not interested in the details. Lewis left after no more than one minute in the precinct. Nobody had asked for his name or phone number.

On Friday morning, Lewis testified, he saw in the newspaper a hot-line phone number for people with information about the case. He called and two detectives eventually came to his home to take a report. Since the defense planned to argue that the police had told the kids what to say on the videotapes, it was important to the prosecutors to establish that witnesses such as Lewis did not file detailed reports until after the videos had been made.

Lewis, thirty-one, was tall, thin and WASPish, with straight blonde hair cut short. He worked in a commercial bank in midtown Manhattan.

As he approached the pumphouses on the north edge of the reservoir, Lewis testified, he heard somebody say "Ready!" and spotted two boys in football stances on the side of the jogging path. Somebody threw a rock at him but it missed and hit the fence along the edge of the water. "You want to race?" asked the nervous Lewis. "Yeah," said one of the boys menacingly, "we'll race alright."

Lewis began to run faster. Suddenly he saw about five black kids coming up onto the path ahead of him and another blocking his route. "It all happened very quickly . . ." he recalled. "As they were coming up the path I just panicked and I ran. I ran by them and I tried to get by the one that was immediately in front of me. . . . I tried to run between him and the fence. As I went by him, he hit me in my arm." The force of the blow snapped his arm back.

"At this point I was just sprinting as fast as I possibly could," Lewis continued. "Right after I got by him I ran for maybe twenty yards. I looked over my right shoulder, I saw, I'm guessing eight to ten of them, running after me . . . I ran for another hundred, hundred and fifty yards until I didn't hear footsteps behind me."

Lederer showed the jury two photos of a deep, dark bruise extending from Lewis's right shoulder to his elbow. X-rays revealed no broken bones. Lewis didn't know what he had been hit with, but the jury was to hear lots of testimony about a pipe being used on the joggers that night.

David Good, a thirty-four-year-old geotechnical engineer, next testified that he was running around the reservoir when he encountered a group of perhaps ten black kids. One shouted, "You better run faster than that!" Within seconds the kids were throwing sticks and stones at the runner and a large branch hit Good's leg. He kept running but turned around to call the youth who hit him "a miserable piece of shit."

On his way to the Central Park stationhouse to report the incident Good came across a male cop on a scooter. He told the officer what happened. The cop said he'd already heard about the gang and drove off toward the reservoir. He did not take Good's name and detectives didn't locate the witness until May.

The next witness was Robert Garner, a thirty-year-old research analyst for British Airways who spoke with a pronounced English accent. At five feet eight inches and weighing approximately 140 pounds, he was smaller than Malone, Lewis or Good, but the jury would soon see that, considering what happened to John Loughlin, greater size was not likely to have protected Garner from the beating he took when he was waylaid by a group of fifteen to twenty kids on the northern side of the reservoir.

There was a lot of yelling, Garner recalled. He thought somebody shouted "Merry Christmas!" before he was hit with a rock. Once the gang had him surrounded, a tall kid began punching him in the face and chest while others held him.

"I may have fallen down. I'm not certain of that," said Garner. "But I spoke to the one who was hitting me. I said, 'What do you want from me?' He said, 'Money of course.' They laughed." It seemed to Garner the kids were having a good time.

When they realized he had no money one of the kids said, "Get outta here!" Garner ran as fast as he could until he reached the sidewalk on Central Park West. From there he walked home. He didn't report the incident to police until nearly two weeks later.

"Mr. Garner," asked Lederer, "at the time . . . what was your feeling about what was happening to you?"

"I was terrified," he replied. "I thought I was going to die."

The most dramatic testimony came from John Loughlin. A former U.S. Marine, Loughlin taught physical education at a public school in a rough neighborhood in upper Manhattan. Standing six feet four inches and with an athletic build at 190 pounds, Loughlin had been an imposing presence to the kids who saw him jogging slowly around the reservoir. Several of the defendants had told Lederer that they thought he might be a cop because he was wearing a green fatigue jacket and camouflage pants. They were going to leave Loughlin alone until Jermain Robinson got up the nerve for a confrontation.

Loughlin was running a route he had followed for years when he saw a gang beating up Garner. "It looked like someone was in trouble there, so I stopped," he testified.

Before Loughlin could see what was going on down in those shadows below the track he heard a voice close to him. "What are you lookin' at? What are you, one of those vigilantes?"

He did not respond, said Loughlin, but at least two defendants had told Lederer that the guy in the army jacket had said something that angered Robinson. (The jury would later hear McCray say on his video that Loughlin said "something like he thought he was bad.")

"Here is one of those vigilantes," Robinson called out, and three or four kids shouting "Vigilante!" began walking toward Loughlin.

"And what is the next memory that you have?" Lederer asked.

"The next thing I remember," said Loughlin, "I was face down on the ground and being hit in the back of the head twice." Loughlin put up his hand to guard his head and felt the slamming force of a smooth, blunt object. It could have been a baseball bat, he said. Loughlin lost consciousness, and his next memory was staggering up to an auxiliary police car. His Walkman radio was gone.

The prosecutors set up another easel between the witness stand and the jury box, balancing on it a white board approximately three feet high and five feet wide. On this board they attached, with Velcro stickers, eleven nine-by-fourteen-inch glossy, color photographs of Loughlin's various injuries. Burns had tried in vain to keep the graphic photos out of evidence on the grounds that "they are only calculated to inflame the passions of the jury against the defendants." Lederer countered that the photos were necessary to "describe the assault" since Loughlin's memory was limited to the blows that knocked him out.

The witness stood beside the easel with a microphone in his hand and, one by one, pointed to the photos and described the injuries they depicted. Several jurors were shaking their heads or wincing as Loughlin detailed the bloody damage done to the back of his head, both shins, his right arm, an ankle, his right knee, his back and his rib cage. Most dramatic were the bruises around both eyes, which were described the next day in *Newsday* as looking "as if they had been outlined with charcoal."

"As you sit here today, on June 27, 1990," asked Lederer, "do you suffer any lasting injuries as a result of the attack on April 19, 1989?"

"Yes," he replied. "Continuing pain in my right knee, difficulty moving it, and pain in . . . the left side of the back of the head."

The last task the prosecutors had for Loughlin was to tell the jury about the lineup in which he had identified Robinson. This sparked another bench conference, at which Joseph argued that the identification was irrelevant to the guilt or innocence of his client. Furthermore, he said, the prosecutors were only seeking to use this evidence "to bolster the credibility of a witness they may later call."

"What about that?" asked the judge.

"To be honest," Lederer replied, "I hadn't looked at it that way." She offered to agree to an instruction to the jurors that they should not add any weight "to the testimony of Jermain—if he testifies" because of the identification.

Her purpose in offering the lineup testimony, Lederer explained, was to counter the defense Rivera had described in his opening statement. She reminded her adversaries that Rivera had told the jurors that the police had dictated to Santana the details of his incriminating statement. But Santana had told the cops as early as the afternoon of April 20 that Robinson had beaten Loughlin. The police, however, did not know who Robinson was at that time and didn't pick him up until the afternoon of April 21. Therefore, Lederer said, Loughlin's identification of Robinson proves that Santana was telling the truth.

"Is it your position that this testimony is only offered so far as Santana is concerned?" asked Galligan.

No, replied Lederer. McCray and Salaam had also said Robinson beat Loughlin—though they only knew Robinson as "the kid with the gold caps"—so the identification confirmed the accuracy of their statements as well. The judge allowed the lineup testimony.

As the first week of trial drew to a close, the jury heard a few final details about the horror show at the reservoir. An auxiliary police officer testified that Loughlin sat in the back of his car until transportation to the hospital was arranged.

"We proceeded back to the precinct and we had to hose down the back seat of the car and the outside, where he had touched the handle and such," said Anthony Falese.

Why? asked Lederer.

"It was very messy. There was blood all over."

The next witness was Mark Carlson, a police officer who interviewed Loughlin as he sat in Falese's car. After a while the cops had given up on the ambulance they had called and had driven Loughlin to St. Luke's Hospital.

Lederer asked Carlson to describe how Loughlin looked when he first saw him. "He was bleeding heavily from the head area," said Carlson.

"The person you described was bleeding from the head? Did you notice anything about the head of the person?"

"It was heavily soaked by blood."

There was no reason for Lederer to ask the question a second time, just to get what was essentially the same answer. Perhaps she was hoping that Carlson would repeat the phrase he had used at the pretrial hearings. In response to a similar question about Loughlin's appearance, Carlson had responded, "It looked like he was dunked in a bucket of blood."

CHAPTER 9

MATTERS OF EVIDENCE

THE AFTERNOON SESSION OF TUESDAY, July 3, WAS DEVOTED TO THE testimony of witnesses who had found Paula Harris writhing in a mud puddle four hours after her assailants had left her for dead. Lederer's central witness in this connection was the first police officer on the scene, patrolman Joseph Walsh. After establishing his credentials— twenty years on the force, the last ten in the small, relatively quiet Central Park Precinct—Lederer had Walsh recount the early morning hours of April 20, 1989.

He and his partner, Robert Calaman, had parked their unmarked car at the intersection of the East Drive and the 102nd Street Crossdrive at about 1:30 A.M., testified Walsh. They were drinking coffee when two Latino men came running up to the car, shouting excitedly about a guy down in the woods having been beaten and tied up. They were pointing down the grassy hill that slopes away from the crossdrive, northward into the dark ravine. As the men led the way, Walsh continued, he drove the car down to the footpath and headed west until he could see, in the high-beams, a body moving in the mud just off the broken pavement.

Call an ambulance, Walsh told his partner; call a sergeant. When he got out of the car and approached the victim Walsh realized the men were mistaken. It was not a guy but a woman, with a dirty bra around her chest, pushed away from her breasts; otherwise she was naked.

"She was lying face up and she was kicking violently," Walsh said. "The first thing I saw was, just, she was severely beaten. Her head, one of her eyes was really puffed out, almost closed. She had cracks in the side of her head. The side of her head was cracked, sort of covered with blood."

As he continued Walsh's voice came close to cracking. "I tried to tell her who I was. I was telling her, 'We are police officers. Who did this to you? Can you speak to me?' I was trying. There was no response."

On closer inspection Walsh realized the cloth that was tied around the woman's wrists—locking her open palms together in a praying position in front of her face—was also wrapped around her neck and stuffed into her mouth. He pulled the material out of her mouth, which loosened the tension on her throat and also freed her arms to move away from her face. "So now she was struggling, still struggling, moving her hands up and down, trying to bust them loose."

The jury sat in rapt attention as Walsh continued his description. "She seemed to be in some type of shock. I was looking at her face. She was looking right at me. She seemed to be not seeing me. She seemed to be looking right through me. She seemed to be kicking. I kept telling her, 'Please calm down.' I put a yellow blanket on her; she kept kicking it off."

Lederer showed the officer a filthy, long-sleeved shirt that looked as though it had been tie-dyed with a dull brown and rust-colored mixture. He identified it as the cloth that had bound and gagged the victim. He stood up to face the jury box and twirled the garment into a tight rope.

Is there anything different about that shirt now? asked Lederer.

"It's dry now," Walsh responded, "and it was soaked with blood. Now it's sort of brown; that night it was red."

Lederer produced a photo of the shirt, spread out on a neutral background. It was deep red, so dark that one could not read the Coca-Cola insignia on the front. Yes, said Walsh, that's what it looked like when I found it. The photo was circulated among the jurors.

After having loosened the shirt so the Jogger could breathe more easily, Walsh had decided not to remove it completely. He apparently thought it best to leave any further ministrations to the ambulance crew he had hoped would arrive soon. But the ambulance was a long time coming. "How long had you been there before an ambulance arrived," Lederer asked Walsh.

"Approximately 25 minutes," he said. (A paramedic would later explain that the ambulance was originally sent to the corner of 102nd Street and Second Avenue, five blocks east of the park.)

The two men who had found Paula Harris—Carlos Colon and Benicio Moore—had testified earlier that afternoon. Both unemployed construction workers, they had been drinking on the West Side and were walking back to their East Harlem homes when they heard moaning sounds in the darkness and saw the victim beside the footpath. The body was covered with mud. Moore later described it as looking "like a monster."

Both men testified that they began to run as soon as they saw the body. "Why?" Lederer asked Moore.

"Because I knew it was somebody hurt," he said, "a human being, and I ran to get some help. If [Walsh] wasn't there I would have made a phone call and get the cops."

Colon had testified: "I don't know who, you know, the person that did that to that lady, I don't know if he was still around. So I was not going to stay there to find out!"

All three defense counsel questioned Moore, Colon and Walsh, despite the fact that their cross-examinations allowed the jury to hear this terrible story over and over again. None of the defense lawyers seemed to have a coherent objective, with the exception of Mickey Joseph's demonstration, using Lederer's map of the park, that the Jogger was found several blocks north of the spot where his client, McCray, claimed the rape took place. Peter Rivera risked alienating the jury with his suggestion that Moore and Colon might have been the assailants. He pressed them on their drinking, why they had run from the body, why the cops had detained them for a few hours for questioning. Finally, over Lederer's objection, the judge allowed Rivera to ask Moore, "Did the police ever take blood samples from you on this case?" The answer was no.

The prosecutors were going to call a string of medical experts and laboratory technicians, beginning on July 5, to describe the extent of Harris's injuries and the results of hundreds of tests performed on items of physical evidence. This group of experts was preceded by a fight with the defense team over the admissibility of a set of charts the DA had prepared to bolster the scientific testimony.

The exhibits were big, about four feet by six feet, and fancy, with black backgrounds and lettering in white, green, yellow and pink. They were divided into grids like giant sheets of graph paper, with lots of horizontal and vertical columns. Impressive and expensive, the charts were state of the art in the growing field of litigation support: exhibits designed by consultants to help trial lawyers make their cases more visually compelling to jurors. And they scared the hell out of the defense lawyers.

The charts illustrated the results of tests conducted on blood samples, hair samples, semen samples and clothing seized from the suspects or found at the rape scene. In the extreme left column, for example, a slide with a smear from the Jogger's vagina was listed. Following the color-coded boxes across the board, jurors could see when the sample was taken, when and where it was tested and by whom. On the far right, in the column labeled "Conclusions," were little magnetic covers. The intention was that a witness describing the results of a test performed on that slide at Metropolitan Hospital, for example, would remove the cover and the words "positive for sperm" would be revealed.

The prosecutors had commissioned the charts to help the jury and themselves. There were so many tests done on so many items—some with conflicting results—that they were concerned the jurors would be confused about the evidence. For example, a slide containing a smear from Harris's rectum that was examined at Metropolitan Hospital tested negative for sperm. When that slide was tested again by the police department's lab, it came out positive for sperm. Expecting that the defense would attack the reliability of their scientific evidence, the prosecutors hoped the charts would reinforce their interpretation of the results.

While it was certainly true the state had conducted hundreds of tests, the prosecutors were still left with a paucity of physical evidence. The best Lederer could do with respect to the three defendants on trial was prove that there was semen in McCray's underpants and mud on his clothes that might have come from the park, and semen on Raymond Santana's sweatshirt and underpants. These charts, however, would undoubtedly give the jury the false impression that the prosecutors had a virtual mountain of physical evidence.

At a bench conference, Joseph and Bobby Burns expressed alarm at the prospect of the jury seeing the charts. Rivera chose to sit out the debate. (Indeed, Santana's lawyer would rarely open his mouth at bench conferences, apparently preferring public performance to the complex legal wrangling that actually would determine the course of the trial.) The defense lawyers conceded that the charts might be appropriate as tools for the prosecutors to use during summation. They argued strongly, however, that there was no justification for bringing the charts in as evidence, in themselves, of anything.

"You can't lighten her burden," Burns told Galligan, "by, in effect, manufacturing a piece of evidence."

Joseph told the judge the exhibits could mislead the jury. "The bottom line is, it's not evidence. It's a summary. It does say 'positive for sperm' but cannot say whose sperm. . . . This chart merely attempts to take what a witness is saying and then boil it down to one word, and then allow the People to have that one word displayed before the jury. . . . That's improper and prejudicial," Joseph concluded.

Galligan decided not to permit the charts in evidence "at this time," reserving judgment on whether they could be used later. Lederer never offered them again. The defense had won an important battle.

Later on July 5 the prosecutors called Robert Kurtz, the surgeon who had supervised Harris's care during her seven weeks at Metropolitan Hospital. DA Tim Clements began his examination by asking the doctor to describe the patient's condition when she was brought into the emergency room at about 2:30 A.M. on April 20.

"She was critically ill and just barely alive," said Kurtz. The victim was in deep shock, her blood pressure so low that technicians could not get a complete reading of it. Her body temperature was eighty-five degrees. She was unable to breathe on her own so a technician stood at her side squeezing an airbag sixteen times per minute, pumping oxygen down a tube in her throat.

As she lay in the emergency room, Harris continued to flail her arms and legs. Her wrists and ankles were wrapped in gauze and tied to the gurney to prevent her from hurting herself. Kurtz explained this activity not as an unconscious response to imagined attackers but as a result of severe brain damage. This jerking movement "is characteristic of her having been deprived of the function of . . . both halves of the brain that control all her higher functions, all her thinking, her ability to feel things, her ability to move her extremities."

The patient was bleeding from five major cuts across her forehead and scalp, four on the left side and one on the right. There were other cuts under the scalp, said the doctor, and several skull fractures. "She lost an amazing amount of blood. . . . Most people having lost 80 percent of their blood—they're dead."

Even without this blood loss, however, the woman's life was in immediate jeopardy from extreme swelling of her brain, caused by blows to the head. "About a quarter of the patients with brain swelling of the extent she had would die right out," said Kurtz. "Or there is substantial risk it would result in intellectual or emotional damage that is very severe."

Clements showed the doctor a photo of Harris's head taken by a detective at the hospital on April 20. It was the same photo that had shaken Kharey Wise during his first video session with Lederer. Kurtz described the injuries in the picture after it had been passed among the jurors. Many had winced looking at it.

The prosecutor also displayed large drawings of a head, depicting the same type of injury Harris suffered to her left eye socket. "That fracture," Dr. Kurtz told the jury, "was the result of a tremendous force exerted against her eyeball, which caused [the bones] to explode." He used the diagrams to explain the complex surgery he had performed to rebuild that portion of the patient's face, putting her eyeball back in place as a jeweler would a gem that had been forced from its proper setting. The surgery, Kurtz concluded, "eliminated much, though not quite all, of her double vision."

The doctor's further testimony of Harris's return from the brink of death, rising out of a deep coma, was the stuff of perfect melodrama. It was delivered in a detached tone. Kurtz recalled the day Harris was able to read and understand the words "yes" and "no" on flash cards as encouraging evidence that she was recovering from the brain damage. There was the day she finally began to eat by herself, though she would only take yogurt and ice cream.

Only once did the forty-eight-year-old surgeon betray emotion. Describing the anxious moment when, twelve days after admission, his patient was taken off the respirator to see if she could breathe on her own, Kurtz recalled: "That was, for me, one of the worst moments I had in taking care of her." He spent many hours afterward, he said, sitting at her bedside watching for any sign that her breathing was again obstructed.

Nearing the end of his questioning, Clements asked Kurtz about fluid in Harris's uterus that had been revealed by a CAT-scan. Examination of the vagina and uterus determined the fluid was not blood, said the doctor, and a pregnancy test proved negative, so it was not the result of gestation. In his opinion, said Kurtz, the only other possibility was semen.

Finally, to establish the evidence he needed for the charges of attempted murder and assault with depraved indifference to human life, Clements asked Kurtz whether the injuries to Paula Harris were life-threatening.

"Certainly they were," said the doctor. "She hung onto life by a thread. I think it's close to a miracle that she survived."

———

During his cross-examination of Kurtz, Rivera established that the amount of fluid in Harris's uterus—about a half-teaspoon—was less than the average ejaculation.

Beyond that, the defense lawyers dwelled on the fact that there were no injuries to the victim's genitalia or rectum. They tried repeatedly to get Kurtz to agree that forcible intercourse with a struggling woman would result in some evidence of physical trauma in those areas. But the doctor replied that such was not necessarily the case. In fact, he said, the majority of rape victims suffer no physical injury at all. "The compulsion they are subjected to doesn't seem to involve physical force," said Kurtz. "In my experience, it involves the threat of physical force."

Burns asked whether the doctor had ever seen a rape victim with injuries in the genital area.

"Yes," said Kurtz.

"Would it involve those situations where the victim fought back, put up a fight?" asked Burns.

"Not necessarily related," said Kurtz. "It's more dependent upon what the rapist does than the victim."

Rivera asked whether "rough sex" would cause trauma. Kurtz asked the lawyer what he meant by rough sex.

Rivera elaborated. "Would consistent and persistent sexual acts being performed on one individual, would that cause trauma?"

"It might not," said the doctor.

"And if the same person was fighting back, being held and continued to fight back, is there a possibility of trauma?" asked Rivera.

"It doesn't really have much bearing," said Kurtz. "You don't fight with your genitalia. You fight with your arms, your legs and your fists."

By the time they were finished with the surgeon, the defense team had only complicated its problems. The lawyers were suggesting that the absence of genital and rectal trauma raised doubts about whether Harris had been gang-raped. But the medical expert had rejected that theory. The more Kurtz was pressed, the more convincing became his counterargument. A seasoned expert witness, the doctor often turned in his chair to address the jury directly.

Ultimately, the questions posed by the defense lawyers had dramatized precisely the image they sought to dispel from the jurors' minds: an innocent woman overpowered by a gang and raped continually, despite putting up a fierce struggle.

In their daily press conference on the sidewalk, the defense lawyers seemed not to notice the damage they'd done. "The testimony of Dr. Kurtz does not establish beyond a reasonable doubt that she was raped," said Burns, "or that it happened the way they say it happened."

Interspersed among the expert witnesses who testified during the next several days were police officers who had been involved in the early stages of the case, collecting evidence or tracking down suspects. Among these witnesses was Detective Ramon Rosario, who had been the first detective to get a look at Paula Harris.

Rosario took the stand on July 6 and told the jury that he didn't need a doctor to tell him what had happened to the woman he saw naked and unconscious in the emergency room at Metropolitan Hospital on the morning of April 20. Rosario, in his fifth year of working the midnight shift in Manhattan, had taken one look at this victim and decided she'd been beaten over the head with a blunt instrument and dragged some distance, probably before being raped. The bruises on her knuckles told him she had fought back.

When Rosario learned from the patrolmen at the hospital that five kids had been picked up the previous night and charged with another assault in the park he called the Central Park Precinct. It was about 3:00 A.M. Informed that the kids were still at the stationhouse, Rosario had told the desk officer to hold them for questioning. He had then called his supervisor, Rosario recounted, and told him "we had a serious case here."

Patrolman Eric Reynolds had been preparing summonses ordering each of the teens in custody to appear in Family Court, with Santana and Lopez to answer an unlawful assembly charge and the others to answer for the assault of John Loughlin also. Juveniles can only be released into the custody of a parent or guardian. If Reynolds released the kids to their families individually, however, he would have to show up in court the next morning, as would their parents. But if he released them all together he could give them a future court date. So he told the assembled parents they would wait a while longer for Santana's family to arrive. Rosario's call had come in while they were waiting.

Now Rosario told the jury that, later that morning, Reynolds and he, and two detectives from the Sex Crimes Unit, had gone to Antron McCray's apartment. McCray, who was not among the boys arrested the previous evening, had been fingered early that morning by Kevin Richardson. The cops told the boy's father, Bobby McCray, that they wanted his son to come down to the precinct for questioning and that, since the boy was a juvenile, his parents had to come also. The father agreed, Rosario said.

Because the rules of evidence generally prohibit a witness from testifying about what someone else said (though there are many exceptions), Lederer could not have the cop repeat Bobby McCray's response verbatim. If he had the jury would have heard that the father had not only agreed to the trip but had suggested that the cops put his son in a lineup, so they could see that he was guilty of nothing.

Before they left for the precinct, Rosario testified that he had asked Bobby McCray whether it would be all right for the boy to put on the clothes he had worn the night before. The father again agreed and Antron went into his bedroom to change. He returned, said Rosario, in jeans and a hooded sweatshirt that were "caked in dried mud."

On his cross-examination of Detective Rosario, Joseph established that his client was not advised of his rights before going to the precinct. "You didn't advise the McCrays at that point that they might want to have a lawyer meet them at the Central Park Precinct or anything to that effect, did you?" asked Joseph.

"No, sir," said Rosario.

The police are not required to read the *Miranda* warnings unless they intend to question a suspect who is in custody. A witness, even if he is a *potential* suspect, who agrees to an interview without having been arrested can be questioned indefinitely without first waiving his rights. Under the circumstances described by Rosario, in which the McCrays agreed to accompany the police without their son having been arrested, there was no requirement to read the boy his rights at the apartment. The jurors, however, might not be aware of such technicalities and some might resent the cop taking advantage of unwary parents.

Joseph next wanted to counter earlier testimony from other cops that indicated that some of the defendants at the Central Park Precinct the previous night had not seemed to take their predicament very seriously. But none of that testimony had implicated his client and now, seeking to fix something that wasn't broken, Joseph got into trouble.

Was Antron crying in the car on the way to the precinct? Joseph asked.

Yes, said Rosario.

When Joseph finished his cross-examination, Lederer used her redirect examination to ask Rosario what he had said to the boy in the car. Joseph, knowing from the pretrial hearings what Rosario would answer, objected on the grounds that, since he had not raised the issue on cross, the prosecutor was prohibited from asking about it now. But Lederer argued that Joseph's question about McCray's crying had opened the door through which she could ask about what happened in the car. Galligan agreed.

"I told his parents," said Rosario, "to tell Antron to tell the truth no matter how bad he feels it is. No matter how bad, whatever happened, to just tell the truth. And to just let him know they love him, that they're his parents and no matter how bad it is, or whatever happened, that they will still love him."

Then what happened? asked Lederer.

"I observed tears in Antron's eyes," said Rosario. "He rested his head on his mother's shoulder and she in turn embraced him with one arm."

Having jumped into this hole, Joseph did a decent job of climbing out with his re–cross-examination. "Did you know Antron was being brought to Central Park Precinct to be questioned about some very serious crimes?" he asked.

"I knew he was going to be questioned regarding an attack," said Rosario. "I didn't know if he was a victim, a witness, a suspect. I didn't know what he was at that point."

The answer damaged the cop's credibility, so Joseph asked it again.

"I assumed he was not a suspect," the detective responded.

It was hard to believe. Why would Rosario give his tell-the-truth speech to the parents of a witness, let alone a victim? The detective had to know McCray was a suspect, Joseph was advising the jurors, otherwise why would he bring three cops to the apartment with him? And why would he tell the boy's parents they had to come to the stationhouse, too? And why, if the kid were not a suspect, would Rosario have him put on the clothes he wore to the park the previous night?

Rosario was followed by two detectives from the Crime Scene Unit, through whom the prosecution put into evidence two dozen photographs depicting, among other things, blood on the asphalt of the 102nd Street Crossdrive, drag marks in the grass leading to the woods beside the roadway, and a trail of blood stretching more than two hundred feet down to the muddy spot where Harris had been found. The series of photos also included aerial shots, in one of which a detective identified the towers of Schomburg Plaza overlooking the northeast corner of the park.

The physical evidence that was shown to the jury on July 9, 10 and 11 also included half of a brick and a triangular rock with jagged edges. The rock, said Detective Robert Honeyman, was stained with blood and had hair stuck to it. The brick was embedded in the dirt at the rape scene. In a bench conference with Judge Galligan, Joseph tried to keep the brick, which had no blood on it, out of evidence. There was no proof it was the brick used in the assault of Harris, as described by Santana and Salaam.

Lederer argued that the brick's proximity to the blood-spattered ground where Harris was found was enough to make it relevant. "If you had a stab victim and they found a knife beside the stab victim, and you weren't able to find blood on the knife," she said, "I don't think you can keep the knife out of evidence when the defendant says, 'I stabbed her.' "

"The difference," Joseph countered, "is that a brick, there may be numerous bricks throughout Central Park. And, in fact, this officer testified that this was one of several bricks that he saw in the area. And he selected this one for whatever reason."

Joseph had logic on his side but Galligan ruled for Lederer. A color photo of the brick ran on the cover of *Newsday* the next day.

The prosecutors also introduced three more photographs of Harris's injuries, bringing to four the number the jury had seen thus far. Several jurors were shaken by the pictures, which were even more graphic than the one they'd seen the previous week. In these photos, taken by Detective Honeyman approximately fourteen hours after the attack, blood and puss were still oozing from the victim's stitched-up head wounds. The photos also depicted open cuts and raw scrapes virtually covering the rest of her body. Emily Sachar described the jury's reaction to the photos in *Newsday:* "Migdalia Fuentes, a secretary at the United Nations, bit her lip and swallowed hard . . . Ben Neal, a mail and filing clerk, pursed his lips tightly together and shook his head . . . George Louie, a picture framer, covered his mouth with his hand."

The following day the prosecutors called Doctor Vernard Adams, a forensic pathologist from the city coroner's office, to testify about more photos. On the easel in front of the jury box they displayed thirty color photos depicting extensive injuries to Harris's naked body. Her legs, from ankle to hip, were scratched as though she'd been set upon by a pack of rabid house cats. Above her right thigh, near the pelvic bone, was a round, crimson wound the size of a silver dollar, several layers of skin scraped away as though with heavy-duty sandpaper. Only the soles of her feet were unscathed.

The defense had tried to keep these photos out of evidence, too, on the grounds that they were inflammatory. Furthermore, Joseph said, nobody disputes the seriousness of the injuries. But Galligan, noting that "it's the burden of the People to prove their case beyond a reasonable doubt," had not been swayed.

The jurors, occasionally glancing at the seemingly bored defendants, listened in horror as Lederer slowly guided Adams through the whole series of photos, eliciting a description of each injury and suggesting potential causes. In this exercise Lederer linked virtually every mark on the victim's body to some aspect of her theory—based on the defendants' statements—on how the attack was carried out. There was, for example, a narrow cut on the woman's upper right thigh. Could that cut have been caused by a zipper? asked Lederer. Adams said yes.

The long cracks in the skull and a star-shaped abrasion on the left cheek, said the doctor, were caused by a blunt object.

"When you say a blunt object," asked Lederer, "are the injuries that you've just described consistent with being struck with a rock or a brick?"

"Yes," Adams replied.

Lederer held the jagged, gray rock, on which a large brown blood stain was visible, in her small hand. Could it have been this rock? she asked.

"Yes," said Adams.

Moments later she showed the doctor the brick. "Could that brick have been used, or a brick like that have been used, to cause the injury you just described?"

"Yes."

CHAPTER 10

DEMONSTRATORS AND DNA

———

BY THE THIRD WEEK OF TRIAL MICKEY JOSEPH'S CONSTANT AND OFTEN fruitless battles at the bench to keep damaging exhibits out of evidence and dangerous witnesses off the stand were frustrating him. But Joseph never let his vigor wane. Like any conscientious trial lawyer, he was carefully building a record that a colleague could later use to mount a credible appeal if McCray were convicted. Each time Judge Galligan issued a significant ruling there was the potential for reversible error. If the defense had not first objected to the ruling, however, the defendant's appeal could be weakened by that neglect, especially if the question were a close call.

Joseph found himself carrying more of the burden at bench conferences in this trial than he had expected. Unlike Rivera, Burns participated in the frequent sidebar conferences but he had limited skill in that critical area, despite having practiced criminal and civil law for three decades. On the few occasions when he had a valid legal position, Burns was unable to make a coherent argument. Joseph realized very early that he would have to do his best to make an appellate record for Salaam and Santana as well as his own client. He did not criticize his co-counsel, but several months after the trial Joseph did remark:

138

"When you're playing shortstop, it's nice to know that if they hit the ball to second or third base, somebody's going to get it." That security was something Joseph, a reliable journeyman who would never be a star in the New York bar, did not have in the Central Park case.

On July 11 the DA put Patrick Garrett on the stand. The young business school graduate was a vice-president in the corporate finance department of Salomon Brothers. His desk was next to Paula Harris's.

The prosecutors had called Garrett to tell the jury about Harris's routine, about the fact that she had failed to keep an appointment with him on the night of April 19, and about his identification of her the next morning at Metropolitan Hospital. They also wanted him to describe the lasting effects of her injuries. Joseph again objected and everybody made another trip up to Galligan's bench.

Nobody was disputing her identity, Joseph argued, and nobody was disputing the seriousness of the injuries, so how was this testimony relevant?

Lederer noted that Rivera had suggested that the two men who found Harris at 1:30 A.M. might have somehow been responsible for the assault. But Garrett would testify, Lederer said, that Harris had left work at 8:00 P.M. and had failed to keep a 10:00 P.M. appointment with him, thus establishing that she had been incapacitated sometime during the period that the defendants were in the park. (Since Raymond Santana and four others were not picked up until about 10:30 P.M., this testimony would also put a dent in the allegation of many defense Supporters that the suspects were already in custody when the Jogger was attacked.)

The prosecutor also reminded Burns that he had claimed in his opening statement that the police were under immediate pressure to solve the case because the victim was an affluent white woman. Garrett's testimony would show that the cops had had no idea who Harris was until he identified her at about 10:00 A.M. on April 20. (This testimony could as easily have come from a detective as from Garrett, but Lederer was quickly coming up with as many justifications as she could think of to call her witness.)

Garrett would also testify, Lederer told the judge, that Harris's face was so swollen and disfigured he found it difficult to recognize her. Furthermore, he had noticed on many occasions since she returned to work that she had problems with vision and equilibrium, often bumping into people and walls. "She can't walk a straight line," said Lederer.

That was the testimony that really worried Joseph, who argued passionately that it was irrelevant because Dr. Kurtz and the photographs had already established the severity of the injuries. "It may be something of interest to the newspapers and the networks, and it may be something that might cause the jury to have greater prejudice against the defendants because this woman has suffered further," said Joseph, "but it's not necessary [to prove] serious physical injury." Joseph went so far as to promise the judge he would not argue in his closing remarks that the injuries to Harris were not serious.

It worked. Galligan asked Rivera and Burns if they intended to challenge the severity of the injuries in their summations. Both said they would not. The judge decided to permit Garrett to testify about identifying Harris "as long as we're not going to go into any blood and gore." As to evidence that the Jogger still suffered the effects of her injuries, he forbade Lederer to raise the subject. "I think the proof has been established at this time or it never will be," said Galligan. "I don't see any point in it."

Now in his fourth year with Salomon Brothers, the boyish, twenty-nine-year-old Garrett was in all likelihood making more money than the judge or any of the lawyers in the courtroom. On the stand he told the jurors that he and Harris met when they were rookies at the investment bank and they had become good friends. They had shared a two-bedroom apartment for eighteen months. In February of 1989 the pair gave up the apartment and each moved into a smaller one alone. No, he said in response to Lederer's question, they never dated.

They had arranged to meet at her apartment on East 83rd Street on the night of April 19 so he could look at a stereo she wanted to sell. When she left work at 8:00 P.M., Harris said she was going to run first and would see Garrett at 10:00 P.M. He worked until 9:30 P.M. and then went uptown. When he got to Harris's apartment at 10:00 P.M. she was not home. He walked to the corner and called her number from a pay phone, leaving a message on her answering machine.

The next morning, Garrett testified, he got to work at eight o'clock. Harris, who was usually at her desk by that time, was not in yet. Her secretary didn't know where she was. Garrett and others at the bank got worried and contacted the authorities. Perhaps an hour later he got a call from the police, who asked him to go up to Metropolitan Hospital.

Garrett was greeted by a detective who showed him the snapshots of Harris lying unconscious on a hospital bed, her face horribly disfigured, her head in bandages. "He asked if I could identify the Jogger from the pictures and I said no, I could not, and that I would like to see her," Garrett testified. "At that point we went up to her room and I spent ten, fifteen minutes in her room and identified the Jogger."

Lederer asked him, "And on what did you base your identification of Paula Harris?"

"Well," Garrett responded, "it was actually difficult to identify her, as well as I know her . . ."

"Objection!" shouted Joseph.

"The question is," Galligan interjected, "what did you base it on?"

"I looked at her for ten minutes," explained Garrett, "and then I looked at—the police officer showed me her ring. I knew it was her ring and I could tell that it was Paula."

On cross-examination Burns tried to inject the Boyfriend Theory, though it was hard to see any logic in his questions that might help Salaam's case.

You don't know what time she got home that night, do you? asked Burns.

No, said Garrett.

You don't know what time she left her apartment for the park, do you?

No, said Garrett.

You don't know whether she actually got to the park at all, do you?

No, said Garrett.

Burns then asked three times whether Garrett and Harris had dated, "in terms of boyfriend, girlfriend dating."

No, said Garrett, becoming visibly angry. His eyes narrowed and his head tilted slightly downward from the elevated witness stand, fixing Burns in a cold, hostile stare.

"During the time that you and she lived together, would it be fair to say you dated other people?"

"Yes."

"Would it also be fair to say during the time she lived with you Ms. Harris dated other people?"

"Yes."

"During the time you lived together—I'm sorry, lived as room-mates—did you date more than one person?"

Galligan sustained Lederer's objection to the question.

"Did Ms. Harris date more than one person?"

Again the judge sustained the prosecutor's objection.

"Thank you, Mr. Garrett," said a smiling Burns, returning to his seat as the witness did his best to conjure up a look that would kill the lawyer.

Shortly before Garrett had begun to testify, the Reverend Al Sharpton had walked into the courtroom and sat with the Supporters. By the time Garrett finished, Sharpton was asleep.

New York's Criminal Procedure Law, unlike those of such states as Washington, Vermont, Iowa, Missouri, and Florida, does not require the prosecution to tell the defense before trial what witnesses it intends to call. In accordance with the *Rosario* ruling, however, the law mandates that each witness's prior written or recorded statements be turned over to the defense after the jury is sworn and before opening statements are delivered. Consequently, Lederer and Clements, who had approximately fifty witnesses in the wings, had given the defense nearly two thousand pages of documents between the start of jury selection and the first day of trial. (Since the lawyers were in court every day, of course, the material had to be studied at night or on weekends, if it was going to be studied at all.)

The so-called *Rosario* material included prior statements by Jermain Robinson and Clarence Thomas, but not a word from Paula Harris. This did not necessarily mean the Central Park Jogger would not testify. It simply meant Lederer had refrained from taking notes during their meetings over the previous year. While the defense lawyers expected Harris to take the stand, they had no way of knowing if or when she would appear.

A few hours after Patrick Garrett's testimony the prosecutors called Junith Thompson, a gynecologist who had examined Harris on the morning she was admitted to Metropolitan Hospital. During a bench conference in the middle of Dr. Thompson's testimony, the prosecution indicated that it was going to call Harris.

After taking the witness through a recitation of her examination and the gathering of vaginal and rectal smears for testing, Clements asked: "Doctor, as part of your practice do you prescribe birth control?"

"Objection!" Joseph and Burns shouted in unison.

At the bench Galligan asked the prosecutors, "Where are we going?"

"New territory," said Lederer. She told the judge that Clements would have the doctor explain how a diaphragm is used to prevent semen from entering the cervix and, ultimately, the uterus. There would be testimony, said Lederer, that Harris had consensual sexual intercourse three days before the attack and that she had used a diaphragm on that occasion. Logically, therefore, the semen in the smear from her cervix and the fluid in her uterus, which Dr. Kurtz identified as semen, could not have come from that consensual partner. Since she had not had sex after April 16, the semen found in her body on April 20 had to be the result of rape.

Joseph objected to Thompson's testimony on the grounds that there was nothing on the record about Harris having used a diaphragm. We've been told the boyfriend is not going to testify, said Joseph in reference to earlier bench conferences, and we've been told the Jogger's memory about the period prior to the attack is unreliable. So where is this testimony going to come from?

"It seems to me," said Galligan, "the only person that can testify to that would be the boyfriend or the girlfriend."

"Or the girlfriend," responded Lederer.

In his cross-examination of Dr. Thompson, Rivera emphasized that a diaphragm is not a foolproof method of contraception. The device would only block semen from entering the cervical canal, the witness agreed, if it was the right size, was in good condition and was properly placed. Joseph had Dr. Thompson acknowledge that there were no signs of physical trauma to the genital area. Burns then asked, "Isn't it true that you found no . . . clinical findings which establish that a rape had been committed?"

"I can't say that," Thompson replied.

It was now clear that Harris would testify. Her appearance, even with amnesia restricting the evidentiary value of her testimony, was certain to have a powerful emotional impact on the jury. The news that she would offer substantive testimony, limiting the possible sources of the semen in her body, made her potentially devastating to the defense.

Even so, Rivera was not dissuaded from his simple strategy. Out on the sidewalk at the end of the day he told the press, "It will be our contention that she was not raped." He was asked whether the defense lawyers would call their own medical expert. "Yes," said Rivera. They never did.

During the lunch break on July 12 there was more activity on the sidewalk than the usual defense press conference. As Lederer and

Clements left the building at 111 Centre Street they were accosted by about a dozen demonstrators chanting, "No justice, no peace!"

It was a familiar refrain, made popular in recent years by the followers of Sharpton, who had been in court again that morning. The reverend was not among those following the prosecutors up the street. This group was the lunatic fringe of the Supporters. It did not include relatives or friends of the defendants, but was a cadre of agitators who seemed to spend much of their time protesting injustice to African-Americans at one courthouse or another.

"Who is this mystery woman?" one yelled. "What was she doing in the park," shouted another, "scoring drugs?" Still others demanded, "Where's the boyfriend? Where's the boyfriend? The boyfriend did it!" Several people began shouting the Jogger's name repeatedly, in the hope that it would be picked up by the nearby microphones of television and radio reporters who were interviewing defense lawyers or following the motley procession.

This scene became an almost daily occurrence as the prosecutors walked between the courthouse and their offices across the street, escorted by at least four bodyguards. Lederer routinely led the group, although on days when the crowd seemed particularly ugly she was placed at the center of a circle of men. In the mornings and evenings the entourage usually included paralegals pushing two large racks of files, similar to shopping carts, stuffed with documents and exhibits. Clements had a recurring fear that someone would overturn the carts, throwing the state's case into temporary chaos and possibly triggering violence.

It wasn't long before the extremists shifted the focus of their hatred from Paula Harris to Elizabeth Lederer. There were those who saw the prosecutor not only as a surrogate for the victim but as the embodiment of white oppression. Lederer continually had to shake off shouts of "witch," "bitch," "white devil," "slut" and "whore," as well as death threats, from people who were only a few feet away.

Eventually some protestors brought their venom into the courthouse. From that point on Lederer regularly found herself running a gauntlet of verbal abuse between elevator and courtroom. On more than one occasion the threats got so bad that the security men urged her to let them sneak her out of the courthouse through an obscure, private exit. Lederer refused, saying the prosecution would not be intimidated. We're going out the front door, she insisted.

The results of the DNA tests performed at the FBI laboratory were more beneficial to the defendants than the state. The prosecutors knew, however, that if they did not call Special Agent Dwight Adams to testify the defense would. And the district attorneys could not afford to have the jury think they were trying to hide evidence they themselves had commissioned.

Ever since the DNA report had been turned over to the defense the previous December, the prosecution had tried to put the best possible spin on the disappointing results. "Inconclusive" was the word District Attorney Robert Morgenthau's press spokesmen had used repeatedly and it was the term Lederer chose in her opening statement. But that was really a matter of interpretation.

There were four critical semen samples tested: one from the crotch of the Jogger's running tights, one from her sock and one each from Q-Tip swabs that were used to extract fluids from her cervix and rectum. These samples had been chemically treated to reveal the unique DNA pattern in the semen. Each pattern was then compared to the DNA pattern in blood samples taken from fourteen males, including the three defendants on trial.

Four tests were performed on the semen from the cervical swab, agent Adams now testified. Three had resulted in "no reading" and one revealed "a very weak result." Because that pattern was so weak, Adams had decided to make "no interpretation" about whether it matched the DNA in any of the known blood samples. "I chose to call this a 'no conclusive result,' " Adams testified.

The agent did, however, compare the faint DNA pattern in the semen from the cervix to the stronger pattern he found in the semen on Harris's sock. "They appeared to match," he said. But the sample from the sock, said Adams, definitely did *not* match any of the known blood samples. Hence the theory that the male who left his mark on the sock had also raped Paula Harris and got away.

As for the other two samples, Adams testified that the semen on the rectal swab did not contain enough DNA for him to get a reading. The semen on the victim's running tights, he said, matched the blood sample from one Kevin O'Reilly.

The jury had no way of knowing who O'Reilly was. He had simply been listed by Adams as one of fourteen males whose blood was analyzed. At this point in the trial the only names on that list the jurors could be expected to recognize, in addition to the three defendants, were Kevin Richardson, John Loughlin and Antonio Diaz. (Loughlin and Diaz were tested so the prosecutors would know whether any blood found on the defendants' clothing had come from them.) The jurors were likely to assume, however, that the others were kids in the gang McCray, Salaam and Santana had been running with on the night of April 19. (In fact, seven of them were.) For all the jury knew, O'Reilly was one of the defendants who would be tried later.

This was exactly what Mickey Joseph did *not* want the jurors to think. It was not enough that his client had been ruled out as the source of the semen in the crotch of Paula Harris's tights. Joseph wanted to make it crystal clear that the semen came, not from a rapist, but from her boyfriend.

At the bench Joseph asked for a stipulation to inform the jury that O'Reilly was Harris's boyfriend. Lederer was uncomfortable with the idea of compromising the victim's privacy any further, but there were no grounds on which to fight Joseph. To leave the impression that the only semen the FBI was able to identify came from somebody other than a voluntary sexual partner was clearly prejudicial to the defense.

Galligan approved the stipulation, which, at Lederer's insistence, included the statement that the blood was taken "for comparison purposes." Clements read the stipulation to the jury, concluding, "Kevin O'Reilly is the boyfriend of Paula Harris."

In subsequent weeks O'Reilly's name occasionally surfaced in the sidewalk chants of Lederer's hecklers.

When Joseph got his chance to cross-examine Dwight Adams, he was ready. He had consulted his own DNA expert and learned that, when comparing known and unknown samples, it is easier to declare a non-match than a match. The complexity of DNA testing is such that a match cannot be declared unless the patterns appear identical in several aspects. If, however, during the testing it is determined that the patterns do not match in one or two of those aspects, that information is sufficient to exclude the possibility that the samples came from the same source.

Joseph used his questioning of Adams to remind the jury that the semen on the victim's sock and running tights definitely did not come from his client.

Turning to the semen on the cervical swab, Joseph asked: "In that test . . . am I correct in understanding you were able to get a DNA pattern?"

"That was the pattern I described as being very weak, or faint," said Adams. "Yes."

"Okay," said Joseph. "But it was a pattern you were able to visually observe?"

"You can visually observe two distinct bands," said Adams, reminding the jury: "But they are very weak and I got no other results."

"I understand," Joseph replied. "But from those two bands would you agree with me that you can see they are different than the pattern of DNA for Antron McCray?"

"Yes, sir," said the agent.

Joseph was so pleased with the answer that he repeated the question. Then he asked if it were not also true that the faint DNA pattern from the cervical swab was sufficient to exclude all of the men who provided blood samples.

"That's correct," said Adams.

Just in case anybody on the jury had missed the significance of this testimony, Joseph asked, "Would you agree with me that DNA is a science that is of assistance in excluding, as well as establishing, a connection?"

"Absolutely," Adams replied enthusiastically. "I have worked in excess of 600 sexual assault cases and, generally, in 25 percent of those I have excluded the individual accused of depositing the semen."

This testimony jolted the press corps, which had long ago accepted the DA's contention that the DNA tests were "inconclusive." As a matter of science, it was now clear that the FBI's results were not "inconclusive" at all, despite the insistence of Adams and the prosecutors that the term was appropriate. In fact, the results proved conclusively that the semen in the victim's cervix did not come from her boyfriend or any of the six defendants charged with rape. In the *Daily News* the next day Lizette Alvarez described the new information as a "revelation, wrested from an FBI expert under cross-examination."

"Prosecutors have said all along that DNA 'genetic fingerprint' tests of semen found in the Jogger's cervix were too weak to interpret," wrote Alvarez on July 14. "But FBI agent Dwight Adams testified yesterday that he did make out a faint DNA pattern in one of four tests he conducted. That pattern, he said, did not match the semen of the three defendants currently on trial, the three others to be tried later, or the Jogger's boyfriend."

Now the defense team had to hope the jury would feel as misled by the prosecutors as the media did. If they were lucky, one or two jurors might even hold a grudge.

CHAPTER 11

THE PEOPLE CALL
PAULA HARRIS

HER ANXIETY OVER PUTTING PAULA HARRIS ON THE STAND THE NEXT morning was enough to keep Lederer up all night on Sunday, July 15. How would her star witness, still recovering from the beating she had endured nearly fifteen months before, handle the strain?

It is never easy to convince a woman who has been raped to walk into a courtroom and face her attacker again, describing to strangers the details of a nightmarish violation of her entire being. In this case the threat such an experience presented to the victim's emotional and psychological well-being was intense. Most often the courtrooms into which sex crimes prosecutors coax their witnesses are relatively empty, containing perhaps supportive friends and relatives, maybe the defendant's family and a couple of trial buffs. But Lederer was asking Harris to get up in front of more than one hundred people, of whom half were journalists in the business of exploiting her experience, and many of the others were defenders of her assailants, openly hostile to her and resentful of everything she represented.

The prosecutors had discussed sparing the reluctant Harris this ordeal but Lederer had decided it would be too risky. The videotapes were compelling but a coercion defense might raise enough doubt in the minds of some jurors to cause problems. The photos and medical testimony had certainly established the severity of Harris's injuries but they did not conclusively prove rape or sodomy. The best hope of keeping Harris off the stand had been if the DNA tests had proved one of the defendants was a rapist. Since the tests failed to do that, however, jurors could interpret the results as working in favor of the defense, especially after Joseph's cross-examination of the FBI expert.

The only way to prove that the unidentified semen in her cervix had not come from a voluntary partner was to ask the Jogger. "You only get to do it once," Lederer would subsequently explain. "It would not have helped later to say, 'Maybe it would have turned out better if we had called her.'"

In addition to the critical evidence only Harris could provide about her sex partners and use of a diaphragm, there were sound strategic reasons to put her on the stand. Until she appeared in court Harris existed only as a character: the Central Park Jogger. The jurors, and everybody else in the courtroom, had heard her name spoken by lawyers or witnesses dozens of times each day but they had seen no face, heard no voice to go with that name. Even the explicit photos of her battered body and bruised face did nothing to pierce the anonymity of the Jogger. To the jurors, as to the public, she was the abstract innocent victim.

The Jogger's privacy, so carefully preserved by her friends, family, colleagues and Lederer, had become a liability to the district attorney since the trial began. It seemed that the prosecutor was not representing a person to whom the jurors could relate but an assortment of photographs. Behind those photographs lurked the image of a privileged yuppie whose life was discussed as though it existed in a space and time that were foreign to the courtroom.

Lederer understood the importance of giving any jury a victim to avenge. Even in homicide cases, she did everything possible to make the victim a real person in the minds of the jurors. Now she had to bring the Central Park Jogger to life, to take her down from that pedestal constructed by the media and show her to the jury in all her human frailty.

"She had been labeled as an investment banker," Lederer later recalled. "People think investment bankers have ice water in their veins . . . I thought, let the jury see that she walks and talks. . . . This is who she is."

It was also in the prosecutor's interest to show the jury that the miracle recovery described by Dr. Kurtz and trumpeted relentlessly by the press corps was sadly overstated. Harris, at twenty-eight years old, had not reached the peak of her promising life on April 19, 1989. The jurors had to be shown that such a peak was now forever unattainable. The great potential in this woman, who was described by a Wellesley economics professor as "probably one of the top four or five students of the decade," had been irrevocably reduced. One source in the district attorney's office had stated that she lost twenty points off her IQ.

Harris was afraid to testify, afraid for her physical safety and embarrassed at the prospect of discussing the most intimate details of her life. The experts at Gaylord Hospital, where she had undergone rehabilitation, had advised that the preservation of her anonymity was vital if she was to adjust to a normal life again. But Harris had come to trust Lederer, who had visited her during her months in the Connecticut hospital, and the prosecutor trusted her own judgment. Lederer had put many rape victims on the witness stand and she had learned from them that testifying can be a healing, validating experience. She had seen victims transformed by standing up for themselves in a courtroom and fighting back, regaining a measure of the dignity stolen by the rapist.

———

"The People call Paula Harris," said Lederer, immediately bringing down on the courtroom an absolute silence. All eyes turned to the door beside the jury box through which witnesses entered the well.

A minute went by; then another. The press and spectators began to murmur. "What's wrong?" juror Harold Brueland later said he had wondered. "Is she crying? Is she getting sick?"

Another minute went by. Lederer became nervous herself but she knew it would take Harris some time to arrive. The prosecutors had sneaked the Jogger into the building that morning and secreted her in a jury deliberation room on the sixth floor, one level below Galligan's court. She was having trouble climbing that flight of stairs, thought Lederer; that accounted for the delay.

When the door opened and the thin woman in the deep purple business suit stepped over the threshold, escorted by a court officer, everyone in the room, including the defendants' Supporters, fell silent. The total quiet would remain for fifteen minutes, save for the clear, strong voices of Lederer and her witness.

Harris walked the dozen or so steps to the witness stand, her head bobbing slightly as with a palsy. Her escort supported her arm as she unsteadily climbed the three steps to the chair. As she answered questions she looked straight at Lederer, her brown eyes fixed in an unnaturally wide stare.

She looked bewildered, thought juror Brueland, like a frightened rabbit. She looked like an injured bird, thought Lederer.

As the witness spoke in a clear, confident voice, Lederer's initial apprehension gave way to pride. The veteran prosecutor felt a surge of excitement like nothing she had ever known.

Everybody in the room was transfixed. Even the defendants, laconic teenagers who acted uninterested through most of the trial, sat straight and took notice.

It was her habit to run alone, as many as six or seven times a week, Harris explained. She ran at night because she usually worked from 7:30 A.M. until 7:00 or 8:00 P.M.; there was no time to run before work or at lunch. Her typical workout was six or seven miles. It was an excessive schedule for a noncompetitive runner, though it squared with the many profiles written during the previous year of Harris as a compulsive, control-obsessed personality.

"Do you recall going jogging in Central Park on the night of April 19, 1989?" asked Lederer.

"No, I don't."

"Do you have any memory whatsoever of what happened to you in the park on April 19, 1989?"

"No, I do not."

To those who looked at Paula Harris sitting in that chair, calmly answering questions, it was hard to imagine she was the same woman whose body was depicted torn and broken in the photos that had been displayed the previous week. Her sandy hair was clipped short, parted on the left side, and she was alert, apparently in full command of her faculties. She had a long straight nose and a small mouth. If one saw her on the street one might say, there's an attractive young woman with an unfortunate scar. The flaw was a thin but jagged white line that traced a half moon around her left eye—the one Dr. Kurtz had rebuilt—beginning above the eyebrow and encompassing the high cheekbone. The eye encircled by the scar was slightly out of kilter with the right eye. There was a less obvious scar on Harris's lower lip, as well as scar tissue under the straight hair that swept across her forehead.

Those who had seen pictures of Harris taken before the assault said she had been very pretty. Juror Rafael Miranda thought she was still beautiful. Others thought she looked too thin, gaunt even, and much older than her thirty years. Juror Migdalia Fuentes later described her as "a frail little thing."

The last thing she remembered taking place on April 19, said Harris, was a phone call she'd made at about 5:00 P.M., canceling a dinner date because she still had a few hours of work to do.

What, asked Lederer, is your next memory after that phone conversation?

"I remember waking up in the hospital on a Friday evening, late in May. . . . It was the weekend of Memorial Day."

Lederer had the witness identify the tights, the bloody shirt and other clothing found at the rape scene before asking whether Harris recalled the days before April 19.

"Yes, I do."

Now the prosecutor had to dispel the notion that the unidentified semen came from somebody other than a rapist. It is technically improper to ask a witness leading questions but Lederer had decided to see if she could get away with it. She did not want Harris to have to explain the details of her sex life, so she phrased her questions, as much as possible, in a way that permitted the witness to answer yes or no. The defense did not object.

"Did you have sexual relations with anyone prior to April 19?"

"Yes, I did."

"When was that?"

"On Sunday, the 16th of April."

"Did you have sexual relations at any time between the morning of April 16 of 1989 and the time of your last memory, at approximately 5 P.M. on April 19?"

"No, I did not."

"Who were you with on the morning of April 16?"

"Kevin O'Reilly."

"Who is Kevin O'Reilly?"

"He is my boyfriend."

"Did you use any form of birth control on that day?"

"Yes, I did."

"What did you use?"

"I used a diaphragm."

"Did you follow the prescribed use of a diaphragm?"

"Yes."

"Did you also use the necessary precautions for the removal of the diaphragm after you inserted it on that day?"

"Yes."

"Did you have vaginal intercourse on that day?"

"Yes."

The DNA test had failed to identify the semen in the rectum but Lederer could use Harris's testimony to establish at least that it was not a lover's. "Did you have any other form of intercourse with Kevin O'Reilly on that day?"

"No, I did not."

Lederer needed to explain to the jurors why O'Reilly's semen was on the tights Harris had worn running in the park three days later. So she asked whether Harris had gone to Central Park later on the morning of April 16. When the witness said yes, the prosecutor asked under what circumstances. At this, Mickey Joseph objected.

During the ensuing bench conference, Harris was asked to step down from the stand, a routine precaution to prevent the witness from being influenced by the debate among the lawyers. As she stepped unsteadily away from the final stair and walked the short distance to the doorway, all eyes followed as Harris drifted to her left and bumped into the big map of the park that was balanced on an easel.

At the bench Joseph told Judge Galligan the fact that Harris had gone to the park on April 16 was not relevant to the crimes that occurred on April 19. While he was not a proponent of the Boyfriend Theory, Joseph could not sit idly by and let Lederer close the loopholes through which an alternative theory might be argued.

The primary reason to call Harris at all, said Lederer, was to explain the presence of her boyfriend's semen on the tights she wore on the night of the crime. "She will testify," Lederer told the judge, "that after having vaginal intercourse with Kevin O'Reilly on the 16th she went to Central Park and wore the tights on which the stain was found. . . . And that's how the stain everybody used to trigger this attack on Kevin O'Reilly came to be there."

"Number one," Joseph responded, "I think it's an incorrect statement to say that *everybody* used it to attack Kevin O'Reilly."

"I withdraw that," said Lederer, whose protective instincts toward Harris were showing.

"I don't see the relevance of her running in the park on April 16," repeated Joseph.

The judge didn't see the relevance of the running either. "But putting the tights on seems relevant," said Galligan. "I'll allow it for that reason."

When Harris returned to the stand, Lederer asked her to describe any lasting effects of the injuries she suffered.

"I have problems with balance when I am walking," she testified, "and coordination. At times as I'm walking down the hall or down the street I'll veer off either to the right or to the left. I also have a great deal of trouble going down steps and I have to hold onto the bannister, or if there is another person there I'll grab onto them. I also have lost my sense of smell completely and totally; that hasn't come back at all.

"I also suffer from double vision," Harris continued, "and I compensate for it when I'm reading by holding papers, whatever I'm reading, over to the left. And it takes a fair amount of concentration to focus on what I'm reading and try to make the vision just one instead of two. And it seems to be worse at night when my eyes are more tired. And also if there is a situation where there is a great contrast of light and dark, such as in a movie theater, it's worse there, or if I'm in a car in the evening."

A row of seats behind the press corps on the prosecution side of the room had been reserved for Harris's friends and colleagues. Occasionally, during pauses between questions, she glanced at them and smiled. Otherwise her gaze was locked on Lederer.

Finally, the prosecutor asked again whether Harris had "any memory whatsoever" about what had happened on the night that changed her life forever.

"No," she repeated, "I do not."

Neither Joseph nor Rivera saw any percentage in cross-examining Harris. It was hard to imagine a more sympathetic witness. Besides, her credibility was unimpeachable and she had given no factual testimony that could be rebutted. The best thing the defense could do was to let her get out of the jury's sight as soon as possible.

Burns wasn't so sure. When his turn came, he fiddled with papers for two or three minutes before turning to the witness and saying, "I have no questions, Miss Harris."

"Thank you," she replied.

That the defense had made the right decision was obvious to the jury. Harold Brueland, for example, later said he would have considered it "a cruelty beyond imagining" to cross-examine Harris. The Supporters did not agree. When the defense lawyers left the building for lunch they were surrounded by an angry crowd on the sidewalk. Many chanted "Sellout!" Why, they demanded, was the Jogger spared the third-degree many rape victims are subject to?

Under New York law the victim of a sex crime has the right to ask the trial judge to close the courtroom to the press and public during the victim's testimony. Galligan would surely have granted such a request. Harris and Lederer had discussed this option and Harris decided against it. She said she did not want to antagonize the press corps.

Although the media had proved insatiable in uncovering and reporting the minutiae of the Jogger's life, it had continued to withhold the one item that most concerned Harris: her name. Even the *Amsterdam News,* the black weekly that had printed her name off and on in the early days, did not use it once the trial began. If the media were suddenly to reverse this generally observed policy, Harris would become an immediately recognizable celebrity. It is highly unlikely that editors would have abandoned the practice of protecting her anonymity if their reporters had been banned during her testimony. But the longstanding policy of protecting the identities of sex crime victims was being reevaluated throughout the industry at the time and Harris was unwilling to take the risk.

One thing Harris didn't have to worry about was photographs. That summer New York was in the third year of an experiment allowing television and still cameras in courtrooms at the discretion of trial judges. Galligan had permitted cameras during some of the early pretrial proceedings. On the eve of trial, however, he had ruled that no cameras would be allowed.

With the exception of Rivera, the defense lawyers had opposed the presence of cameras. Galligan had taken no position until Lederer put her objection on the record. The DA's office did not generally try to bar cameras but Lederer had several witnesses, in addition to Harris, who were camera shy. Benicio Moore and Carlos Colon, the men who had found the Jogger in the woods, lived in East Harlem and they feared for their safety if they should become recognizable on the streets as witnesses for the prosecution.

Without cameras, television newscasters and the tabloids had relied on sketch artists to provide daily scenes of the action in the courtroom. A half-dozen artists filled the front row on the side of the room shared by the prosecution table, witness stand and jury box. On the morning of Harris's appearance Galligan granted Lederer's request that the artists be forbidden to sketch Harris during her testimony. After she left, the artists took up their pads again and drew Harris from memory, complying with Galligan's order by obscuring the features of her face.

The extensive coverage of Harris's testimony was celebratory. "Lady Courage," shouted the front-page headline in the *New York Post.* The *Daily News* announced, "She Didn't Weep, She Didn't Shudder." *The New York Times* also played the story on its front page, rare treatment for a local criminal trial, and carried yet another profile of the Jogger inside under the headline, "Smart, Driven Woman Overcomes Reluctance." The story, by M. A. Farber, retold much of the personal information that had been reported during the previous year. That information included the fact that Harris had once been diagnosed as suffering from anorexia nervosa, an eating disorder bordering on self-starvation.

Nobody was more impressed with Harris's demeanor than Lederer. As she stood there and watched Harris discuss the havoc wreaked on her life, without a trace of self-pity, the prosecutor was inspired yet again by the inner strength she had come to recognize in this woman. Many months later the emotion Harris had stirred in her was still evident. Lederer recalled that day in court: "I think it was really a way of saying, 'You didn't get me.' It was one of the most moving things I've ever seen."

The prosecutors had not saved Harris's emotionally powerful appearance for the end of their case. It had been scheduled to precede the playing of the videotapes. They wanted the jurors to have a clear picture of Paula Harris in their minds as they watched Antron McCray and Raymond Santana coolly describe the assault on the victim they called "the lady jogger."

Detective Harry Hildebrandt of the Manhattan North Homicide Squad took the stand on July 18 to give the jury his version of the interrogation of McCray. Hildebrandt and his partner, Thomas McCabe, had sat down with the fifteen-year-old and his parents in the youth room of the Twentieth Precinct at 3:15 P.M. on April 20. At the last minute a sergeant had come in and asked if Detective Carlos Gonzalez could sit in on the interview. Gonzalez was with the Central Park Precinct squad, which wanted to prevent the Homicide hotshots from running away with the case.

As Detective Rosario had a week earlier, Hildebrandt described the

McCrays as extremely cooperative. Confident that their son could not have done anything very serious, they wanted to get to the bottom of the situation as quickly as possible.

After reading the boy his rights, said the detective, he had asked what had happened the previous night in the park. McCray spoke for twenty to thirty minutes, describing his sojourn in the park but saying nothing about a female jogger. Hildebrandt said the kid was very nervous. "He was fidgeting, moving around in his chair, constantly moving around, wiping his face, looking down at the ground. He became silent at periods of time."

When Antron had finished his story, Hildebrandt testified, he asked his father, Bobby McCray, to step into the hall. "It seems to me like your son is holding something back," said the detective. The father agreed, said Hildebrandt, "and he stated that he can tell when his son wasn't being completely truthful."

The second time around, Hildebrandt testified, the boy admitted punching "the bum" (Antonio Diaz) in the chest and hitting John Loughlin in the legs with a pipe. But he still seemed recalcitrant. At one point, Hildebrandt said, Antron's mother, Linda McCray, told the boy to tell the officer everything he knew. "We brought you up better than this," the cop quoted the mother as saying.

What about the female jogger? the detective asked Antron.

I don't know anything about a female jogger, said the teenager.

Hildebrandt testified that he again took Bobby McCray into the hallway. "I said to Mr. McCray that I felt his son was still holding something back and that he seemed to be embarrassed. And maybe he was embarrassed because his mother was in the room." Again the father agreed, said Hildebrandt. "Then he suggested that his wife leave the room; maybe we can get this thing over with."

The detective stated that Bobby McCray then said to Antron: "I'm glad we had your mother leave the room. Because maybe you feel funny talking about what happened. But now, please, tell them what happened."

"He described exactly how the female jogger was attacked, who hit her," Hildebrandt testified. "How he kicked her. How her clothes were ripped off and how different individuals, including himself being number three, jumped on top, followed by other individuals."

Hildebrandt had put McCray's statement into writing and it had been signed by the boy and both parents. Lederer had the detective read the statement aloud before it was passed among the jurors. As the white-haired policeman spoke in flat but clear tones the jurors were offered the corroboration Lederer had promised of the testimony given by her early witnesses. "We went after this guy and girl on a bike-for-two," recited Hildebrandt, "but they got away from us."

Hildebrandt next gave the prosecutors a means to introduce the videotape, stating that he had been at the taping session.

Before the tape was played Galligan delivered an instruction to the jury designed to comply with the *Bruton* ruling, which the lawyers had debated before trial when Galligan had granted the district attorney's request to try the defendants in groups. The judge told the jury that a statement made by a defendant outside the courtroom can only be considered as evidence against that defendant, not against any other. Galligan further explained that there were places on the videotape where McCray's voice was obscured by a high-pitched beeping sound. He warned the jurors not to speculate about what the defendant might have said in those instances.

The defense team objected to the instruction. "My position is that the defendants are prejudiced by being tried jointly," said Joseph. By highlighting the editing of the written and taped statements, he added, Galligan's instruction increased the likelihood that the jurors would assume—correctly—that the omitted portions were references to code-fendants. (Post-trial interviews with jurors revealed that Joseph was correct.)

Two twenty-three-inch television monitors were wheeled into court, one placed in front of the jury box and the other facing the defense table. It was a hot day and, as usual, the air-conditioning in the courtroom, which had no windows, was not up to its task. One juror waved an Oriental fan in front of his face throughout the proceedings. A technician popped the videotape into the VCR and the voices on the soundtrack filled the room.

"When first, when we seen her, we thought it was a man," said McCray's image on the screen. "That's when we all charged her."

The jurors heard Lederer's voice ask, "What were the names of the people who charged her?"

"Me, Clarence, Kevin, and um, um, Tony, Steve and [BEEP]." The sound had replaced Santana's name.

McCray, seated at the defense table, watched the tape. "We charged her," he said. "We got her on the ground. Everybody started hitting her and stuff. She was on the ground. Everybody stompin' and everything. Then we got, each—I grabbed one arm, some other kid grabbed one arm and we grabbed her legs and stuff. Then we all took turns getting on her, getting on top of her."

"Did anybody have a weapon?" asked Lederer.

"Yeah, a black pipe," he responded, spreading his hands about sixteen inches apart.

"Who had that pipe?"

"At first, I don't really know, but I think [BEEP] had the pipe. I don't know." This time the tone replaced the phrase "the tall black kid," which the prosecutors had removed to prevent incrimination of Salaam.

The lady had been hit with the pipe in the head and the ribs, said McCray, before she was stripped. McCray identified the boys who then mounted her as himself, Clarence Thomas, Kevin Richardson, a Puerto Rican he didn't know and "BEEP." The jurors did not hear him say "the tall skinny kid." They might wonder whether he had named Santana, Salaam or both.

McCray's voice was soft and, as Hildebrandt had noted, he fidgeted and often wiped his face with his empty, open hands. He would occasionally glance toward his parents and then look at the floor.

As the tape played Lederer followed along with a transcript, looking up now and then to study the reactions of jurors. Some of the panelists seemed to be straining to understand the boy's unclear diction. Migdalia Fuentes and Edith Milton looked sad, exchanging a few words and weak smiles at one point. One alternate shook his head whenever the beeping sound came on. Brueland, Richard Peters and George Louie watched intently from the back row while, up front, Pedro Sanchez and Charles Nestorick seemed to be fighting off sleep. At one point juror Rafael Miranda made eye contact with some reporters and raised his eyebrows in an exaggerated manner. He resumed watching the tape and, in response to something McCray said, suddenly jerked his head back as though punched. The Supporters were unusually quiet.

On the video McCray denied having penetrated Harris, insisting that he only rubbed his penis against her to feign intercourse. "My penis wasn't in her. I didn't do nothing to her. . . . I was just doing it so . . . everybody would just, like, know I did it."

When they were finished raping her, said McCray, "BEEP" hit her in the head with the pipe, "then we left her there."

"After you were all done," asked Lederer, "somebody still hit her in the head?"

"Yeah."

"She wasn't moving anymore by this time, was she?"

"No."

When the tape stopped several jurors took long looks at McCray, who had turned his head from the television set and was staring at a wall behind the bench.

Nothing on the videotape gave any indication that the statement had been coerced. The kid's parents were on the tape, listening to the reading of the *Miranda* rights, silently watching their son admit his complicity in a brutal rape. The boy seemed nervous, but why shouldn't he? Not only was evidence of duress lacking but McCray seemed almost eager to help Lederer fill in the details.

Joseph's strategy for countering the impact of the tape was to persuade the jury that McCray's admissions were not truly voluntary. The judge would tell the jury at the close of the trial that an involuntary statement must be rejected, even if true. If Joseph could demonstrate that the cops had induced the McCrays to cooperate by making the kinds of promises or threats that could cause a person to falsely incriminate himself, the jury would theoretically have to discard the confession. That was the law, even if the jury believed such tactics had caused self-incrimination by a guilty party.

In his cross-examination of Hildebrandt, Joseph scored several points, hitting hard on important inconsistencies with the testimony of Detective Gonzalez, whom the jury had heard several days earlier. The credibility of both cops was damaged as a result and a foundation was laid for Joseph's defense.

Hildebrandt said it was Bobby McCray's idea to have his wife leave the room. Gonzalez had said that was suggested by the detectives.

Hildebrandt, who had taken the boy's written statement, testified that McCray never said he penetrated the victim. Gonzalez had testified that Antron *did* admit penetrating the Jogger.

Hildebrandt denied that McCray cried during the interrogation; Gonzalez had said he did.

Hildebrandt said Linda McCray returned to the room before he put the statement in writing; Gonzalez had said she returned afterward.

Both policemen testified that they had taken no notes and both denied it was their intention to get a statement from McCray. Hildebrandt said he had not even known that McCray was a suspect. The detectives also denied having talked before the interrogation about what each knew of the case, although both had interviewed other suspects earlier. (Gonzalez had, in fact, participated in an interrogation in which Kevin Richardson said that McCray had raped the Jogger.) In a scenario that was repeated with several other detectives, they also claimed to have posed virtually no questions. They simply asked, "What happened?" and McCray had spontaneously spilled his guts.

None of this rang true to the jury. By the time Joseph was finished with Hildebrandt several jurors, including Brueland, Louie, Peters and foreman Earle Fisher, had considerable doubts about whether either detective had told the truth. "People don't just make confessions because they've got to get it off their chests," said Brueland later. "They have to be somehow maneuvered into that situation where it makes sense to say something."

Through questions put to Hildebrandt and Gonzalez, Joseph posited an alternative theory of how the interrogation was conducted that many jurors found more credible.

"Isn't it a fact that when you went into the hallway with Bobby McCray, Antron's father, you told him that you knew that Antron was in the park?" Joseph asked Hildebrandt. "And that Antron could go to jail unless he was going to talk to you, unless he was going to assist you? Didn't you tell him that?"

"No."

"Isn't it a fact, detective, that Mrs. McCray wasn't asked to come back into the room until this entire written statement was put on paper?"

"No."

"Isn't it a fact that you didn't want her back in the room until it was on paper because she was the one who kept telling you not to harass her son; and not to keep calling him a liar? Isn't that why you didn't want her in the room?"

"No."

During his earlier cross-examination of Gonzalez, Joseph had exposed a significant inconsistency between the cop's pretrial testimony and what he was telling the jury. Gonzalez testified at trial that after Mrs. McCray left the room her son spoke for thirty to thirty-five minutes, finally admitting his role in the rape. "And no questions were asked of him?" asked Joseph.

"Right," said the cop.

The defense attorney then read from the transcript of the pretrial hearings, quoting Gonzalez's earlier version of this episode. "When the mother had left, I would say we were inside the room for an hour and fifteen minutes before he started making his third statement, in which he also did not implicate himself in the Jogger," Gonzalez had testified. "And then we started questioning. That's when he broke down and started giving specifics."

Joseph also pointed out mistakes in McCray's version of events. McCray said the rape took place near the reservoir rather than the 102nd Street. Crossdrive and he described the Jogger as wearing blue shorts instead of black tights. These inconsistencies, and others which Joseph would later emphasize, bothered one juror deeply. Ronald Gold thought that perhaps the kid was pushed into confessing to something he hadn't done.

On her redirect examination of Hildebrandt, Lederer tried to explain away some of the holes in his story that had been exposed by Joseph. But Gold couldn't get those nagging inconsistencies out of his head. Over the next few days the prosecutors focused their efforts on Salaam, but in Gold's mind, at least, McCray's guilt was far from proven.

CHAPTER 12

A LAWYER
SELF-DESTRUCTS

————

THE CASE AGAINST SALAAM WAS WORRISOME TO LEDERER and Clements. No written statement, no video, no physical evidence and no witnesses placed him at the rape scene. Under the terms of the plea bargain they'd made with Jermain Robinson, the prosecutors could call him to testify that he had seen Salaam hit a male jogger with a pipe at the reservoir, but that wouldn't help with the higher charges of attempted murder and rape. Salaam, fifteen years old at the time of the crime, had made an oral confession without a parent present. Would the jury accept the word of detectives that they had acted in good faith, believing Salaam was sixteen? If the jurors were inclined to acquit the kid, thought Lederer, they could certainly use that error to justify their verdict.

The prosecutors were relying almost entirely on the credibility of Thomas McKenna, a member of the Manhattan North Homicide Squad who had been a detective for twenty-two years. Some cops love to get up on the witness stand and regale a jury with their exploits. McKenna was not one of them. Nor did he like the attendant waiting around courthouse hallways. This did not mean, however, that he wasn't a good witness.

Several jurors later said they found McKenna highly credible, his candor standing in marked contrast to the guarded manner of other detectives. Lederer called McKenna to the stand on Monday, July 23. His testimony followed a brief appearance by Detective John Taglioni, who told the jury that Salaam had said he was sixteen years old, making him an adult under the law, when Taglioni picked him up at Schomburg Plaza on the night of April 20. Salaam produced a transit pass with a date of birth that proved he was sixteen, said Taglioni.

McKenna picked up the story from there, describing the interrogation he had conducted on the third floor of the Twentieth Precinct. The detective acknowledged that he had immediately asked Salaam about the assault of the female Jogger and that he told Salaam he *knew* that he had been in the park the previous night. He also admitted tricking the suspect with a lie about having found fingerprints on the Jogger's tights. If those are your prints, said the cop, you're going down for rape. Upon hearing this, said McKenna, Salaam blurted out: "I was there but I didn't rape her."

In McKenna the jurors were finally seeing a detective who wasn't afraid to admit having taken an aggressive role in obtaining a confession. His credibility was a big boost for the prosecution. If the jurors accepted everything else he was saying, they'd have no reason to think McKenna did not honestly believe Salaam was sixteen. And if they could forgive the cops that mistake, they'd convict.

Still, since Salaam never signed a statement, the prosecutors had no documents to put into evidence. McKenna had taken brief notes in a steno pad during the interrogation, which was cut short when he was informed that Salaam's mother and an attorney were asking about the boy. The next day, at the prosecutor's request, McKenna prepared a handwritten report recounting what Salaam had told him. Finally, two days later, the detective filled out a police department form describing the interview. But all of these documents were inadmissible under the hearsay rule. In the absence of Salaam's signature, the papers themselves did not constitute statements by Salaam but rather statements by McKenna. Unlike the cases of McCray and Santana, therefore, in this case the jurors would have no incriminating paperwork on Salaam with them in the deliberation room. They would have to rely on their memories of what McKenna had said about Salaam's involvement, or have his testimony read back.

After leading McKenna through the preliminaries of the interrogation, Lederer asked what Salaam had told him about the events in the park on the night of April 19. Technically, coming from the cop, Salaam's spoken words were also hearsay, but McKenna was permitted to repeat them because an exception to the hearsay rule allows into evidence an admission of guilt made by a defendant to another person. Such an admission is considered inherently reliable because a person is not expected to tell a lie that is against his own interests.

The cop recited the familiar story about Jermain Robinson clothes-lining the bum, Tony Montalvo taking his food, somebody else pouring beer on his head while others kicked and punched the man. Then the gang moved on.

"He said at this point he was with a group of people, he doesn't identify them," testified McKenna. "They saw a bike with a man and a woman on the bike, a tandem bike. He said he stepped, they stepped out on the road, they tried to stop them. But the man who was on the front sped up, to him it looked like he was coming right at Yusef. And he stepped out of the way and the man, somehow or another, managed to get through the crowd of people. . . .

"He said the next thing he remembers is that he saw a female jogger coming down the path," continued McKenna as the jurors listened closely. "Kevin ran out and stopped her. She started to struggle with Kevin. He said he stepped up to her and he hit her with a pipe. He said she went down, but she was still struggling. So he hit her with the pipe again. He then said he then went down on the floor and he was feeling her tits. He said her shirt was on but then Kharey took her shirt off and lifted it above her tits and he started to feel her breasts again.

"He said then somebody took her pants off but he doesn't know who took the pants off," continued McKenna, needing no prompting or direction from Lederer during this long monologue. "And Kevin got on top of her and, to quote him, 'Kevin started to fuck her.' He said Kevin got off and Kharey got on and Kharey fucked her. He said then Kharey got off and two other guys, but he doesn't know who they are, they got on her and they fucked her. He said then he just, he just left."

After Salaam and Robinson beat up John Loughlin, continued McKenna, they heard sirens and ran out of the park. The detective was about to recount a conversation between Salaam and Robinson on the subway going home when Bobby Burns objected, on the grounds that he'd only been asked what Salaam had said about his activities in the park. Once again, the lawyers paraded to the bench.

"What's he going to testify to?" asked Galligan.

According to what Salaam told the detective, Lederer explained,

Robinson had said he committed the assaults as revenge because a group of white guys had once beaten him up. In response, she continued, Salaam had said for him it was just something to do, it was fun.

Galligan was troubled. "How is the statement that somebody else said it was racial, how is that pertinent?" the judge asked.

Lederer maintained that it was pertinent because it explained the context in which Salaam described the wilding as fun.

A debate ensued in which Joseph argued that, while Salaam's end of the conversation might be admissible, Robinson's statement about his own motivation was not relevant.

Lederer pressed her argument. "They're discussing the crimes that they've just committed," she said. "They just spent an hour in the park beating people up!"

"I understand that," replied the judge, "but how does that allow hearsay?"

Galligan explained that he was "just a little concerned" about the remark, despite the fact that it "is not alleged to be the statement of Yusef, so we're not attributing to him any racial motive." The judge told the lawyers he'd rule on the objection after lunch.

When they returned from the break, the prosecutors again tried to convince Galligan to allow the testimony. "It's being offered," said Clements, "so the jury has some context in which they can understand Yusef's explanation for why he was in the park."

But Galligan didn't see any logic in the prosecutor's position. How did Robinson's state of mind explain the motivation of Salaam? "I don't understand it," said the judge.

Indeed, it was hard to reconcile the prosecution's effort to introduce such a clearly inflammatory remark with repeated public protestations during the previous year from the DA's office—including a press conference on the topic conducted by Robert Morgenthau himself—that race was not an issue in the case.

Galligan ruled that McKenna could not repeat Robinson's statement. It was the only testimony the prosecutors tried to elicit that suggested any of the kids had a racial motive for the assaults. (In an interview after the trial Lederer asserted that she didn't want the statement introduced for any reason other than to establish context for Salaam's response. "I think we were just as happy *not* to have race come in," she said.)

When Lederer resumed questioning McKenna she asked what Salaam had told him about leaving the park and getting on the subway.

"He said in the course of the ride uptown he had a conversation with the others and then they got off the train, they went home," said McKenna. "I asked him why he got involved with this, how could he get involved in this. And he said to me, 'It was something to do. It was fun.' "

Did he say anything further about weapons? asked Lederer.

Yes, said the detective. He said the pipe had come from Kharey's house and that, at some point during the night, he dropped it and another kid picked it up. "He also said he had a knife, which he took from his house."

The day had begun badly for Burns, opening with a bench conference at which Lederer asked Judge Galligan to hold him in contempt of court. It was a request she had made before and one she would make again before the trial ended. The cause of Lederer's consternation was Burns's propensity for asking improper questions in defiance of the judge's orders. This was a device Burns used to let the jury know that, contrary to what the BEEP in the videotapes might lead them to believe, neither McCray nor Santana had implicated his client by name.

The DA was also angered by Burns's apparent contempt for the proceedings. His cross-examination of Taglioni was typical. Burns repeatedly made disparaging comments about the detective's answers. When he asked, for example, if the cop had been given a physical description of Salaam before he went up to his Harlem address, Taglioni said he had a "partial" description.

"What were you told?" asked Burns.

"He was a male black," said Taglioni.

"Wow," replied Burns, to the delight of the snickering Supporters in the gallery.

Burns's uncharacteristic conduct grew out of extreme frustration. The DA's case against Salaam was weak and he was struggling to get the jury to look at it objectively. His client, who had made no written statement or videotape, was sandwiched between two kids who had sealed their own fates as soon as Lederer switched on the video camera. Burns considered Galligan's rejection of his motion for a separate trial a grave judicial error that the appellate courts should correct. In the meantime, however, Salaam's family was counting on him to keep the kid out of jail, and to that end Burns was desperately grasping at any straw.

As powerful as McKenna's testimony was, Burns could at least take solace that the prosecutors had little else against his client. If he could cast doubt on McKenna's credibility, the state's case was vulnerable. Burns decided to attack on two fronts. First, he would deny Salaam had ever made the incriminating statement. Second, he would try to convince the jury that the cops had improperly questioned Salaam, knowing all along that he was under age and purposely keeping him isolated from his mother while trapping him with the fingerprint ruse.

The trick in this defense was to walk the fine line between what could be mutually exclusive claims. On one hand Burns was arguing that an innocent kid had been coerced by corrupt cops through isolation and deception. On the other hand, he was claiming the kid had made no incriminating statement. So the jury was essentially being asked to believe that McKenna and his allies tried to trap the kid and, having failed, resorted to fabricating a statement. Such a defense would require masterful cross-examination and careful preparation of one's own witnesses. A skilled lawyer might pull it off.

But Burns made virtually every mistake imaginable in his cross-examination of McKenna. His repeated efforts to rattle the detective were so poorly designed that they gave McKenna opportunities to enhance his own credibility or further implicate Burns's client.

On the fingerprint trick, for example, Burns asked: "Did you believe that it was possible to get fingerprints from some satiny cloth surface?"

"No, I did not," said McKenna.

"Well, you told it to him like it was something that he should believe," said Burns. "Isn't that true?"

"If he was guilty he would believe it," said McKenna. "He would believe it, I guess, if his prints were on the pants. . . ."

"But that was a lie, am I correct?" asked Burns.

"It's a fib," said the cop, "a non-truth."

Burns asked the detective to define the difference.

The difference, McKenna explained, is that a lie might hurt someone and a fib will not.

Not content to leave the jury with a memory of having heard McKenna recite Salaam's oral statement once, Burns made a monumental error by introducing into evidence all of the paperwork related to his client. This included three pages from McKenna's steno pad, his handwritten report recounting Salaam's statement, and the departmental form he'd filed about the interview. In offering these damaging documents, which the prosecutors had had no grounds to introduce, Burns was in effect waiving his client's right to object to them. Joseph's objection was overruled, presumably because the papers did not specifically incriminate McCray, who had not been named by Salaam.

Lederer, of course, had no objection to what would prove to be one of her luckiest breaks. Burns had gone so far as to have sixteen copies of the documents made so they could be distributed among the jurors and alternate jurors. Now the panelists would have the equivalent of a written statement from Salaam available during deliberations. But before the documents could be distributed Robinson's remark about "getting even" with whites had to be deleted. Burns even fumbled this clerical task, causing a delay in the proceedings and prompting Galligan to say to him, "Let's stop acting like a clown." The court finally recessed for the day so Burns could get clean copies of the paperwork.

Burns's strategy in introducing the documents was to highlight inconsistencies among them. The chronology of events in the steno pad and McKenna's handwritten report were different, for example, and there were lots of details in the report that were not in the notebook. Burns also pointed out that neither the paperwork nor McKenna's pretrial testimony included the assertion that Salaam believed the tandem bike was aimed directly at himself. This, Burns suggested, had been added by the detective at trial to bolster the testimony of cyclist Gerry Malone. McKenna easily explained most of these discrepancies, however, and the damage done by the documents far outweighed any doubt Burns hoped they would cast on the cop's credibility.

On Tuesday Burns continued to blunder through his cross-examination of McKenna, eventually asking a question which even he recognized—too late—as disastrous.

"Would it be fair to say, Detective McKenna, that aside from Yusef's statement to you in relation to the female jogger, you didn't know whether it was true or not? Is that correct, Detective McKenna?"

"Mr. Salaam told me it was true."

"But aside from that statement, you can't—as you sit here right now—tell these jurors that that's a true statement, is that correct?"

"No, I won't say that, counselor. I would say that I could say that [it is true]."

Instead of running from this clear sign of trouble, Burns pressed on, apparently blind to the fact that he was giving the detective a rare opportunity to express an opinion about a defendant's guilt. "What is the basis for your saying that it was true?" he asked.

"As I sit here today, there are certain things that Mr. Salaam said to me on that date that now prove, yes, he was there. Because there are certain things that were done at the scene of that crime, according to Mr. Salaam . . ."

Burns belatedly panicked. "Judge, I object!" he shouted.

"Let him answer," said Galligan calmly. "You asked him."

"According to Mr. Salaam," continued McKenna, "certain things he did and certain things testified to about the young lady, not proved, and came out through the investigation having been founded. There must have been some basis, there must have been some basis for his knowledge of the crime, for me to now sit here and tell you, yeah, I think he was there. I don't know what his participation was, because he told me what his participation was. I didn't know. And I tell you right now: He was there and he told me what happened. And today, as I look at the case as it is, it's there and he was there."

Lederer could not have scripted a better answer.

Joseph was flabbergasted. "Judge, may we approach?" he asked.

"No," said Galligan, "you can save your trip for another time."

Burns pressed on until he was making such a mess of the record that Lederer joined Joseph and Rivera in objecting to his contorted line of questioning. Finally Galligan began to sustain objections and consented to a bench conference.

Joseph demanded a mistrial. The question asked by Burns, said Joseph, elicited testimony "that otherwise would not be admissible" concerning evidence that McKenna learned subsequent to the interrogation. That evidence, said Joseph, "substantiated the truth of the confession. . . . I think that though he was specifically talking about Yusef's confession, I think it has an effect on all of the statements."

The jury has already been told, said Galligan, that any testimony from McKenna related to Salaam's statements to him could only be considered as evidence against Salaam. The mistrial motion was denied.

Lederer capitalized on every mistake Burns had made when she conducted her redirect examination of McKenna. First, she had the detective read aloud his report on Salaam's statement. As the jurors read along with the copies provided by Burns, they noticed that McKenna had left out a detail when he described the statement earlier: In the written report McKenna stated that Salaam told him someone hit the Jogger with a brick but he didn't know who it was.

Next, Lederer took the opportunity to ask McKenna about an interview of Al Morris that he had conducted before questioning Salaam on April 20. It was Morris, one of the Schomburg boys who was in the park but denied having been at the rape scene, who had given Salaam's name to McKenna in the first place. Lederer had hoped to have the cop testify on direct examination about what else Morris told him, but Galligan forbade it on hearsay grounds. Then Burns had foolishly asked McKenna about Morris, establishing that the kid had said nothing to implicate Salaam in the rape, but inadvertently informing the jury at the same time that a witness had placed Salaam in the park. Worse, by asking about Morris's statement Burns had effectively waived any grounds on which the defense could object to Lederer's inquiring about the same subject. Joseph, knowing full well what Lederer was now going after, was furious.

The prosecutor asked McKenna what Al Morris had told him about the events of April 19.

"He said that he entered Central Park with a group of friends . . . and that someone in the group had stated that they wanted to wild some joggers," replied McKenna.

Lederer's case against Salaam closed on Wednesday with the brief testimony of Detective Joseph Neenan. In the early evening of April 21, said Neenan, he escorted Salaam to the men's room at the Twenty-fourth Precinct. As he was washing his face, said the detective, Salaam asked: "How much time am I looking at for what happened?"

Reverend Calvin Butts, pastor of the Abyssinian Baptist Church and the most influential black minister in New York, had been sitting with the Supporters during McKenna's testimony. Butts had been belatedly drawn into the case. In the weeks immediately following the crime he was among a group of Harlem clergymen who had refused to make a donation to a bail fund for the defendants. He later explained the clergy's reluctance to Felipe Luciano in *Manhattan Lawyer* magazine.

"So many of the victims of crime are black senior citizens, who are members of these churches," said Butts. "When they're injured, when they're mugged, when their doors are kicked in, when they're raped, they lose compassion. They get fed up. They've become skeptical, particularly regarding the Central Park defendants. . . . They're saying maybe these guys are guilty, and maybe they're believing the media. There is a sense of compassion but they're tired. . . . They're raising their grandkids because their kids are on crack or dying of AIDS."

By the time that interview appeared, on the eve of the trial, the black media had helped raise skepticism about the state's case and the ranks of the Supporters had grown. Butts was criticized on his own radio call-in show for his initial refusal to help the defendants' families.

Now, accompanied by more than a half-dozen fellow clergy, he had come to court to demonstrate his support for the defense. The lack of physical evidence created reasonable doubt, Butts told a reporter, and therefore "these boys should not go to jail." The political climate had changed dramatically since May 1989, when Butts had told *Newsweek:* "This incident shows that there is an infatuation that our young people have with sex and violence."

In the week before McKenna testified, the jury had heard detectives John Hartigan and Bert Arroyo describe Raymond Santana's first interrogation, which began at 1:40 P.M. on Thursday, April 20, fifteen hours after he'd been picked up with Steve Lopez on Central Park West. At the end of that three-hour session Santana signed a statement describing the reservoir assaults, admitting his participation in the beating of Loughlin. He didn't mention a female jogger.

Santana had been accompanied during the interrogation by his grandmother, Navidad Colon. The boy's father, Raymond Santana, Sr., showed up at the Central Park Precinct at about 5:00 P.M., after finishing his shift as an orderly at a nearby hospital. When the father arrived, the detectives showed him Raymond Junior's statement and told him they believed the boy knew more than he was admitting. (Hartigan had been told by Richardson that morning that Santana helped strip the Jogger and held her arms while McCray raped her.) While the cops were discussing this with his father, Hartigan testified, Raymond asked if he could speak with the detective alone. The elder Santana granted permission, according to Hartigan, and left the room with the grandmother and Detective Arroyo.

Hartigan testified that once he and Santana were alone, the boy admitted participating in the rape. "I explained to him that he couldn't tell me these things without his parents being present," Hartigan testified. "That he would have to talk to me, he would have to tell us, while his father was still in the room. He can tell us these things and not to be ashamed, that his father would understand."

Hartigan went outside to get Santana's father and grandmother but they were nowhere to be found, having disappeared when Arroyo left them to go to the men's room. In their absence Hartigan added a paragraph to the bottom of the statement Santana had already signed.

After talking with his father, Hartigan wrote, Raymond Santana stated that he saw Kevin [Richardson] struggling with a white woman, ultimately tripping her over his leg. "Steve came over and was holding her arms with his legs," the addendum continued. "Antron came and started ripping her clothes off. Antron pulled her pants off and she was screaming. . . . Kevin pulled down his pants and had sex with her. When she was on the floor I grabbed her tits. . . . I did not have sex with her."

At the bottom of the page Hartigan told Santana to write, in his own hand, "The above statement is in addition to the statement I made above and is true." The detective and Santana then signed the addendum. But Santana's grandmother had refused to sign the original statement, saying she did not know how it would affect the boy, and now the addendum carried no guardian's signature either.

———

Peter Rivera spent more than two hours attacking the credibility of Hartigan's testimony, suggesting through his cross-examination that an interrogation of a rape suspect is by no means the smooth, polite type of encounter that Hartigan—and Arroyo before him—had described. Although Hartigan, a senior member of the elite homicide task force, was not the least bit shaken by Rivera's accusatory and aggressive manner, the lawyer did manage to draw the jury a plausible picture in which Santana's immigrant grandmother and naive father had been manipulated into submissive roles while the young suspect was frightened and badgered into confessing.

"Did you ever turn to my client and ask my client if he ever fucked Paula Harris?" asked Rivera.

"No, I did not," said Hartigan.

"Did you, or any of the other detectives, ask my client if he was looking at Kevin Richardson's dick?"

"Never," said Hartigan calmly.

"Did any of you call my client a faggot?"

"No."

To this sordid scenario Rivera soon added a suggestion that the boy may have been coerced by threats of physical torture. "Your questioning of Raymond Santana was very civilized, is that correct?" he asked.

"Yes," said Hartigan.

"You never raised your voice?"

"No."

"You never had any cattle prods that you were holding as you were asking questions . . . ?"

"No."

"You never had any stun guns or any nightsticks that you were banging on the table as you were questioning Raymond, is that correct?"

"That's correct."

While these accusations struck most jurors as a desperate tactic, Rivera's less sensational suggestions seemed credible to many on the panel. Hartigan, for example, denied telling Santana that McCray and Richardson had informed on him and that, to protect himself, Santana should therefore tell the cops everything he knew about what his friends had done. That strategy seemed plausible to the jurors, who had seen television cops use it often.

Furthermore, the notion that the police had created a hostile, intimidating environment by mocking the boy's masculinity rang true to some of the gay men on the jury. Rivera returned to that line of questioning near the end of his examination.

When you spoke with Raymond "out of the presence of his parents and Detective Arroyo," said Rivera, did you ask him again if he'd had sex with the Jogger?

"I never asked him any questions as to what he did," said Hartigan, giving an answer that had by now become familiar from the cops on this case but which many jurors later said they could not believe.

"And you never turned to Raymond and told Raymond the reason he didn't have sex with her was because he's a faggot?" asked Rivera.

"No."

"Was it at that point that Raymond turned and said, 'All I did was grab her tits'?"

No, said Hartigan.

Lederer called Detective Michael Sheehan on July 25 to set the stage for the playing of Santana's videotape. After five weeks and nearly fifty witnesses, the DA was ready to rest her case and she wanted to end it with a bang. Santana's tape was even more graphic and chilling than McCray's.

Sheehan's credibility, like McKenna's, was enhanced by his candor and confidence. He loved the cops-and-robbers game, he loved the chase, and he loved telling war stories. In fact, Sheehan had developed a second career, after twenty years on the police force, as an actor specializing in police roles. His best performance to date had been in a television movie about the Robert Chambers trial, in which he portrayed his real-life boss, Lieutenant Jack Doyle, commander of the Manhattan North Homicide Squad. Sheehan, forty-two, was the perfect type for such parts, a big man with classic, black-Irish good looks, born and raised in upper Manhattan.

Lederer had Sheehan pick up the story of Santana's series of interrogations where Hartigan had left it the previous week. Sheehan testified that he had arrived at the Central Park Precinct on the evening of April 20 with instructions to take Santana to the Twentieth Precinct. It was then, Sheehan testified, that Hartigan told him to find the kid's father and take another statement in his presence.

Sheehan and two colleagues, August Jonza and Rudy Hall, had an eventful ride across town with Santana in the back seat of the car. Earlier that day, Sheehan testified, the detectives had conducted a fruitless search for the pipe that had been used to beat Loughlin and Harris. On the way over to the Twentieth Precinct they discussed making a detour to take another look around the wall that borders the west side of the park. That, said Sheehan, was when Santana spoke up, saying: If you're looking for the pipe, I can show you where it is. Santana then directed the cops up to Columbus Avenue and 100th Street where, he said, McCray had ditched the pipe after using it to break light bulbs under a scaffold that covered the sidewalk. But again, the cops couldn't find the pipe.

Back in the car, Sheehan testified, Santana told the cops, "I had nothing to do with the rape of that lady. All I did was touch her tits."

Long before Lederer asked Sheehan to read aloud Santana's second written statement—this one having been witnessed and signed by the boy's father—Joseph and Burns knew their objections were hopeless. But the record had to be preserved for a credible appeal.

At the bench, Joseph objected on the grounds that his client should have been granted a separate trial. He argued once again that the deletion of McCray's name from Santana's written statements (and his video) was not sufficient to protect his identity from the jurors, who could not help but assume that the phrases were references to either McCray or Salaam. Joseph presented Galligan with case law that, he said, held that a joint trial was impermissible if the editing of a defendant's statement did not absolutely prevent incrimination of a codefendant.

Burns made the same argument, noting that in Salaam's case the damage was more severe and clearly prejudicial. Regarding the assault of Paula Harris, said Burns, Santana insists that the only people at the scene were himself, McCray, Richardson and Lopez. But the elimination of McCray's name gave the jurors the opportunity to wrongly assume that Santana *did* implicate Salaam in the rape. Salaam's right to a fair trial, at least on the charges related to Harris, said Burns, was "irretrievably compromised by inviting the jury to make a choice." The implication that either McCray's name or Salaam's had been deleted, said Burns, was entirely unfair given the fact that "the district attorney knows full well that it's not my guy, it's the other guy."

As he had many times in the past five weeks, Galligan overruled this objection. Sheehan read the written statement and, through him, the prosecutors introduced the videotape. To the lawyers and the press corps the tapes had become old hat, losing much of their emotional impact with repeated viewings. To the jurors, however, the tapes were new and their power to shock was evident on the faces of nearly all the panelists watching the television monitor.

Santana had been in custody for twenty-eight hours by the time he sat down with Lederer and Sheehan to make his videotape at 2:20 A.M. on April 21. By then the fourteen-year-old had told his story over and over again, under the mistaken belief that he was talking himself *out* of trouble. In truth, however, he incriminated himself further with each retelling, adding details that helped solidify the state's case against him and his pals.

In contrast to McCray's meek manner on videotape, Santana, who had a streetfighter's reputation at Junior High School 117, came across as a smart aleck, the kind of kid who would show disrespect to teachers and other adults just to get a rise out of them. Santana did his case no good by portraying himself on the videotape as a leader of the gang, even taking a headcount—thirty-three—when the Taft boys and the Schomburg boys merged before entering the park. Santana described seeing a bunch of guys across a ballfield beating up on somebody, but claimed that when he and a friend named Jason called out, this group of about twenty-five boys suddenly stopped what they were doing and ran to Santana's side. After leaving the park, Santana said, as the boys were walking up Central Park West, "I was up front. Steve was like a half-a-block behind and the kids was like . . . a block behind him." (When Lederer had interviewed Lopez she had asked whether Santana was the leader of the group. "He was tryin' to be," snorted Lopez.)

Santana's defiant attitude on the tape was not likely to make a favorable impression on the jury, but Rivera could at least be thankful that among the few incriminating statements Galligan had suppressed before trial was one his client had made shortly after his arrest. Hours before Paula Harris had been found, Officer Powers told the five kids in the juvenile room, "You guys shouldn't be out here beating up on people. You should be out with your girlfriend." In response, said Powers, a snickering Santana had turned to Lopez and said, "I already got mine."

On the videotape Santana seemed bored and impatient as he described how "a bunch of us went to Central Park to rob bicyclists and joggers," how Jermain Robinson viciously pummeled Loughlin—"He was tryin' to murder the man!"—and how Richardson raped "some lady." Perhaps he had told the story so many times in the past thirteen hours that Santana saw another recitation as simply the role he was supposed to play in this melodrama the cops were directing. Now they wanted him to fill in this lady DA, to tell her the story he'd been telling them all day and night. Maybe Raymond Santana shared the attitude of his father, who had sat silently at his side during the video session. In the courthouse hallway one day the elder Santana was asked why he hadn't demanded a lawyer rather than let his son make the videotape. He thought it was too late, the father explained, because Raymond had confessed earlier in writing. He thought the video was just a formality, he added.

Most of the jurors watched the video in horror, though Ben Neal, Charles Nestorick and foreman Earle Fisher fell asleep during the thirty-five-minute tape. McCray and Salaam watched with keen interest, while Santana intermittently looked at the wall and his own image on the screen. Lederer watched the jury.

While Richardson raped the Jogger, said Santana, Lopez was kneeling on her arms. Santana demonstrated the victim's position for the cameraman, reaching both arms back over his head with his wrists together.

"And what was he doing with his hands?" asked Lederer.

"He was coverin' her mouth, but every time she. . . . He was smackin' her, he was sayin', 'Shut up, bitch!' Just smackin' her."

"And did she keep screaming?" asked Lederer.

"Um hmm. And he just kept smackin'."

"Did somebody stuff something in her mouth?"

"No," said Santana. "He picked up the brick and he hit her with the brick twice."

"After he hit her in the head with the brick," said the prosecutor, "did she stop screaming?"

"Yeah," said Santana coolly. " 'Cause she was like, shocked."

When Lederer asked Santana on the tape whether he had actually seen Richardson's penis penetrate the Jogger, Rivera smiled, hoping the jury would see the question as bolstering his theory of how Hartigan had pushed the kid into a confession. This was, however, a faint hope. The jurors were more likely to note Santana's voluntary self-incrimination: As he described Richardson's raping of the Jogger, Lederer asked, "Were you watching?"

"No," said Santana, adding smugly, "I was grabbin' the lady's tits!"

Santana claimed that he didn't see anybody else get on top of the woman because he left the park when Richardson finished. Lederer asked why he left.

"They told me to leave, so I left."

"Who told you to leave?" she asked.

"My conscience told me to leave," said Santana irritably, "that's what told me to leave."

———————

Rivera's rambling, four-hour cross-examination of Sheehan had little impact, other than to alert the jury to discrepancies between his client's version of events and the prosecution's. Santana, for example, said the rape followed the reservoir assaults rather than preceding them. Also, Santana said the woman was not bound or gagged, he saw nobody sodomize her and he was unclear about the location of the rape, placing it near the reservoir, as had McCray.

Bobby Burns was correct in thinking the jury had understood his implication when, a week earlier, he had defied Galligan's orders and asked Hartigan whether Richardson, in his written statement, had placed his client at the rape scene. Lederer's objection had prevented the detective from answering, but the jury understood Burns's message: The answer would have been "No."

When his turn to cross-examine Sheehan came up, Burns hoped to make the same point again, since Santana had never said Salaam was at the rape scene, either. Although the judge had taken the precaution of previously ordering Burns not to repeat the tactic, the frustration was too much for the lawyer to bear. After a few brief questions put to Sheehan, Burns turned to the bench and loudly said, "Your Honor, pursuant to your direction, I will not ask any questions concerning the redacted material in Santana's account."

A furious Lederer demanded, for the second time in four days, that Burns be held in contempt of court. Galligan told Burns he considered his conduct "outrageous" and said he might very well hold him in contempt at the end of the trial.

So that Thursday ended for Burns as badly as Monday had begun. For the prosecutors, however, it was another milestone. Shortly after Sheehan left the courtroom, Lederer rose and announced, "At this time, the People rest."

CHAPTER 13.

THE COERCION
DEFENSE

AS HE OPENED THE DEFENSE CASE ON FRIDAY, JULY 27, MICKEY JOSEPH'S task was to answer the one essential question raised by his client's videotape: Why would Antron McCray confess to crimes he hadn't committed?

McCray's parents were present, after all, throughout his interrogation. Would they have let the detectives force their son to falsely incriminate himself? Joseph's answer was that they would, if the cops had promised to let the boy go if he agreed to incriminate himself and testify against the other suspects. Now Joseph had to convince the jurors that such a deal had been made, despite the denials they had already heard from detectives Hildebrandt and Gonzalez.

Joseph's cross-examinations had done considerable damage to the credibility of the detectives, highlighting important contradictions between their accounts of the interrogation. But that the police might be lying about their encounter with the McCrays did not necessarily mean the boy was also lying about his involvement in the wilding spree. To establish his client's innocence, Joseph would have to rely on his own witnesses.

At the pretrial hearings Burns and Rivera had made the mistake of calling all the witnesses they would use again at trial. This not only provided a preview of their trial testimony, but it gave the DA a chance to rehearse her cross-examinations. Joseph, however, was smarter than his co-counsel. He had not expected Galligan to suppress the videotapes anyway, so he had called no witnesses at the hearings. Now Lederer, like the jurors, was about to see McCray's parents testify for the first time.

———

"They told him, 'Tell me what I want to know. Put yourself right with them and you may be a witness and go home.' If not, he is goin' to jail."

"Did they say that to him after they were calling him a liar about the woman?" asked Joseph.

"Yes they did," said Bobby McCray.

Antron McCray's stepfather was thirty-five years old, had a tenth-grade education and was manager of a parking garage. Bobby McCray was active in his community, coaching a successful team in a local youth baseball league. On the witness stand he seemed nervous and angry. The stenographer had trouble understanding his thick speech and asked him to repeat several of his answers.

Joseph had prepared his witness well. McCray's answers were consistent, delivered without hesitation. He told a story that followed the structure of the testimony given by detectives Hildebrandt and Gonzalez. There had been three parts to the interrogation, interrupted by two hallway discussions among himself and the detectives. Before the third session his wife was asked to leave the room and only then did Antron incriminate himself regarding the female Jogger.

Beyond that outline McCray and the policemen differed on all the crucial points. In the father's testimony the boy had said he witnessed the assaults on "some gentlemen" in the park but had not participated. He had insisted he knew nothing about any woman. The boy had been yelled at and badgered until he and his mother were in tears. His wife was told to leave the room not to relieve Antron's shame but because she was trying to shield her son from this coercion.

Joseph asked McCray whether he had objected when Detective Gonzalez asked Linda McCray to leave. "I didn't have no right to say anything," he replied matter-of-factly. "I was in the precinct."

Early in McCray's testimony Joseph won an important victory at a sidebar conference. The prosecutors argued that Bobby McCray should not be allowed to testify that Antron had told the detectives he was not involved in the rape. To allow the defendant's denial into evidence through the father's testimony, DA Clements argued, undermined the hearsay rule. Lederer added: "I think if Antron wants to put that evidence before the jury, he can testify to that." Joseph did not intend to put his client on the stand and resented this attempt to force him to do so. If the police can testify about what Antron said, he asked the judge, how come the father can't? How can he testify to coercion if he doesn't say what his son said? Galligan ruled for the defense.

Eventually, said McCray, he ordered his son to incriminate himself in the reservoir assaults and the rape because the detectives had persuaded him that Antron would not be a credible witness against the others unless he admitted some involvement.

Bobby McCray described his private conversation with Antron. "I said, 'I know you're telling me the truth. You tell these people what they want to hear and you'll go home.' "

"What did your son say?" asked Joseph.

" 'I wasn't there. I'm not going to lie,' " answered McCray.

"What happened next?"

"I got upset and angry, and threw a chair across the room, because I was trying to get my son to tell a lie," he replied. (The detectives had said they'd heard a loud noise, like furniture moving, when McCray and his son were alone in the youth room.)

When the interrogation resumed, said McCray, the detectives questioned his son repeatedly about the rape. The cops were yelling, "Stop bullshitting! Stop bullshitting!" stretching their arms across the table to point their fingers into Antron's face.

The boy continued to assert that he knew nothing about any woman, despite his father's urging, now in the presence of the detectives, that he cooperate. "I kept insisting," said McCray, " 'if you don't tell them what they want to hear, you are going to jail.' "

Finally, said McCray, his son, in tears, capitulated to the combined pressure from himself and the cops. "He said, 'Okay . . . forget it.' "

Since there was no hiding from the videotape, Joseph next offered the jurors a perspective from which they could view it as fitting into his defense. Why would the boy's parents consent to the taping unless they believed there was something in it for them? "Did you sit there throughout the entire video and not say anything?" he asked McCray.

"Yes."

"Why?"

"Because I already told the police my son is going to cooperate and be a witness," said McCray.

After the taping, added McCray, he was surprised to learn that his son was not free to go.

Joseph asked McCray what he had said to the detective he'd made the deal with.

"I said, 'What the fuck is this? You told me we can go home. . . . We have been here a long time.'"

"What did he say?" asked the lawyer.

"Just sat there looking at me like I was crazy."

"Then what happened?"

"We still remained," said McCray, concluding his direct testimony with a tone of defeat in his voice.

———

Joseph had tried to prevent Lederer from cross-examining his witnesses, saying the task should be left to her co-counsel, Tim Clements. Joseph told the judge that it would be improper for Lederer to question anyone who had appeared on the videotapes, because she had participated in making them. The defense lawyer's argument was based on what is called the unsworn witness rule, which is intended to prevent a prosecutor's personal credibility from being injected into a case as additional evidence against the defendant.* "Miss Lederer is now going to examine this witness about an area that she is a witness to," said Joseph after McCray's direct testimony. The judge overruled the objection, saying it was the conduct of the police, not Lederer, that was in dispute.

Lederer's attack on Bobby McCray's credibility was simple and direct. If Antron were innocent, if he had not been at the rape scene, then how was his story so rich in detail and why did it correspond

---

*There was conflicting case law on the issue, but prosecutors who had taken confessions from defendants had sometimes been disqualified in New York on these grounds. In one such case the defense had argued that the prosecutor had violated the defendant's rights when taking the confession. As a result, the prosecutor was prohibited from delivering a closing argument, on the grounds that this circumstance would improperly inject the prosecutor's personal credibility into the case. In another case, a prosecutor who took a confession from a defendant was barred from trying the case at all. "In short, [both cases] hold that even if the prosecutor who took the confession from defendant did not testify, the defendant would be denied a fair trial if the court were to permit the prosecutor to argue to the jury that his conduct did not violate the defendant's rights" (*People* v. *Lloyd Paperno,* Appellate Division, Supreme Court of New York, 1980).

closely to the stories of the other defendants? Because, answered McCray, the police had told him what to say. Quoting extensively from a transcript of his son's videotape, Lederer hit McCray with a series of questions that established precisely the opposite.

"When Antron was asked about who raped the Jogger, did the police tell him to say it was 'a black guy,' then it was 'a Puerto Rican guy with a black hood'?" she asked.

"No," said McCray. "They told him that Kevin Richardson admitted to raping this person, okay?"

"Mr. McCray, what I asked you was: Did the police ever tell Antron McCray two people, who he couldn't name, had raped her?"

"No, they didn't."

McCray answered "I don't recall" to the next three questions, which concerned his son's detailed description of the beating of John Loughlin.

Then Lederer asked him: "Did the police ever tell Antron that he had to say something about someone named Steve getting hurt?"

"No."

"Did the police ever tell Antron that if he was asked, did anyone take any money or jewelry or anything from the woman, that he should say, 'No, I don't think so, no'?"

"No."

"Did the police ever tell Antron, when he was asked to describe the pipe that was used . . . to gesture, to show the size of that pipe?"

"No."

"Did the police ever tell Antron that he had to gesture to show how he held down the woman's arm while she was being raped by others?"

"No."

Lederer asked seven more detailed questions, eliciting a "no" to each one. At that point, she changed direction. "You went in that room with Antron and you told him to lie, is that true?"

"Yes."

"And you told him to lie because you believed that that was how he would avoid going to jail, is that right?"

"Yes, it was."

"You understood the *Miranda* warnings?"

"Yes, I did."

"Mr. McCray, did you honestly believe, after Antron McCray admitted to the police that he was on top of that Jogger, that he held her down while other people raped her, that he hit her and assaulted other people in the park, did you honestly believe, after he signed that statement, after you signed that statement, that he would be permitted to leave that precinct?"

"Yes I did," he said, "because he told them what the police told him to say."

Returning to the content of the teenager's video, Lederer asked a short series of questions that culminated when Bobby McCray, confused now by his inquisitor's sudden jumps from one tack to another, revealed more than he had intended. "And he described what happened in the park on that night?" asked Lederer.

"Yes he did."

"And he gestured with his hands to show the size of the weapon?"

"He talks with his hands because we all talk with our hands," said the father. "That's normal."

"That's normal behavior for Antron?" asked Lederer.

"To talk with his hands," said McCray, "yes."

"And that's the way he was talking on that tape?" she asked.

"Yes."

"I have nothing further," said the prosecutor, pleased with McCray's inadvertent admission that his son had indeed been at ease during the taping of the video.

———

Linda McCray was so short, barely five feet, that the microphone in front of the witness stand obscured her face from the gallery. In a halting, frightened voice, stopping frequently to catch her breath, she told a story that coincided with her husband's.

She had been crying throughout the interrogation, she said, as the detectives cursed her son and repeatedly called him a liar. "I told them, 'He is tellin' you what he knows. He said he wasn't there.' " Eventually, she testified, the Puerto Rican detective told her it would be best if she left the room.

Why did you agree to leave? asked Joseph.

"I was scared," she replied. "I was upset. I didn't know what to do. They were the police. I just left." When she was brought back to the room later, said Ms. McCray, the detectives showed her Antron's written statement and her husband told her to sign it, so she did, without reading it. She was equally acquiescent later as she silently endured the videotape session.

Ms. McCray also testified that she was present when the detectives took her son to Central Park after the video had been completed and there asked him more questions about the female Jogger. Lederer's objection cut off this line of questioning, with which Joseph hoped to inform the jury that his client, when taken to the rape scene, denied having been there before.

Arguing against Lederer's objection at the bench, Joseph told Galligan: "At Central Park Antron said something to the effect of, I don't remember the exact words but, 'I'm not lying anymore. I don't know anything about any woman.' And I think that is relevant in light of the issue that has arisen as to whether the statements were coerced."

"I think it probably is, too," said Galligan, "but not through this witness."

The only way that testimony would be admitted, Joseph knew, was through Antron McCray. And he was still determined not to give Lederer a chance to cross-examine the defendant.

Lederer was as methodical and aggressive in questioning Linda McCray as she had been with her husband. But the mother was a fragile, sympathetic figure who had spent each day since the trial started in the hallway, reading a small Bible. She carried the book in a blue canvas bag adorned with a pair of hands folded in prayer, below which was the legend: "The family that prays together, stays together." If Lederer pushed this sad woman, who cried sporadically throughout her testimony, to the breaking point, she would risk alienating the jury.

"You were not in Central Park on the night of April 19, were you?" asked Lederer.

"What?" said the surprised witness. "No."

Having testified that she had not read the written statement, Ms. McCray took the position that the first time she heard anything about her son committing a rape was during the subsequent video session. Lederer was incredulous. "You let your son say these things, it was the first time you ever heard that, and you sat there and didn't say a word?" she asked. "Is that right?"

"Right," said Ms. McCray. "Because my husband told me the police told him, told him that if he do cooperate, play ball with them and be a witness, he can go home. And if he didn't, he'll go to jail. My husband believed them and I believed them because I wanted my child to go home." She was crying now, the desperation evident in her small voice. "Understand?" she asked Lederer. "I wanted my child to go home. That's all."

As the brief cross-examination neared its conclusion, Lederer returned to the questions that had upset Linda McCray during discussion of the videotaping. The witness now sat on the edge of her seat, shaking and shouting her answers through tears.

"Did you honestly believe," asked Lederer, "that if Antron McCray sat down and said, 'I held her down while four other people raped her; I raped her; I hit her; I kicked her; I beat someone with a pipe,' did you honestly believe . . ."

"Objection!" shouted Joseph. "This is just being asked for effect."

"Objection is overruled," said Galligan.

"Did you honestly believe after he described what he did that he would go home?"

"I believed in what the police said to my husband," she answered. "I know my child wouldn't do nothin' like that."

"You weren't in the park on that night, were you?" demanded Lederer.

As Joseph again shouted an objection, and Linda McCray insisted "I know my child!" Galligan cut off Lederer's questioning. "She answered that a couple of times," the judge said.

"I know my child!" the mother repeated.

Lederer pressed on in spite of Galligan. "Mrs. McCray, that was the first time that you heard Antron say that?"

"Judge!" cried Joseph. "Argumentative!"

"Sustained," said Galligan, telling Lederer sternly, "We have been all through that."

The prosecutor was finished and Joseph, after a few clarifying questions, rested his case.

Bobby Burns, having badly botched his cross-examination of Detective McKenna, got a last chance to rescue his client, Yusef Salaam, on Monday, July 30. Before calling the first of his witnesses, however, Burns rose in open court to complain to the judge about the paucity of seating for spectators.

It is unfair, said Burns, that the press should have five rows of seats "in this cramped, itty-bitty courtroom" while the public lined up outside and waited hours to get into the trial. Galligan simply noted that the seating arrangements had been the same since June 18 and he was not about to change them now.

Burns had a valid point, but it was no coincidence that he chose this morning to suddenly take on the role of advocate for the Supporters, who were present in strength because a special guest was coming to the trial. Shortly after the session got under way, Al Sharpton and Vernon Mason walked in with Tawana Brawley. Although her allegation of a racist gang-rape had long ago been rejected by a grand jury, Brawley was still a *cause célèbre* in the black press.

Burns staged a replica of the defense he had used at the pretrial hearings. First he called Salaam's older sister, Aisha, to testify that her brother had told the cops, when they came to his apartment in Schomburg Plaza on the night of April 20, that he was fifteen. Next Burns called Salaam's aunt, Marilyn Hatcher, and her fiancé, Vincent Jones, to say that they had arrived at the precinct before Salaam's mother, and had repeatedly told the police that the boy was only fifteen.

On cross-examination Lederer poked holes in the credibility of each witness, establishing that they could not have known at the time that Salaam's age would become an issue and would therefore not have made such a big deal of his juvenile status. She also drew an admission from Ms. Hatcher that Burns's witnesses had met as a group before the pretrial hearings, implying that their testimony could have been carefully coordinated to avoid contradictions.

Despite the pretrial record, which clearly showed that David Nocenti's testimony had done Salaam more harm than good, Burns again called his client's "Big Brother," who winked at Salaam after taking his seat on the stand. Nocenti's description of his argument with DA Linda Fairstein about whether he could talk to the suspect at the stationhouse supported the notion that the investigators had been hostile to the defendant's family. But he offered nothing else to help Salaam's cause.

When she cross-examined Nocenti, Lederer used his testimony to cast doubt on virtually every point raised by Burns's other witnesses. The following exchange was typical:

"Did you ever hear Sharonne Salaam, Marilyn Hatcher or Vincent Jones ever tell anyone that Yusef was 15?" asked Lederer.

"No," Nocenti replied.

Discussing Nocenti's testimony later one juror said of Burns: "What kind of lawyer would set up the case and then have a key witness kill it?"

The media were watching Burns closely. With his dreadful handling of McKenna, Burns had diverted the public's attention from the sensational daily testimony to the relative skills of the defense lawyers, a rare concern for anyone other than aficionados. The black press was especially harsh on the defense team. The Brooklyn weekly *The City Sun*, for example, accused all three attorneys of capitulating to a racist conspiracy to convict the innocent youths.

During the lunch recess on Monday, Tawana Brawley had exchanged pleasantries with Salaam and McCray in the hallway. Out on the sidewalk Sharpton, Mason and Brawley had held a press conference. "Tawana is here today," said Sharpton, "to see how the criminal justice system responds differently for a white victim than it does for a black victim." Sharpton also questioned the competency of the defense lawyers, saying the families of the defendants shared his concern. Upstairs, Mason had disclosed that he was helping Yusef Salaam's mother prepare for her upcoming testimony.

On Tuesday, Sharonne Salaam took the stand and told the jury that immediately upon arriving at the stationhouse she had told Fairstein that her son was fifteen, and that she would not grant permission for him to be questioned. Fairstein had told her, she said, that she could see Yusef, but had stalled for nearly an hour while the interrogation proceeded without his mother's knowledge. The witness was contentious during Lederer's cross-examination and refused to budge from her story.

When Joseph and Rivera learned on Tuesday afternoon that Burns would have the defendant testify next, they begged their colleague to change his course. Both lawyers were trying to keep the jury focused on what happened in the police stationhouses, not in Central Park. That would be impossible with a defendant on the stand. And if Lederer got the better of Salaam, it would suddenly be *their* clients who suffered from guilt by association.

Burns, however, was resolute in his belief that jurors want to see defendants proclaim their innocence, that they are suspicious of a suspect who hides from a prosecutor's questions. His decision sparked a new wave of media criticism.

Yusef Salaam walked confidently from defense table to witness stand in a well-tailored, double-breasted, blue-gray suit. His hair had been recently and stylishly cut, shaved from the sides and back of his head, high and flat on top. Like everyone in the Salaam family he was tall and carried himself with class. As he sat down he placed the two books he'd been carrying for the past few days on the railing beside him. Perhaps the jurors could read the titles on the spines: the Koran and *Ninety-nine Names for Allah*. He was remarkably self-disciplined for a teenager, sitting straight and still with his hands neatly clasped in front of him on the railing.

"Yusef," asked Burns, "were you in Central Park on the night of April 19, 1989?"

"Yes, I was."

One by one, Burns elicited from his client denials of each incriminating statement attributed to him by Detective McKenna. Did you hit a female jogger with a pipe or with your hands? Burns asked.

"I never touched a female jogger," said Salaam. "I never saw a female jogger in the park." His voice was deep and steady, his enunciation clear.

Much of what he had told McKenna, said Salaam, was secondhand. He was just repeating the stories he'd heard that afternoon around Schomburg Plaza, like the one about Jermain Robinson beating up a guy in an Army jacket. In this way Burns took many of the details from McKenna's testimony and cast them in what he hoped was a harmless light.

"Why did you enter the park?" asked Burns.

"I thought it was going to be fun," said Salaam.

"Did you have fun while you were in the park?"

"No."

The defense might have stopped at that point, leaving the jury with the theory that Salaam had gone to the park with his friends but, like more than a dozen other teenagers, had left when the serious trouble started. Burns might also have left the jurors with the impression that McKenna had perhaps taken advantage of the phony birth date on the bus pass, knowing he could use it later to justify having isolated the boy from his mother. The jury had already been told by several policemen that the brass—from captains and inspectors up to the citywide chief of detectives—was all over the case as soon as it hit the media. Maybe McKenna had thought he'd get himself a piece of the glory by twisting, just a little, what Salaam had said.

But Burns wasn't one to leave the jury with "maybes." He wanted to answer all of their potential questions, and for some reason he expected twelve presumably sensible people to believe the story his client was about to tell.

Salaam said he went into the park with a group of about fifty kids, including Kevin Richardson and Kharey Wise, "to walk around." Within minutes of entering the park, however, he lost track of his friends and never saw them again that night. Tracing his route for the jury on the big map beside the witness stand, Salaam said the gang was walking up a grassy hill when he inexplicably took off alone down a dirt path into the woods. He wandered aimlessly around the park, coming across a bum lying on the ground—"I thought he was dead"—and witnessing an assault as he ran past the reservoir. From there, he said, he left the park.

Salaam's explanation for his query to Detective Neenan seemed to stun his lawyer, as it did everybody else in the courtroom.

"Did you ask the detective," Burns asked him, " 'How much time am I facing?' "

"Yes."

"And what were you talking about?"

"I was just talking about how much time am I facing because they were questioning me," said Salaam calmly. "I thought I was being arrested for being in the park late."

"I'm sorry," said Burns, "being in the park?"

"Late."

"What?"

"Late."

"Late?"

"Yes," said Salaam. "I didn't know . . . if they close at a certain time or not."

Lederer seemed as flabbergasted as Burns, with his client's credibility in shreds, wrapped up with a series of questions demonstrating that Salaam was neither a stranger to, nor uncomfortable with, violence. Contrary to McKenna's testimony, Salaam denied he had carried a knife into the park. But Burns apparently wanted to explain why the knife had come up at all during the McKenna interrogation, so he asked Salaam whether he had been carrying a knife earlier that day. Yes, said his client.

"And why did you have that knife?" asked Burns.

"I had it for cutting," replied the teenager.

Salaam explained that his friend, Eddie de la Paz, had an argument with a guy who wanted to date his sister. Eddie thought the guy was too old. "This kid was shorter than me," said Salaam, "but he was kind of stocky." Salaam, a knife tucked into his jacket, had intervened in the dispute, trying to convince Eddie to leave it alone. When the other kid got a look at Salaam, he ran away.

Salaam said he put the knife back in his apartment before going to the park but admitted that he had brought along a twelve-inch pipe. He lost the pipe, he said, when it fell out of his pocket at some point during his solitary journey.

Where did the pipe come from? asked his lawyer.

After the dispute with the stocky kid, said Salaam, he and Eddie went up to Kharey Wise's apartment and told him about it. Eddie then went into Wise's apartment, got the pipe, and gave it to Salaam.

"And why did you carry the pipe?" asked Burns.

"He just told me to hold it for him," said Salaam, "and I forgot I had it."

"And is that the same pipe that you lost in the park?" asked Burns.

"Yes."

The attorney turned toward the prosecution table and said, "Now he's your witness, Miss Lederer."

A prosecutor is expected to destroy a defendant who has the gall to testify and Lederer knew every lawyer in town would be watching her cross-examination. When she walked into the packed courtroom on August 1 she noticed more than the usual number of familiar faces. The gallery included such luminaries as Deputy Chief Administrative Judge Milton Williams, the highest-ranking judge in the city, and John F. Kennedy, Jr., a rookie prosecutor that year in Morgenthau's office.

Lederer wasn't sure she could satisfy the expectations of her audience. She knew there was no way she could do a cross-examination of this witness that would be as devastating to his case as his own direct testimony.

Trusting the jury to reject Salaam's story, Lederer concentrated on exposing him as the malicious, belligerent person she believed him to be. The jurors must be shown that the gentlemanly teenager in front of them was a tough, explosive character, capable of cracking a woman's head open with a pipe. To accomplish that she would have to draw Salaam out, get him angry, give his hostility a target.

Lederer began by leading up to a question that might expose a critical hole in the state's case if it remained unanswered: Why would Salaam have pretended to be sixteen? How was it to his advantage to represent himself to the cops as an adult?

With a few questions she established that Salaam's mother had sent him directly to bed on the night of April 19 because he'd come in at 10:30, at least an hour after she had expected him home. When the police had come looking for him on the night of April 20, Ms. Salaam was not home. Salaam knew, Lederer suggested to him, that Al Morris, who was sixteen, had been questioned earlier and released without his parents' being notified.

"Isn't it true that you thought that if you went to the precinct with the police before your mother came home that your mother might not find out that the police were questioning you?" she asked.

"No," said Salaam. "I just went with them."

"And didn't you know that if you told the police that you were 16 years old they would question you in the absence of a parent?"

"No," he replied. Salaam had damaged his credibility in earlier testimony, and his denials were not what mattered. From the prosecution's point of view, the important thing was that the jury hear the questions.

The antagonism between witness and questioner was obvious. Salaam, his back straight, his hands still neatly folded, gazed coolly at Lederer.

There was a rapid series of questions about whether detectives had searched Salaam at his apartment. Lederer pressed for details. Salaam claimed he could not recall them. She mocked his answers. "That did not make an impression on you?" Lederer asked sarcastically. "You cannot recall whether they gave your wallet back?"

"You're talking so fast," Salaam said calmly, "I can't really understand you."

Lederer took the witness back to his earlier testimony about walking up the hill with fifty other kids, from whom he was suddenly separated.

I got tired, explained Salaam, and fell behind. When I got to the top of the hill they'd gone on ahead.

The prosecutor dwelt on that for a little while, suggesting the absurdity of this big, healthy teenager becoming fatigued within five minutes of walking into the park. This line of questioning quickly deteriorated into an argument, with Salaam displaying some of the defiance Lederer wanted the jury to see.

"You were with that group as you started to walk up the hill, isn't that right?" she asked.

"I was behind them," said Salaam.

"Were you with them?"

"I was behind them."

"Were you with them?"

"I was behind them."

Lederer was going over Salaam's route through the park again when he repeated what he'd told Burns about seeing "a man laying on the ground."

"Is that the person you thought was dead?" asked Lederer.

"Yes."

The man in question, of course, was Antonio Diaz. If Salaam hadn't seen the gang beat him up, why had he assumed he was dead? "How did you know he wasn't sleeping?"

"I didn't know if he was sleeping, either," replied Salaam. "I thought the person was dead. That was my train of thought right there."

"And you didn't go over there to look?"

"No."

"You decided he was probably dead?"

"Yes."

"And you decided to run away?"

"Yes."

"Did you go call the police?"

"No."

"Did you go over to see if he was bleeding?"

"No."

"You just decided to run away from him?"

"If I touched this person," Salaam protested, "my fingerprints would have been on him."

For most of the cross-examination, which stretched over an hour without any break in intensity, the lawyer and witness exchanged taunts.

"Do you always carry a pipe in your pocket?" asked Lederer.

"No, I don't," said Salaam. "I don't have a pipe of my own."

At another point, when Salaam gave her an evasive answer, Lederer asked whether he had understood the question.

Yes, said Salaam.

"Can you answer that question?" she asked.

"I just did," he replied.

It was common for Lederer to keep her arms folded across her chest as she questioned witnesses, sometimes raising her left hand to her cheek. As her examination of Salaam became increasingly heated, she seemed to wrap her arms more tightly around herself, almost as though she were in a straitjacket. She leaned slightly forward, intermittently taking a step toward the witness stand and back again. Occasionally, when he spat one of his contemptuous answers at her, Lederer would jerk her head very slightly to one side, as if to shake it off before pressing on.

She took Salaam by surprise with a series of questions based on Kharey Wise's videotapes. "Isn't it true you were present with Kharey at the scene of the rape?"

"At the scene of who?" said a startled Salaam. "The rape?"

"The rape," said Lederer.

"I wasn't with Kharey," he replied. "Only time I saw Kharey was when he went inside the park. I don't know what he did after that."

"Isn't it true you were with Kharey when, in Kharey's words, you were playing with the female jogger?"

"No, it isn't."

"And isn't it true that you were trying to silence her?"

"No, it's not." They were stepping on each other's words now, with Lederer launching a new question as soon as Salaam said "No" and Salaam denying the accusations before she had finished her sentences.

"And you were covering her mouth?"

"No, it's not."

"And you were laughing . . ."

"No!"

". . . at the scene of the rape? Isn't that true, Yusef?"

"No, it's not true!"

Mickey Joseph objected and requested a bench conference, at which he made a motion for a mistrial. It was prejudicial to all of the defendants, he told Galligan, for the DA to ask questions based on the statements of Wise. She had now told the jury, said Joseph, that a codefendant who was not on trial had confessed, in detail, to the rape with which Salaam, McCray and Santana were charged. It was, he said, a violation of the *Bruton* rule, which prevented the out-of-court statements of one defendant from being used against another. Moreover, he added, Wise's admission took on added credibility because the jury knew it was Lederer who had taken the statement to which she was alluding. Burns and Rivera joined the motion.

Lederer argued that Salaam, who had chosen to testify, admitted going into the park with Wise. "I am asking him about statements or information that I have on what he did in the park." If the court found her use of the phrase "in his words" objectionable, said Lederer, she would change the form of the questions.

The judge accepted Lederer's position, denying the mistrial motion on the assumption that the jury did not know Wise was a codefendant.* Galligan ruled that Lederer could ask about Salaam's alleged activities but could not refer directly to any statements made by Wise.

When she resumed Lederer hit Salaam with other facts that had turned up during the investigation. "Do you recall telling Michael Briscoe . . . as you saw police cars driving by . . . to chill out . . . they're just going to the place where we beat up the bum?"

No, said Salaam.

"You never handed out four or five knives to the people going into the park?" she asked.

No, said Salaam.

None of this seemed to faze the boy, who remained hostile but controlled, brushing off the prosecutor's accusations. McKenna had testified that the only other cop present when he questioned Salaam was Rudy Hall, a black detective. Salaam claimed there were four detectives in the room.

"What did they look like?" asked Lederer.

"Four detectives," he replied.

"What did they look like?" she repeated.

"White men."

"You don't know anything besides white men?" she asked.

"White big men."

"Do you know what color hair they had? Whether they wore glasses?"

"All I know is they were white men," he answered.

In closing, Lederer went back to Salaam's testimony about running away when he saw Diaz on the ground. She would use this to set up her kicker.

---

*Judge Galligan was mistaken. Many of the jurors had made that simple deduction.

"You said you ran because you didn't want to be blamed for killing someone you didn't kill?" she asked.

"Yes."

"You didn't want to take responsibility for that?"

"I don't think anyone would want to take responsibility for that," he replied.

"Isn't it true that you're testifying here today because you don't want to take responsibility for a woman you damn near killed?"

"I didn't near kill anybody," he insisted.

The Supporters were delighted that the defiant black youth had stood up to the white prosecutor. But the steel nerves they so admired represented the very quality that gave the jury pause. Salaam had been much too cool. Wouldn't a teenager, in his first trouble with the law, facing five to ten years in prison for a crime he didn't commit, be more confused and frightened? Why wasn't he up there begging them to see the terrible mistake that had been made?

Beyond Salaam's curiously detached manner was the substance of what he told the jurors. Like nearly everybody else who listened to his testimony, they barely believed a word he had said. The *Post* concisely summed up the city's reaction with a headline on the next day's front page: "Salaam Baloney!"

The afternoon was waning as Salaam resumed his seat at the defense table. Court would adjourn in little more than an hour, yet Peter Rivera approached the bench and told Galligan he could put on his entire defense in that time. This was not necessarily good news for his client, Raymond Santana.

Like Burns, Rivera was about to present precisely the same case he had shown the prosecution at the pretrial hearings. And, like Joseph, he had only two witnesses: the defendant's grandmother, Navidad Colon, and his father, Raymond Santana, Sr. Rivera hoped their testimony would convince the jury that these simple Puerto Rican guardians of his client had been cynically manipulated by shrewd detectives who had then coerced a confession from the boy.

Rivera called Santana's grandmother to counter the testimony of detectives Hartigan and Arroyo about the initial interrogation of Santana at the Central Park Precinct. The *Miranda* rights and the first few questions put to Santana had been translated by Arroyo into Spanish for the grandmother's benefit. If you're going to translate the whole interview, Hartigan had said to Arroyo, we're going to be here all night. At that point, both cops testified, the grandmother told them that she understood English. Arroyo had stopped translating and the interrogation had proceeded in English for about three hours. Rivera hoped the jury would believe Colon did not understand English, that she had simply bent to Hartigan's will and that her grandson, therefore, had not had the adult protection to which he was entitled.

Judge Galligan smiled ever so slightly when Colon, testifying through an interpreter, said she did not speak English. At the pretrial hearings she had answered a couple of simple questions put to her in English before the interpreter had a chance to translate them.

As it happened, Rivera's case took longer than he had expected. Lederer did not get a chance to cross-examine Colon until the next morning, when she established that the grandmother had told reporters who came to her apartment after the crime to leave her alone—in English. Under the prosecutor's questioning, Colon was eventually forced to concede that she understood some English.

Out in the hallway during his mother's testimony, the elder Santana discussed the potential impact of the trial on his son. "Even if he's found not guilty," he said, "this will be a lesson to him."

To which Sharonne Salaam responded: "What lesson? That Puerto Ricans shouldn't go into the park?"

"Remember, that's a white park," cautioned Santana Senior. "They don't want us in there. Whenever a black boy goes to the park he gets arrested. Always consider that." This inclination to submit to authority was precisely what Rivera hoped to show the jury when he put Santana Senior on the stand.

Santana and his father were not close. When the boy's parents had split up some years earlier, Raymond lived in the Bronx with his mother, whom a teacher described as, at best, neglectful. When his mother became gravely ill, Raymond's father went to court to get custody of the boy. As a result Raymond moved to East Harlem, where he shuttled between the apartments of his father and grandmother. His eighteen-year-old sister had remained in the Bronx, where she was raising her own baby.

The defendant's father looked meek and at times bewildered as he answered Rivera's questions. His testimony, however, did little to support the coercion defense, except that he said fourteen-year-old Raymond had been handcuffed to the bars of a holding cell at the Twentieth Precinct.

Rivera did not address Detective Hartigan's contention that, before his son's admission to involvement in the rape, the father had given the detective permission to speak with Raymond alone. In the absence of a denial, the jury could be expected to assume that Hartigan had told the truth.

Rivera succeeded at least in bringing out helpful testimony about Detective Sheehan's late-night excursion to the rape scene with Santana and his son. After taking a second written confession from Santana, Sheehan had driven the boy and his father home, where he waited while the elder Santana fetched a change of his clothes for his son, who was going back to the stationhouse with the detective. On the drive between the precinct and East Harlem, Sheehan had made a detour to the scene of the crime.

Over Lederer's objection, Galligan permitted the father to tell the jury about the conversation he overheard between Raymond and Sheehan. Down in the ravine below the crossdrive, Santana related, the detective had said to his son, "Raymond, you was here." To which, said Santana Senior, the boy replied, "No. I never been here." Raymond then pointed toward the reservoir, added Santana, saying he had only been on the other side of the park.

———

On cross-examination Lederer made short work of Santana's father. At one point she asked whether Raymond Junior had voluntarily signed the statement he had given Sheehan at the Twentieth Precinct. "No," said the father. "He didn't understand what he was saying." But the witness was easily dislodged from that position.

"Did someone force Raymond Santana to sign that statement?"

"No."

"Did anybody force you to sign that statement?"

"No."

The father's credibility was as easily damaged. He had testified that Sheehan did not read the *Miranda* warnings before taking his son's second statement. To rebut this, Lederer had the television monitor wheeled in and played a short portion of Raymond's videotape, which began with a clear shot of Santana Senior sitting beside his son. On the tape, after reading the boy his rights, Lederer asked whether the detectives had read those rights to him earlier in the evening. Yes, he replied.

"At that time," she now asked the father, "when he indicated that he had been advised of his rights, did you jump up and say: Oh, but

I was there and that didn't happen that way?" Santana was spared having to answer when Galligan sustained Rivera's objection to the question.

The prosecutor made much of Santana's lackadaisical attitude toward his son's predicament. When first notified of his son's arrest, he had waited ninety minutes for a patrol car to take him to the Central Park Precinct, rather than rushing there on his own; he had left the boy at the stationhouse with his grandmother and had gone to work rather than calling in sick on April 20; on a mission to bring food back to the precinct for his hungry son, he had stopped to get himself a meal. Lederer hoped this testimony was sufficient to belie Rivera's contention that Raymond Santana's guardians had been forced to cooperate in a frame-up. This evidence seemed to indicate, rather, that Santana's father was no more concerned about his son's welfare than were the cops.

By the time Lederer was finished, there was little Rivera could do to rehabilitate his witness's credibility. He tried to demonstrate, again, that this was a simple family, as though the father's modest lifestyle would somehow absolve the son.

"Who are the breadwinners in your household?" Rivera asked the elder Santana during a short redirect examination.

"What do you mean?" replied the witness.

"Who works in your household?" said Rivera.

"I do."

"How far did you get in school?"

"Tenth grade."

The fifteen-year-old defendant, who had been taking classes at the Spofford Juvenile Center since his incarceration fifteen months earlier, already had more education than his father.

CHAPTER 14

CLOSING
ARGUMENTS

THE PROSECUTORS CALLED FIVE REBUTTAL WITNESSES TO COUNTER SPE-
cific testimony that had been offered during the defense case. Four of
the rebuttal witnesses were policemen; the last was DA Linda Fairstein.

She seemed relaxed and upbeat when she took the witness stand on
August 6, her long, wavy blonde hair brushed away from her face.
Fairstein handled Lederer's questions about the circumstances surrounding Salaam's interrogation at the Twentieth Precinct with the
ease of an expert witness. She looked directly at Lederer until the
question was completed, then turned slightly to face the jury as she
answered. She was clearly as comfortable in the well as any other lawyer
in the courtroom, despite this unfamiliar role as witness.

Fairstein's nonchalant attitude contrasted sharply with the otherwise tense atmosphere of the courtroom. The Supporters considered
her one of the major villains behind the conspiracy to frame the defendants. The animosity toward Fairstein generated by the packed defense
side of the gallery seemed almost palpable. Sharonne Salaam's angry
eyes burned as she watched from her aisle seat in the third row.

Lederer took Fairstein through the now familiar story of Salaam's
interrogation, conducted by detectives, said the witness, who were

under the mistaken impression that the boy was sixteen. Eventually they came to Ms. Salaam's arrival at the stationhouse.

"Did you have any conversation with Ms. Salaam at that time?" Lederer asked.

"Yes, I did," said Fairstein. "She told me she wanted to see her son. . . . I told her, her son was upstairs with detectives; he was being interviewed by detectives."

Ms. Salaam suddenly leaped to her feet and shouted across the big courtroom: "You're lying! You're lying! Why are you telling all these lies?"

A furious Galligan ordered court officers to remove the woman. Fairstein smiled as the guards escorted Ms. Salaam down the aisle. "You don't have to lie," shouted Ms. Salaam. "My son already took a lie detector test. He's innocent!"

Salaam had indeed taken and passed such a test, which was inadmissible at trial. The judge ordered the jury to ignore the outburst and banned Ms. Salaam from the courtroom for the balance of the trial.

Fairstein's testimony contradicted Sharonne Salaam, who had sworn that Fairstein had assured her at the time that her son was not being interrogated, and that she would be permitted to see him as soon as a room became available. A key element of Salaam's defense was the contention that Fairstein had stalled the mother with this lie while her son was upstairs incriminating himself in the rape.

Bobby Burns tried to emphasize this point in his cross-examination but was frustrated by Fairstein's casual, confident manner. At one point, as he stumbled through a series of poorly phrased questions that Lederer successfully blocked with objections, Burns became argumentative, offending Galligan with the sarcastic tone of his voice.

Galligan rebuked him: "It's not humorous. If you think it's humorous, it's not."

Burns exploded, enraged by Fairstein's apparent amusement at his difficulties. "I haven't laughed in this courtroom," he shouted at Galligan, "I'm not the one." Then, pointing at Fairstein, he added: "This witness here has a smirk on her face! I'm not smiling! This is serious!"

The cross continued but Burns was unable to score any points. Peter Rivera did not fare any better. Seeking to imply something conspiratorial in Fairstein's assignment of Lederer to the case, he only managed to boost the latter's credibility.

"Is Ms. Lederer one of the attorneys assigned to [your] unit?" asked Rivera.

"The best," replied Fairstein, "yes."

Galligan wasn't pleased with this gratuitous plug for Lederer. "Strike out the answer," he told the stenographer. Turning to Fairstein, the judge said, "The question is a very simple question."

"Can you answer the question?" asked Rivera.

"Yes, she is," said Fairstein.

Each caustic exchange between Fairstein and a defense lawyer was taken by the Supporters as further evidence of her prejudice toward the defendants. But it was the jury's assessment of her credibility that mattered. Unless the jurors held Fairstein's flippant attitude against her, the defense team had lost this round.

Mickey Joseph, nearly as thin as Lederer, was standing beside the podium that had been placed in front of the jury box. If he had stood behind it some jurors might not have been able to see the friendly face with the wispy, sand-colored beard. It was the seventh day of August, seven long weeks since Joseph and his colleagues had gathered here to select the jurors he now addressed in earnest tones.

At the start of his ninety-minute summation Joseph reminded the jury that "not one witness" had identified Antron McCray, that there was "not one piece" of physical or scientific evidence to link his client to any crime. The state's case, he said, relied entirely on the teenager's own statements, statements that should be disregarded "because they were obtained improperly, and rejected because they are, therefore, unreliable."

Joseph conceded that McCray had been in the park, had been on the East Drive when the bicyclists were harassed, had been at the reservoir when John Loughlin was assaulted. The boy could accurately describe those events, Joseph argued, because he had witnessed them. Didn't it follow then that the reason he was wrong about so many details of the rape was that he had not seen it?

Why did McCray place the rape at the reservoir rather than the 102nd Street Crossdrive? Why did he say the Jogger was raped where she fell, when the evidence proved that she was first dragged more than three hundred feet into the ravine? Why did McCray talk about having to hold her arms down, when the jurors knew she had been bound and gagged? Why was he wrong about the clothes she wore?

Suppose, said Joseph, that someone who claimed to have seen the assault of Paula Harris had been called to testify at this trial. And suppose that witness described the attack the same way McCray described it. "You people," he suggested, "based on the location and based on the facts, would say that person doesn't know what they are talking about."

Joseph spent a lot of time listing the many inconsistencies in the testimony of detectives Hildebrandt and Gonzalez, emphasizing the gaps he had exposed in the credibility of each with his cross-examinations. But why would those detectives have coerced a confession from his client?

"It's not for me to explain their motives," said Joseph. "But I can tell you this. . . . These detectives knew there was a woman in critical condition in the hospital. . . . There was a lot of pressure on them to solve this case quickly. Media was there; higher-ups were there and they had to solve this case. And the only way they were going to do it was to get a statement."

Was it so hard to believe, asked Joseph, that Bobby McCray would jump at the chance to make a deal with the cops? "That's what he was looking for," stressed the lawyer. "He's being told his son can go home, and that's what he wants to hear. . . . Even murderers cooperate with the prosecution, become witnesses for the prosecution, and don't get prosecuted themselves. . . . You've heard of it and Bobby McCray had heard of it."

More than once Joseph explained to the panel that his client's incriminating statements must be rejected if they had not been made voluntarily. He urged on the jurors a simple test by which they could decide the case without even having to consider whether those statements were true or false.

"The issue is: Do you accept the detectives' testimony to the degree that you can say, it wipes out all reasonable doubt as to the voluntariness of that statement?" asked Joseph.

"And do you disregard, or have you concluded, that the testimony of Bobby and Linda McCray doesn't even raise a reasonable doubt in your mind?

"That's what we're talking about here."

"The attack on the female jogger was so vicious that it cries out for vengeance; that the guilty party be identified and punished," said

Bobby Burns. "But you must agree . . . that the evidence is so conflict-ing, that emotions have run so high, and there are racial overtones that are so powerful, that it is difficult, difficult to get at the truth."

In the world according to Burns much of the case remained a mystery. The evidence, he said, had not even established that Paula Harris was raped. Her use of a diaphragm during sex with Kevin O'Reilly suggested that the sperm found in her cervix and rectum came from an attacker. "Does it establish that beyond a reasonable doubt?" asked Burns.

"This young lady's mind was a complete blank," he continued. "We don't know whether she made a stop before entering the park. . . . We don't know whether or not she came home alone. . . . We don't know the condition of her bed linens, as it relates to sexual activity, on the afternoon, evening of April 19. And furthermore, she can't tell us."

All of this was technically true. There was not a juror, however, who was not convinced by this time that Harris had been raped. In pursuing this line at length, even to the point of resurrecting the discredited argument about a lack of trauma to the victim's genitals and rectum, Burns only succeeded in bringing more bad press down on his own head.

Burns next urged the jurors to put their emotions aside. Harris had been called to testify, he said, for the same reason "those ghastly pictures" of her injuries had been repeatedly displayed. "Those are attempts to catapult you into a spirit of being vengeful."

The DA had to appeal to your emotions, Burns told the panel, because there was no forensic evidence to support what he foolishly referred to as Salaam's "confession." Two small bloodstains had been found on the defendants' clothing, one inside the armpit of Salaam's jacket and another on Raymond Santana's sneaker. Neither stain could be identified. "There is no blood on people's clothing; people who are said to have had sexual relations with her," said Burns urgently. "With all of this blood . . . what happened?"

And where was the pipe? Burns reminded the jury that he had asked a detective about a pipe that was found in the park. Tests on the pipe were all negative—no blood, no skin, no hair nor fingerprints—and it was never put into evidence. "Could that have been the pipe that Yusef lost?" he asked the jury.

After Salaam's testimony, no lawyer in New York would have been able to convince the jurors that the defendant had told them the truth. But Burns had to try. "He could have left out the part about his having a pipe," said Burns, "but that would have been a lie. . . . He was subjected to cross-examination by a skilled prosecutor. . . . Did Yusef Salaam stand up? Did his story remain unaltered? Did he appear to be confused, in error, unsure of himself? Do you think a high school kid who had lied and made up a story—you don't think that would have been exposed?

"But I tell you," continued Burns, "truth is a funny thing. It stands up. You say it, you know it's true, you can stand alone. You can stand alone. Yusef told the truth."

In a long, rambling summation, Peter Rivera insisted that his client had been framed by the sinister forces represented by Elizabeth Lederer and the Manhattan North Homicide Squad, whose members he described as "the real culprits here."

In Rivera's scenario the cops randomly picked Santana, Kevin Richardson, Steve Lopez and Clarence Thomas out of a group of fifteen to twenty kids on Central Park West and framed them for the attack on the Jogger. Once the homicide specialists got to his client, said Rivera, it was only a matter of time before they had him saying anything they wanted him to say. Santana was questioned for almost twenty-eight hours, having had little food and less sleep. Expert detectives such as Hartigan and Sheehan had been getting incriminating statements out of unwilling suspects for decades, Rivera assured the jury. "All they had to do is push the right buttons."

Rivera was alone among the defense lawyers in implying that Lederer had joined the cops in manipulating the defendants. He failed, however, to articulate the case convincingly, relying instead on vague, inconclusive statements about the malleability of teenagers and the leading questions Lederer had asked Santana on the videotape.

Like Joseph, Rivera pointed out several errors in his client's description of the rape, repeating his co-counsel's argument that the kid got it wrong because he hadn't been involved. In fact, said Rivera, Raymond Santana was already in police custody when the rape occurred. And because of the police department's decision to frame these boys, he added, "there is a potential rapist, a potential killer, still out there."

While Rivera had pitched the police conspiracy theory in terms more stark than those offered by his co-counsel, the similarities in their summations were clear. And that was another disadvantage to a joint trial. At separate proceedings any given jury might believe that one bad cop had lied about Salaam's statement, or that two detectives had hoodwinked Bobby McCray, or that three had agreed to frame Santana. Collectively, however, the defense team was asking these jurors to swallow an awful lot. Would they accept the proposition that the dozens of detectives who worked on this case were all corrupt racists? Would they believe that the Manhattan North Homicide Squad was capable of staging such an intricate, complete conspiracy? And would they believe that Lederer, with whom most of the panel was now highly impressed, had been willing to go along with a frame-up?

The defense summations and assorted bench conferences had consumed all of that Tuesday, so Lederer had the benefit of delivering her summation to a refreshed jury the next morning.

"You have seen in the course of this trial the beaten, broken and battered people that the defendants left in the trail of their actions that night in the park," said Lederer, beginning a speech that would span four hours.

"You saw and heard Paula Harris, whose mere survival, the fact that she could even come to this courtroom, is a miracle." The jurors were wide awake and attentive. "Paula Harris," the prosecutor reminded them, "will never be what she was before April 19, 1989."

Lederer's tone was customarily flat and dry. She would rely not on her manner but on her words to evoke the horror of that night. Histrionics were not part of her repertoire and she had seen enough juries to know emotion alone would not win her case. Success depended on her ability to interpret a mountain of testimony in a way that would inevitably lead the jurors to a determination of guilt.

She knew Galligan would later instruct the jury on how to apply the acting-in-concert theory, also known as accomplice liability. In cases of group crimes, the judge would explain, each defendant had to share the intention to commit each offense with which he was charged. So Lederer made sure, early and often, to use language that emphasized her contention that this marauding band of teenagers had acted with the shared objective and practiced unity of a ballet company.

"Antron McCray, Yusef Salaam and Raymond Santana engaged in a spree of uncontrolled violence in the park on that night," said Lederer. "Acting with a joint purpose, acting with an entire group of more than 30 people, they went wild in the park, beating, kicking, using bricks and stones, striking anybody they could find, anyone they could catch. They exploded in a unified burst of violence."

She was describing the humiliation of Antonio Diaz—"they poured his beer on him"—when the demonstration occurred. Three loud cracks, unmistakably caused by a hard object knocking against wood, resonated throughout the high-ceilinged room, just as if Judge Galligan had banged a gavel on his bench. But the sound came from the Supporters' section of the gallery.

Lederer stopped speaking and turned, like everyone else, toward the source of the sound. She saw an entire row of Supporters, including Bobby and Linda McCray, rise in unison and march in silent protest down the center aisle, through the double doors into the hallway. There they formed a circle and said a prayer.

The protestors' long oak bench remained vacant as Lederer resumed her summation, the void seeming to silently mock everything she said. If Lederer was feeling any pressure, however, it did not show. Her argument was methodical and evenly paced. She was remarkably articulate, never stumbling, never hesitant, never even filling a space with an "umm" or an "uh."

Despite the lack of passion in Lederer's presentation, there was an unmistakable undertone of disgust in her voice as she talked about the suspects and their crimes. "Paula Harris didn't have a chance against these defendants," said Lederer. "She was five foot five and about 105 pounds. She didn't have a chance against any one of them, let alone against so many of them."

Seven artists sat in the front row, sketching furiously as Lederer, in a navy blue suit and high-collared, ivory blouse, paced behind a long table that had been placed between her and the jury box. On the table the prosecution's exhibits were carefully arranged: the horrid photos of the injuries Harris and Loughlin had suffered, the rock that had cracked the Jogger's skull, and her once-white shirt, now dyed brown with old blood. In front of the witness stand, obscuring Galligan from the jury's view, was the big map of the park and an easel on which the crime scene photos would soon be displayed. A television monitor and VCR stood ready.

Lederer dismissed every argument the defense lawyers had advanced the previous day. Why was there no blood on the defendants' clothing? Because Harris lost most of her blood from head wounds as she lay in the woods alone for hours after the attack. "These defendants didn't come in contact with her head," said Lederer. "They were on top of her pelvic area and on top of her torso." Each of these defendants stated that Richardson had intercourse with Harris, she reminded the jury, and there was no blood on his clothes, either. But there was, she noted, head hair and pubic hair on Richardson's clothing that, according to an expert's testimony, was similar in many respects to Harris's. (Unlike fingerprints, hair cannot be conclusively matched to an individual.)

As for the fact that McCray and Santana got so many details of the rape wrong, Lederer offered a vivid explanation. "Imagine the frenzy of these teenagers as they were gathering around her, as they were waiting to take their turn. . . . They were reaching in hands to grab her, they were ripping off her clothes, people were kicking her, they were beating her. . . . In the chaos of what was going on . . . the rush to not get caught, the rush to participate, to somehow be involved. Are you surprised then that the defendants, when they're interviewed, don't remember the exact details? What do you think their attention was focused on?"

Forced by the DNA evidence to acknowledge that at least one rapist had escaped, Lederer argued that it did not necessarily follow that these defendants were innocent. The only thing the DNA proved about McCray, Santana and Salaam, said Lederer, was that they did not ejaculate inside the victim. But one did not have to ejaculate to be guilty of rape under the law, she noted. And the jury knew from the defendants' own statements, she insisted, that at the very least they helped others rape Harris. Perhaps, said Lederer, the semen that the FBI couldn't identify came from "the black guy" or "the Puerto Rican guy with the black hood" whom McCray said had raped Harris, or one of the two unknown boys Salaam accused.

Using cold logic, Lederer attacked the coercion defense offered by Joseph. Bobby McCray told you, she said, that he believed things could go one of two ways. If his son denied having been involved in a rape, assault and robbery, he would go to jail. But if he admitted being involved in those crimes, he could go home. "Does that make any sense to you?" she asked.

"Mr. and Mrs. McCray don't want to believe that their son did these acts," said Lederer. "But they weren't in Central Park that night and they don't know all the evidence in this case. . . . And while you may feel sorry for the McCrays, it's Antron who is on trial, not his parents.

And you are not to be swayed by any feelings of sympathy you may have for them."

Describing Salaam's testimony as "an insult to your intelligence," the prosecutor dismissed it with a sarcastic summary. After seeing a man he thought was dead, did he go for help? No. He ran deeper into the park. "Poor, tired Yusef Salaam, who couldn't keep up with his friends," said Lederer, "is now charging full out through the park with a pipe in his pocket."

Santana was not be believed either, said Lederer. She snatched his blue sweatshirt off the table and held it up in front of the jury. The presence of a large amount of semen on the front of this sweatshirt, and under its waistband, she declared, tells you that Santana was on top of Paula Harris, not simply fondling her breasts. Nor did the prosecutor accept Santana's assertion that he left the park after the rape because his conscience bothered him. He only made that claim, and he only placed the rape last in his chronology, she argued, because he knew it would sound worse to admit having continued the wilding after such a violent act.

Throughout this long summation, the three teenagers at the defense table watched Lederer closely, seemingly as interested in her argument as were the jurors. She pointed at the boys periodically. She played sound bites from Santana's and McCray's videotapes twice each. She read aloud Salaam's oral statement as reported by Detective McKenna, the statement Burns had put into evidence. In conclusion, Lederer tied together her simple theme: All of the evidence, all of the testimony, corroborated the statements of the defendants themselves. It was their own words, first and last, that proved their guilt.

"Antron McCray, Yusef Salaam and Raymond Santana had their fun in Central Park on April 19, 1989. Today they have no one to blame for the predicament that they are in but themselves," said Lederer. "They have had a fair trial, ladies and gentlemen, and what they deserve from you now is a fair and just verdict. . . . And the only fair and just and true verdict in this case, based on this evidence, is a verdict of guilty as to each of the defendants on each of the counts."

CHAPTER 15

ALL FOR ONE AND
ONE FOR ALL

THE JURORS HAD A BIG JOB AHEAD OF THEM, THE COMPLEXITY OF WHICH became clear when, following Lederer's summation, they listened to Judge Galligan's long set of instructions on how they should apply the law to the evidence.

The case against each of the three defendants must be considered separately, stressed the judge. To come back with a conviction on any count, each juror had to be convinced, beyond a reasonable doubt, that the state had proven every element defined by the law as an essential component of that crime. Galligan then read the law on each charge, a process that consumed several hours, since there were thirteen felony counts in the indictment.

The charges stemming from the attack on Paula Harris were attempted murder, rape, sodomy, sexual abuse and two counts of first-degree assault. The charges related to the assaults of David Lewis and John Loughlin (and the theft of the latter's headset) were three counts of robbery, three counts of assault and one count of riot. Not all of the charges necessarily had to be considered, explained Galligan, because a conviction on a high felony might negate the applicability of a lower count. If, for example, the panel voted unanimously to convict a defendant of rape or sodomy, they could then ignore the lower sexual abuse charge. Similarly, a conviction on the highest of the three robbery counts would render the other two superfluous, and so on down the line. In this respect the indictment was a veritable Chinese menu, giving the jurors lots of options.

The alternate jurors were dismissed when deliberations began on the morning of August 9. The others, having been sequestered for the first time the previous night, would not be going home for another ten days. The panel, comprising four whites, four African-Americans, three Latinos and one Asian, would spend most of that time in a narrow, cramped room without windows that was adjacent to the courtroom.

George Louie was a loner. A Chinese-American who worked as a picture framer in Greenwich Village, he had not mixed much with his fellow jurors throughout the long trial. While the others commonly formed smaller groups and went to lunch together in nearby Chinatown or Little Italy, Louie kept to himself. He usually ate lunch alone, mulling over the morning's testimony and smoking too much. He had said during jury selection that the case interested him. That curiosity had since grown into fascination.

Louie, thirty-four, had the stereotypical look of a hippie. He was thin, dressed casually and wore round, wire-rimmed glasses. He had a Fu Manchu mustache and his long, straight, black hair was invariably worn in a ponytail. His appearance led the defense team to trust him and the prosecutors to worry. But the lawyers were wrong about George Louie. He had been profoundly affected by the videotaped confessions and the shocking evidence of what had happened to Paula Harris. He went into the deliberations thoroughly convinced of the guilt of each defendant. Though he was smart and articulate, Louie was soft-spoken and not accustomed to taking a leadership role in group situations, but that was about to change.

Louie's most effective and consistent allies were two white government employees: Harold Brueland, forty-seven, a former Methodist minister now working as a computer specialist with the state Department of Social Services, and Richard Peters, a caseworker at the city Human Resources Administration who dealt with drug addicts.

On the other side of the equation, the strongest force pulling swing voters toward acquittal was another white male, Ronald Gold, a former reporter for *Variety* and *TV Guide.* Gold, now retired at age sixty, had also been a speechwriter with the National Gay and Lesbian Task Force. He was quick-tempered, assertive and argumentative.

The most volatile of the swing voters was the enigmatic Pedro Sanchez, a black Latino bus driver who was nearing retirement. Sanchez had said during jury selection that he did not want to serve on this panel, fearing the time off might reduce his city pension. Now he was unhappy about facing an eighth week away from the job, and he would soon grow frustrated as the debate became increasingly dominated by more articulate jurors. According to several jurors, Sanchez had trouble grasping some of Galligan's instructions but, once his mind was made up, he could be as stubborn as anybody else.

One advantage conviction advocates Louie, Brueland and Peters had was simply that they had stayed awake during most of the trial. While anybody could be expected to occasionally nod off in Galligan's hot, windowless courtroom, several jurors had slept too much. As a result, the stenographers were called upon during deliberations to read back reams of testimony. The sleepers included Gold, Ben Neal, Charles Nestorick and foreman Earle Fisher.

Fisher was a retired black man who had been designated foreman in the usual manner in New York state: he was the first juror seated. Fisher, who had a law degree but had never practiced, had most recently worked as a site inspector in New York with the federal department of Housing and Urban Development. As a young man he had worked for the National Association for the Advancement of Colored People and the Urban League.

Neal, an elderly black man, was a mail and filing clerk who had served on juries before.

Nestorick, a single white man, was a customer service representative for New York Telephone.

The other swing voters included Samuel Holliday, a black repairman for Consolidated Edison who had also served on juries previously, and Rafael Miranda, thirty-four, a Dominican maintenance man for the New York Transit Authority.

The panel's two women also shifted from one camp to another as the debate progressed. Migdalia Fuentes, thirty-nine, was a publications assistant with the United Nations Children's Fund. Edith Milton, a quiet, black homemaker, sometimes worked as a clerk at her brother's 7-11 store and was active in her local tenant patrol group.

The first thing foreman Fisher did was put the race question on the table, hoping to clear the air of a potentially divisive subject. Is there anyone, Fisher asked, who thinks race is an issue we should address? Everyone agreed it was not. From that point on, race was not openly discussed, but racial and ethnic considerations did play a subtle role in the ensuing process.

Sanchez and Fuentes, two of the three Latinos on the panel, had been moved by Peter Rivera's sympathetic portrayal of Santana's family. If the boy's father and grandmother had been ineffective guardians of his interests, should his incriminating statements still be considered voluntary? Santana may have been without protectors in the police stationhouses, but Fuentes and Sanchez would be looking out for him in the jury room.

The jury spent four days recreating the wilding spree, retracing the gang's path on the big map and comparing the times at which different witnesses had estimated the assaults. Then they got to the hard part.

Taking one defendant at a time, the jurors considered the lower charges first, reaching relatively easy convictions on riot and the assaults at the reservoir. They hit their first significant stumbling block while debating the theft of Loughlin's radio, a charge some jurors considered frivolous when compared to the enormity of the other events in Central Park. The first round of voting was eleven to one for acquittal.

There was no evidence that any of the three defendants on trial had stolen Loughlin's headset. Indeed, Santana had said on videotape that nobody wanted it because it was just a radio, not a cassette player. Gold, Sanchez and Holliday argued that it was unfair to convict these defendants for robbery because somebody else in the gang might have taken the headset. In response, Louie maintained that, since Loughlin had been deprived of the radio by somebody in the gang, these defendants were guilty of robbery under the acting-in-concert principle, which Sanchez said he did not understand.

On August 13, the fifth day of deliberations, Fisher sent out a note asking Galligan to repeat his instruction on acting-in-concert. Quoting the state penal code, Galligan explained that each accomplice must share in the intention to commit the crime and must "solicit, request, command, importune or intentionally aid" in the criminal conduct that is alleged. Then the judge gave the panel a standard example.

"As in the theater, you have actors with roles of varying importance," said Galligan. "Some have major parts, some have minor parts, but all are players. To be a player it is not necessary that a person be the leading man or that he play the principal role. If his part requires him to do nothing more than walk across the stage, he is a player, despite the unimportance of that role.

"So that even though one person may have committed 99 percent of the acts constituting the crime and another person may have committed but one percent," he continued, "in the eyes of the law they are both equally guilty."

That resolved the stalemate and each defendant was soon convicted of robbery. But the acting-in-concert theory would surface later as a bone of contention. As he reluctantly voted to convict Santana on this charge, Sanchez let it be known that he expected the jury to apply the in-concert principle uniformly; he would not vote to convict the Latino boy of any count unless the two black boys were also found guilty. No specific deal was put on the table but, as the voting continued, no defendant was convicted alone of any charge. From that point on, it was to be all for one and one for all.

The jurors came out into the courtroom periodically to watch the videotapes, reviewing McCray's tape five times and Santana's three times before they were finished. They were all perplexed that these kids could so calmly discuss such appalling violence. But nobody tried to explain the defendants' attitude; that was not their job. In an interview later one white juror, who had voted for acquittal on several charges, speculated that people who commit acts of wanton violence don't see their victims as human beings. To the boys who went wilding in Central Park that night, said this juror, "white yuppies are not people."

The defense lawyers had been right to worry that the editing of the videos would fail to protect their clients from incrimination by a code-fendant. Virtually all of the jurors guessed that Santana and McCray were naming each other or Salaam or both during the portions of the tapes that had been redacted. This led to occasional arguments about the practicality of following Galligan's instruction to consider a taped or written statement as evidence only against the defendant who made it. When it came to the attack on Harris, for example, Gold argued that it was unreasonable not to compare the statements, especially because of the discrepancies among them concerning key details. How, he asked, are we supposed to convict all of the defendants of the same crimes when the evidence against each is so different?

If one defendant suffered most from guilt by association it was

Salaam. Brueland believed that, reading the lips of one defendant on videotape, he had discerned Salaam's name among the litany of those said to have entered the park with the gang. (In fact neither Santana nor McCray had mentioned Salaam's name.) The jurors later claimed they had been able to put such matters aside when voting on each defendant.

The potential influence of the press coverage also sparked a brief dispute. Sanchez commented one day on something he had seen about the trial in the morning paper. Gold upbraided him, saying everybody should follow the judge's instruction not to read about the case. But Sanchez dismissed that concern, saying he couldn't be influenced by the press anyway because he considered everything they wrote a lot of bull.

Salaam's considerable advantage in not having made a videotape had been squandered by his lawyer's faltering and his own testimony. His only reasonable hope was that the jury would dismiss his incriminating statement to Detective McKenna because no guardian had been present. Indeed, some jurors believed DA Fairstein had stalled the boy's mother so the interrogation of her son could continue.

That hope faded, however, when Galligan instructed the jury regarding a statement by a juvenile, emphasizing the letter of the law rather than what the defense counsel considered its spirit. Instead of telling the jury that a guardian must be present when a juvenile is questioned, Galligan said the defendant's age and the presence or absence of a guardian were factors that should be considered. The jurors considered those factors and decided, in effect, that Salaam was capable of understanding and waiving his *Miranda* rights on his own.

As to coercion, none of the jurors thought McKenna's lie about finding fingerprints on Harris's tights was likely to prompt an innocent person to falsely incriminate himself, which was the legal standard required for rejection of the statement.

The jurors also determined that Santana's statements were voluntary, despite the misgivings of Fuentes and Sanchez. The pair was not confident that Santana's grandmother and father had understood the boy's right to counsel. Also, while Fuentes did not believe Navidad Colon had as much trouble with English as she claimed, she thought the entire interrogation of Santana should have been translated for Colon's benefit. Ultimately, however, Fuentes and Sanchez agreed that the police had done enough to safeguard Santana's rights.

As they made their way up the indictment, the jurors' plan for orderly progression began to break down. They had intended to come to a conclusion for all three defendants on a given charge before moving up to the next count. That system had worked on riot, the reservoir assaults and robbery, all counts for which each teen now stood convicted. When the jury reached the sex crimes, however, things began to go awry, beginning with another debate on the acting-in-concert principle.

On the videotapes, which most of the jurors found credible, McCray and Santana denied penetrating the Jogger, as did Salaam in McKenna's account of his oral statement. Lederer had argued, of course, that this trio was guilty of the rape charge under the acting-in-concert principle, since they all admitted helping Kevin Richardson rape Harris.

If the jury's system had remained intact, they would have opened the voting on the rape count with McCray. But Gold was unable to overcome his misgivings about the credibility of McCray's videotape. He steadfastly refused to vote on McCray's culpability regarding any crimes against the Jogger until everything else was settled. He would not be moved from that position.

Santana was next in line, setting the conviction advocates against Sanchez, who said he didn't understand why Santana should be convicted of a rape committed by Richardson. He also expressed the fear that the jurors would look stupid if they voted to convict these defendants of rape and Richardson was later acquitted of that charge at his own trial. This led to another readback of the law on acting-in-concert, after which Louie took Sanchez aside and quietly explained the principle further.

Some jurors were suspicious of Sanchez's repeated flip-flopping on the issue. It seemed as though he chose to understand acting-in-concert when he wanted to apply it to McCray and Salaam, yet he feigned ignorance while attempting to protect Santana. Louie eventually prevailed, however, convincing Sanchez the principle made sense in this case. On the next vote, Santana was found guilty of rape. Salaam, with no protector on the panel, was easily convicted of rape, also.

Sodomy was next but Louie, Brueland and Peters could not muster enough votes for a conviction. None of the defendants talked about sodomy in their statements, except to tell Lederer they hadn't seen anybody commit the crime either anally or orally. Although one lab test had reported a finding of semen in the victim's rectum, another lab had found none. So, Salaam and Santana were acquitted of the charge. As for McCray, Gold was still refusing to take up any more counts against him until all charges against the other two defendants were resolved.

The jurors reached the top count of the indictment, attempted murder, on Wednesday, August 15, the seventh day of deliberations. At the start Louie was alone in calling for conviction, though he soon won over Brueland and Peters. Throughout most of the day the voting held at nine to three for acquittal.

The majority was hung up on whether the DA had proved the defendants had the necessary intent to kill Harris. Unless they intended to murder her, Galligan had explained, there could be no conviction on this charge. The fact that they beat her into unconsciousness and left her in the woods, where she lost three-quarters of her blood, did not in itself constitute attempted murder. But how were the jurors to know what the kids intended? You may infer intent, the judge had explained, from the actions of the defendants, the nature of the injuries and the weapons used in the assault.

Peters did not think the jurors were giving enough consideration to the severity of Harris's injuries, especially after somebody suggested that her attackers only wanted to silence her. He convinced Edith Milton to send for the photos of the woman's battered body. But for a long time the photos sat undisturbed on the table; nobody wanted to look at them again. At the end of the day another note was sent out, this one requesting readbacks of all testimony related to injuries to Harris's head and torso.

As the jurors listened to that testimony the following afternoon, the strain was evident on the haggard faces of Gold, Milton and Miranda. They had spent seven days in the close deliberation room, which was filled nearly wall to wall by two long tables and the surrounding chairs. The smokers were getting on the nerves of the nonsmokers.

Back in that dismal room another vote on attempted murder was six to six. The readback had changed three votes, but only temporarily. Louie couldn't hold the fragile coalition together. Gold, often shouting and interrupting the debate, was persuasively battling for acquittal. The lines kept blurring. Fuentes said boys as young as fourteen and fifteen could not understand that the blows they were inflicting might kill Harris. If they wanted to kill her, said Rafael Miranda, they could have strangled her or cut her throat. Why would they have tied her up, he asked, unless they expected her to wake up?

As the swing voters—Earle Fisher, Charles Nestorick and Miranda among them—shifted sides, the three staunch conviction advocates stood fast. Then Sam Holliday argued that it was by no means clear that any of these three defendants had been present from the start of Harris's ordeal to the end. None of their written or videotaped statements mentioned the binding and gagging. Perhaps, he suggested, McCray, Santana and Salaam were gone by the time the worst of the injuries were inflicted.

This position put reasonable doubt into the minds of Peters and Brueland, who now abandoned Louie on the attempted murder charge. In addition to Holliday's persuasive argument, the hawks saw opportunities for conviction elsewhere. "We were getting a good indication," said Peters later, "that we could get a conviction for assault with depraved indifference" to human life.

One such indication came from Gold, who said he'd vote to convict Santana and Salaam of assault if the others would agree not to press the attempted murder charge against McCray. As a result, Santana and Salaam were now convicted of first-degree assault against Harris and nobody would be convicted of attempted murder. The only charges outstanding were the sex crimes and assault counts against McCray.

Judging by the material the jury was having read back, Lederer was fairly confident that things were going her way. Then at about 5:30 P.M. on Thursday, the eighth day of deliberations, a court officer came out of the jury room with a note that plunged the prosecutor into despair. They wanted to hear again the entire testimony of Bobby and Linda McCray. Somebody in there was buying into the coercion defense.

Both the circumstances of McCray's interrogation and the story the boy told on videotape were deeply troubling to Ron Gold. Joseph's cross-examination of Hildebrandt and Gonzalez convinced him the detectives had lied, but Lederer's questioning of Bobby McCray was equally damaging to his credibility. Antron seemed credible on the video and Gold had no doubt the kid participated in the assaults of Diaz, Lewis and Loughlin. He could not understand, therefore, why McCray was wrong about so many details of the rape; why he seemed to leave out so much.

Because of his doubts about McCray's presence at the rape, Gold was inclined to believe he had fabricated the story to satisfy the cops.

But this, too, presented a problem. He believed the cops had offered Bobby McCray the deal he had described and Linda McCray certainly seemed submissive enough to accept it without complaint. But if the detectives had fed the story to Antron, as his father claimed, surely that story would have been consistent with the evidence. The cops knew Harris had been raped at the crossdrive. Why would they let the kid say it happened at the reservoir?

Gold had also sorted out, from the limited information Joseph had elicited from Linda McCray and Detective Hildebrandt, that the youth had failed to identify the rape scene when he was taken back to the park. He stunned the other jurors when he suggested that McCray, on his videotape, might have been describing a second rape the panel knew nothing about. When his colleagues asked for evidence of this, Gold said the defense was not required to offer an explanation. It was only a possibility, he added, something that might explain McCray's version of events.

The jurors spent the last two days of deliberations debating the points raised by Gold. Louie and Peters hammered at the holes in McCray's defense. Gold hammered at the holes in the police testimony and McCray's account of the rape. The swing voters swung throughout Friday, with Fisher and Nestorick dropping in and out of Gold's acquittal camp.

Several of the conviction advocates thought it likely that the cops had made promises to Bobby McCray so he would urge his son to tell what he knew. They did not think, however, that such a tactic rose to the level of coercion. It made no sense, said Fuentes, that Bobby McCray would tell Antron to confess to a rape that he knew his son did not commit. It just didn't make sense. Many jurors agreed.

By Friday night Gold was hanging tough on the lonely side of eleven to one. He started talking about a hung jury. On Saturday morning, however, he gained an unlikely ally when Harold Brueland cast his vote to acquit McCray of the rape, sodomy and assault of Paula Harris.

Sanchez hit the roof. The thought that the jury might abandon the acting-in-concert principle—after a week of pressing him to accept it—was too much. If McCray is acquitted, said Sanchez, I will withdraw my guilty votes on every other charge in the indictment. Fuentes doubted Sanchez would follow through on this threat but she supported his position. She said that if McCray were acquitted of the attack on Harris, she would have to reconsider her votes to convict Santana and Salaam. Now the deal the jurors had quietly followed was

being spoken of openly for the first time. But Gold, who considered Sanchez irrational, would have none of it.

Brueland had been swayed by Gold's arguments about the inconsistencies in McCray's tape. Maybe, he thought, the cops *did* railroad the boy. But once he went over to Gold's side, he said later, "a whole number of contradictions came flooding back at me." By noon Saturday the other ten jurors had won Brueland back. "You can have a doubt," Brueland finally told Gold, "but you want your doubt to be reasonable."

Having lost Brueland, Gold resigned himself to the fact that he would not change any more minds. He showed the others a note he had drafted to Judge Galligan, declaring the jury deadlocked on the sex crime and assault charges against McCray. Only Miranda, who wanted to go home as badly as Gold did, supported sending the note.

Now it was George Louie's turn to lose his temper. "He raised hell," recalled Fisher, "to think that Ron would even suggest saying to the judge that we were unable to reach a verdict and we were hung." The vehemence of Louie's reaction ensured that nobody else would vote to declare a deadlock.

A few jurors suspected Gold's motive in fighting so hard for acquittal. It was common knowledge among the sequestered panel that he was writing a daily journal about the deliberations. At least one juror thought Gold might be trying to steer the deliberations toward some plot he had in mind. Others rejected that notion.*

Late on the tenth day of deliberations the jurors went out to the courtroom to watch McCray's tape again. Many were physically and emotionally exhausted, perhaps none so much as Gold. The pressure of all those people yelling at him for two days, blaming him for keeping them locked in that dreary place, had mounted. As he watched the tape it seemed to him now that the boy was credible enough about the rape. Maybe he wasn't making it up. Maybe he wasn't talking about a different rape. Who could know?

Back in the jury room Gold was prepared to give up the fight. Let's take another vote, he said. Somebody proposed that the panel look at some other evidence first. Sanchez flipped. If Gold was suggesting a vote, he knew, it could be for only one reason. In frustration Sanchez

---

*After the trial Gold did try to sell his diary, which ran to approximately twenty-five thousand words. It was rejected by *The New York Times Magazine*, *The American Lawyer*, *The Nation* and *The Village Voice*.

kicked a chair across the room. Forget the evidence, somebody said, take the vote.

At 6:30 P.M. a note was sent out, informing the judge that the jury had reached its verdict. Gold, feeling sick and ashamed, marched out with the others to listen as the clerk ran down the ballot and Fisher kept responding, "Guilty. . . . Guilty. . . . Guilty." McCray, Santana and Salaam were each convicted of the rape and assault of Paula Harris; the assaults of Lewis and Loughlin; the robbery of Loughlin; and riot.

Out in the gallery, Bobby McCray cried.

Within a few days of the verdict, Vernon Mason, newly hired to handle McCray's appeal, launched an attack on Mickey Joseph. Mason announced on WLIB, a black radio station, that Joseph had been fired because he had bungled the case. The appeal, he said, would be supported by funds to be raised by Reverend Al Sharpton and Reverend Louis Farrakhan of the Nation of Islam.

Mason represented McCray at the sentencing on September 11, at which time longtime radical William Kunstler officially signed on to replace Burns, who had also been fired. Both of the new defense counsel asked Galligan to disqualify himself on the grounds that he was biased and that his appointment had been improper. Mason said he knew that Robert Morgenthau had personally selected Galligan because Alton Maddox had told him so.

"Is he a confidant of Mr. Morgenthau?" asked Galligan.

Mason pressed the argument that Galligan should step aside with a line that brought a round of applause from the Supporters. "There is widespread—in fact almost unanimous—belief in the black community," said Mason, "that this Court is prejudiced both racially and religiously." Mason delighted the audience again a few minutes later when he described McCray as "an All-American hero."

Both attorneys also argued that Galligan should set aside the verdicts on a variety of grounds, including the lack of physical evidence and the incompetence of Burns and Joseph. The judge did not bother to defend Burns, but he said to Mason: "I defy you or any other advocate to prove Mr. Joseph did anything but an outstanding job." Watching from the back row, Joseph took solace in this remark.

Kunstler, who had told Elliot Pinsley of *Manhattan Lawyer* a year earlier that he would never represent a rapist, enthusiastically took up his new role as Salaam's defender. He picked up on a favorite phrase of the Supporters when he described the trial as "a legal lynching." The defendants' incriminating statements could not be trusted, said Kunstler. "Confessions seem to me to be the least persuasive of all types of evidence, particularly when obtained from children by veteran police officers, particularly white officers filled with the symbols of white manhood, being affronted by a white woman allegedly being attacked sexually by black youths."

When his turn came Peter Rivera followed a more conventional sentencing strategy: He asked for the court's mercy. McCray and Santana each made brief remarks, thanking their families for their support and declaring their innocence.

Yusef Salaam had a lot more than that to say. Throughout the long summer Salaam had become the darling of the Supporters. In the latter stages of the trial he and his mother were often escorted by bow-tied bodyguards from Farrakhan's Nation of Islam.

This trial, said Salaam, has been a test that Allah has put me through, just as He did many great black leaders. "Look at Malcolm X," said Salaam. "He spent time in jail the same as I am doing now. Look at what a great black man he turned out to be before his death. Look at Marcus Garvey. And two of the greatest, Martin Luther King and Nelson Mandela, just to name a few."

Salaam then read a long rap-style poem in which he reinforced his newfound status as victim. "I'm a smooth type of fellow, cool, calm and mellow. I'm kind of laid back, but now I'm speaking so that you know I got used and abused and even put on the news. . . . Some brothers go wildin'," he continued. "We're not down with them. . . .

"The D.A. doesn't want to be wrong and put us on the stand and get the real story told from a righteous black man," said Salaam, suddenly turning to face Lederer and raising his voice. "Yo," he called, "instead of trying to get your name made, it's reconstructing the crime that really pays."

Nearing his conclusion, Salaam invoked the Boyfriend Theory. "It'll be funny if she remembered and said, 'I got hit by my man.'"

Sharonne Salaam beamed with pride as her son spoke. But the last word was Judge Galligan's.

"The intensity of the violence on April 19, 1989, in Central Park is unfathomable," said the white-haired judge, "and no rational mind can explain it. . . . There was a time when young people went into Central Park with baseball bats to enjoy a baseball game; but no more. A 12-inch pipe in the park is now an instrument of fun. . . . There has been no acknowledgment of wrongdoing here, no remorse—only defiance."

With that Galligan imposed sentence on the two designated felonies under his jurisdiction: rape and robbery. He gave each defendant the maximum on each count, three and one-third to ten years, to be served consecutively. But none of the boys would actually do six and two-thirds to twenty years. Under state law the maximum sentence a juvenile could serve for these crimes was five to ten years. This meant the boys would be eligible for parole in five years and, with good behavior, could be confined for no longer than six and two-thirds. (The convictions on four assault counts and riot were set aside.)

Lederer did not like the fact that juvenile sentences were so limited, but she took satisfaction in the knowledge that this trio was going to jail. The prosecutor had never been so totally exhausted. More than a year of fifteen-hour days and seven-day weeks had taken a huge toll. Four days after the verdict the front page of the *Post* had carried a photo of Lederer under the headline: "Secret Agony of Jogger D.A." Timothy McDarrah wrote that she had been involved in a bitter divorce proceeding throughout the trial. Citing an anonymous source, the story stated that Lederer's two-year marriage to Paul Rudden "broke up because she devoted herself to the Jogger case—and ignored him."

Lederer had stopped jogging months ago, in fact she had stopped exercising altogether. She had started smoking again. She had lost weight she didn't need to lose and developed dark bags under her tired brown eyes. What she needed was an extended vacation.

She wouldn't get one. There were three people whom she still wanted to get in front of a jury, and she had already kept them waiting long enough: Kevin Richardson, Kharey Wise and Steve Lopez.

DUE
PROCESS

Part Three

CHAPTER 16

THE DEFENSE
ATTACKS

THERE WERE TWO GOOD REASONS, FROM THE PROSECUTION'S POINT OF view, to sever Steve Lopez's case from those of the other two defendants.

First, if Lopez were tried with Kevin Richardson and Kharey Wise, the emotional impact of their videotapes would be significantly weakened by the erasure of Lopez's name. Both teens had mentioned Lopez repeatedly, agreeing that he was one of the rapists. Moreover, Wise had described Lopez as the instigator of the gang-rape. It was Lopez, Wise had said, who warned the others on the way into the park "not to squeal" if they got caught after "the violence" started. It was Lopez who had said, "Yo, we will rape this woman," when the boys first got hold of Paula Harris on the crossdrive. It was Lopez, Wise asserted, who slashed her legs with a knife and it was Lopez who had called Wise a punk because he didn't rape the victim himself. It was Lopez, finally, who had argued that Harris must be killed so she couldn't later identify her attackers.

If Lopez were tried with Wise, the subsequent editing of the videos would leave Wise's compelling narrative pockmarked with beeping sounds at critical moments. The jury wouldn't know whether the obscured references were to a single boy or several. Just as it had been necessary for Harris to testify in the first trial so the jury would see the victim as a real, living person, Wise's description of Lopez's behavior had to remain intact so that her most vicious assailant would have an identity, too.

Second, the prosecutors were still trying to build a stronger case against Lopez. They had the witness whom Lederer had talked about at the arraignment in May 1989, the kid who said he had seen Lopez rape the Jogger. But was one witness enough, given that Lopez did not incriminate himself? And what if that witness, whose identity was still a mystery to the defense lawyers, should renege on his promise to testify, or crumble under cross-examination by Lopez's lawyer, Jesse Berman? The prosecutors wanted more witnesses. A few detectives were still working the streets of East Harlem. Given time, maybe they'd find somebody to whom Lopez had bragged about the rape. Such things happened all the time. As one detective working on the case put it, "These kids love to strut their shit."

At a brief court appearance in September, Judge Galligan granted Lederer's request to put Wise and Richardson on trial together. She would keep Lopez waiting a while longer.

The contentious tone of the second trial was set during jury selection in October. Each side was permitted the customary number of peremptory challenges, meaning the attorneys could object to the seating of a juror without having to divulge the reason. But when the prosecutors used peremptories to reject three black jurors in a single morning they ran into objections from defense counsel Colin Moore and Howard Diller, representing Wise and Richardson, respectively. Of the four jurors who had been seated up to that point only one was black. Moore, a black civil rights litigator, and Diller, a white veteran of the criminal bar, accused the DA of rejecting blacks solely because of their race.

Galligan ordered Lederer to justify her challenges to the three blacks. The prosecutor offered satisfactory explanations for eliminating two of the panelists. Then, in a move the defense lawyers took as confirmation of their suspicions, she withdrew her challenge to the third juror. The process was completed in seven days. The racial makeup of the panel that would go into deliberations six weeks later was five whites, four African-Americans, two Latinos and one Asian.

The trial got under way on October 22. Lederer presented essentially the same case against Richardson and Wise that she had in the earlier trial. Except for a few changes in the cast of detectives, the state called the same witnesses at the second trial, and they offered essentially the same testimony.

The most significant shift in Lederer's strategy was revealed in her opening statement, which was in all other respects an echo of the one she had delivered four months earlier. At the first trial Lederer had been careful to place the attack on Harris early in her chronology, telling the jurors that it had occurred between the harassment of the tandem cyclists and the reservoir assaults. That jibed with the stories told by two of the three defendants at that trial. Only Santana had claimed that the rape came last.

This time Lederer eliminated the assault of Harris from her chronology altogether. She again retraced the gang's path through the park, from the beating of Diaz to the beating of Loughlin, but she finished that recitation without mentioning the Jogger. When Lederer, as a sort of addendum, did describe what was done to Harris, she gave the jurors no clue when it had happened in relation to the other assaults.

Richardson and Wise had both said on videotape that the rape was the evening's final act; that it followed the beating of Loughlin and that they had left the park immediately afterward. Lederer believed they were incorrect but saw no need to highlight that fact for the jury. By leaving the timing of the rape vague, the prosecutor avoided casting doubt on the credibility of the videos.

Kharey Wise, still in jail after eighteen months because his mother could not raise twenty-five-thousand-dollars bail, grew increasingly agitated as he listened to Lederer's detailed description of the horrors visited upon Paula Harris. At first he was just talking to himself and shaking his head sideways as if to deny what he was hearing. As the prosecutor continued Wise began to shift nervously in his chair, sometimes burying his face in his hands, sometimes pounding his fist against his forehead, all the time quietly mumbling.

When Lederer finished her speech the lawyers walked up to the bench for a conference with Galligan. As Wise watched Lederer cross the well he whispered the word "lies" over and over again. When Galligan called a recess and the jurors filed out of the courtroom, Wise finally reached his boiling point. There were perhaps two or three jurors still to pass through the exit when the defendant began to rise, crying and shouting.

"No! No! No!" the teenager yelled. "I can't take this! Oh, Lord Jesus! I can't deal with this! I didn't do it!"

As Moore tried to calm his client, several court officers rushed to the defense table to hold Wise down in his chair. "No! No!" screamed Wise. "It's wrong! It's wrong! She's lying! Oh, Lord Jesus! That woman is lying!"

———

Howard Diller, sixty, had opened a storefront office in Harlem when he was starting out as a lawyer back in the early 1960s. The uptown office was long gone by the spring of 1989, but a former client from the early days had recommended him to Kevin Richardson's family after the boy was arrested in Central Park.

Diller, who had labored in obscurity for nearly three decades representing petty criminals and drug dealers, had been delighted to find himself at the center of a media circus. The phone never stopped ringing as the best-known print and broadcast reporters in the city lined up for interviews. Diller knew Richardson's modest family, which had secured his services with a five-thousand-dollar retainer, would not be able to come up with much money. But with the kind of publicity the case was generating, it looked like a ticket to instant fame.

At the pretrial hearings Diller had put on the standard coercion defense, calling Richardson's mother, Grace Cuffee, and twenty-four-year-old stepsister, Angela Cuffee, to testify about the circumstances of the boy's interrogation. Diller never hired an investigator, something many defense lawyers do routinely because, he explained later, Richardson's family could not afford the expense.

By the time the case went to trial Diller had decided to offer no more than a token coercion defense. Juries, he reasoned, do not care how the police obtain confessions, as long as the confessions are credible. Didn't the verdict from the first trial prove that?

Diller's strategy was to rely on the letter of the law. In a brief, vague opening statement delivered in a stage whisper, he told the jurors to accept the video as true. Richardson admits no crimes on the tape, he said, and is not even guilty under the acting-in-concert theory. Kevin, said Diller, is a commentator on these events, not a player. "He discusses what other people have done."

The lawyer went on to emphasize the element of the acting-in-concert theory that required intent on the part of each participant. "There is nothing here to show that he had an intent to cause, or to help anyone cause, the great distress that was caused to, at least, two of the joggers here," he clumsily told the panel.

Diller had underestimated the passion the Cuffees brought to their crusade to establish the innocence of Richardson, who was now sixteen years old. At the end of the trial's first day Diller got an earful from Angela Cuffee, who was the catalyst for many of the family's important decisions. His opening had shocked the Cuffees, who did not expect Diller to admit his client was even in the park that night, let alone present during the rape.

Belatedly, Diller realized his approach would not suffice for these clients. "These people think it's a war," he said to a reporter as he walked back to his office on lower Broadway. "Maybe I'm the wrong guy if they want a war."

Delivering an emotional opening in his West Indian accent, Colin Moore exploited the chronology problem Lederer had sought to avoid. Moore relied on the sequence of events that the prosecutors had stressed in the first trial, promising the jury that the state's own evidence would prove Wise's scenario, in which the rape came last, was impossible. Barely fifteen minutes after the attack on Loughlin, Moore noted, several boys were arrested out on Central Park West. The attack on Paula Harris was long over by then, he said.

This position raised two obvious questions, both of which Moore was eager to answer: Why did Wise get it wrong? And, if the gang didn't attack Harris, who did?

His client's four incriminating statements—two written and two taped—were full of contradictions, discrepancies and even fantasies, said Moore, because they are the products not only of psychological duress but of beatings as well. This coercion defense was more sweeping and dramatic than any employed in the first trial. In his opening statement Moore was limited to discussing the anticipated evidence and was not permitted to offer argument. He could not yet give the jury his answer to the second question, which was that the boyfriend did it.

Moore's embrace of the Boyfriend Theory was both strategic and political. Strategically, it gave the jury an alternative theory to weigh against Lederer's explanation for what happened to Paula Harris. But Moore lacked any credible evidence to support his theory and, of course, his client had confessed to the crime. Given those holes, the Boyfriend Theory was an embarrassingly weak alternative. However, it served Moore's political agenda.

At age forty-nine Moore was steadily gaining credibility with leftist

African-Americans as an activist attorney willing to take on the white Establishment. His small practice in Brooklyn was mostly devoted to litigation, much of it arising out of civil rights issues such as police brutality. Whenever possible, Moore would cast his client as the victim of a corrupt and racist system. The notion that the rich, white Jogger had been raped by her boyfriend and that the black youths had been framed appealed to a significant segment of Moore's constituency.

"Ladies and gentlemen of the jury," said Moore in a deep, confident voice that filled Galligan's big courtroom, "there is a victim in this case. There is a victim: Paula Harris. She was the victim of an assault. But there is another victim in this case." Spinning away from the jury box, stretching a long right arm, index finger extended, toward his client, Moore added: "His name is Kharey Wise. He was a victim of police overreaction."

Moore liked to compare his style of oratory to that of a Baptist preacher. Indeed, as he spoke the Supporters, who outnumbered the press and spectators now that the suspense of the first trial had passed, nodded and hummed the sounds of affirmation like a church congregation.

Moore's method of bringing political protest into the courtroom was by no means unique. It was an extension of the time-honored defense strategy of putting the government on trial. Although Moore seemed certain always of where he wanted to take a case politically, he was deficient in many fundamental provisions of criminal law. His first appearance in the Central Park case, for example, had been at the night court arraignment on April 23, 1989, more than two weeks before the case was assigned to Judge Galligan. At that proceeding Moore had argued that there was no evidence—independent of his client's video-taped confession—that Wise had participated in the rape. Judge Charles Solomon had to explain that, when a defendant confesses to a crime, the only corroboration necessary is proof that the crime indeed took place.

But, Moore had replied, Wise's admission that he "played with her legs" while others beat and raped the Jogger was evidence of, at most, sexual abuse. Judge Solomon found himself explaining the acting-in-concert principle to the attorney, and in a startling display of ignorance, Moore insisted the judge was mistaken. "There is certainly no crime of acting in concert to rape," said Moore, "unless one commits the rape."

The judge gave up. "I beg to differ," he replied, moving on to other business.

Now that the case had come to trial, Moore was prepared to argue for his client's innocence on a variety of other grounds. The videotapes were unreliable, he told the jury, not only because they were products of coercion but also because they were factually inaccurate. They must therefore be rejected, he said, and as a result no evidence remained that Kharey Wise committed these crimes. As he neared the conclusion of his long opening statement, Moore told the jurors they would see graphic pictures of the injuries Harris had sustained. "For God's sake," he pleaded, "don't convict an individual only on the basis of photographs."

It is hard to imagine two lawyers with less in common than Diller and Moore. Everything they did, from openings to summations, stood in marked contrast. The most clearcut evidence of their differences, in attitude as well as technique, was in their respective styles of cross-examination.

With few exceptions, Diller addressed the state's witnesses with respect, if not deference. He expressed friendly concern for the joggers and cyclists, asking John Loughlin if he was feeling better now, wishing Gerald Malone "good luck." Diller, a former FBI agent, would phrase questions to police officers so as to indicate that he knew their lingo and understood their responsibilities. He often made little jokes, sometimes at his own expense. Diller's performance said: I'm an insider, an old pro, a nice guy doing his job. If the jury liked the lawyer perhaps they'd look more kindly on his unsavory client.

With the DA's witnesses Moore went for the jugular from the start, accusing—literally or by implication—everybody who took the stand as a co-conspirator in the racist plot to frame his client. He attacked the credibility of every witness on the most minor points, often without the benefit of logic. He was rude, insulting and suspicious of all comers, victims included.

Both defense lawyers avoided the kind of monumental error Robert Burns had made while questioning Detective McKenna in the first trial, but neither was effective as a cross-examiner. Moore scored more often than Diller but he also routinely pushed far beyond the point at which he should have stopped, sometimes opening doors for new testimony that damaged his own case. Several times Moore's poor judgment led him so far from common sense that jurors openly laughed at his questions or shook their heads in wonder. One such instance was the cross-examination of Loughlin.

When the victim's blood-stained pants were put into evidence, Moore questioned his ability to identify his own clothing. "Is that your blood on the pants?" he asked.

"Yes," said Loughlin.

"You can recognize it?" challenged Moore.

"I was there when it got there," said a deadpan Loughlin.

Moore went on to suggest that, since Loughlin had been dressed in Army fatigues and wore "a communication device" in his ears, it was reasonable for the teenagers to assume he was a vigilante. Moore seemed to be agreeing. "What was your purpose in the park that night?" he asked.

"I was jogging around the reservoir," said Loughlin.

"Weren't you involved in some other intelligence activity?" asked Moore.

"No."

Loughlin had characterized as "life-threatening" the blows that cracked his head, causing concussion and the internal bleeding that had left his eyes blackened for several months. Moore showed Loughlin the series of eleven photos of his injuries, inquiring sarcastically about the severity of each wound.

"This nick on your leg, that was life-threatening?" asked Moore.

"No."

"This nick on your foot here, that was life-threatening?"

"No."

"This nick on your knee, that was life-threatening?"

"No."

"This nick above your eye, that was life-threatening?"

"That's not a nick," said Loughlin.

"Well, the cut above your eye, that was life-threatening?"

"It might be."

"Life-threatening?" asked Moore, acting incredulous.

"Yes."

"Has your vision been impaired?"

"No," Loughlin replied, "except when my eyes were full of blood."

Loughlin had explained that he went back to his teaching job after only two days in the hospital, despite great pain and difficulty walking, because, "I felt my appearance would have a good effect on my students."

"So," said Moore, "you think your appearance is more important than your health, Mr. Loughlin?"

The witness, looking contemptuously into Moore's eyes, did not answer.

———

The tandem cyclists, Patricia Dean and Gerry Malone, had married since their last visit to 111 Centre Street back in June. Tall and white, pretty and successful, thirty-year-old Dean represented many of the same things that Paula Harris had come to symbolize to the media. The day after Dean's testimony in the first trial, her photo was on the cover of the *New York Post* under the headline, "One Who Got Away." The archetypal resemblance between Dean and the case's celebrated victim was certainly not lost on the Supporters, and Moore did his best to exploit it when she took the stand on October 26 to tell her story again.

Under Lederer's questioning Dean described the group of about thirty to forty black kids spreading out across the East Drive, making what she called "grunting sounds . . . animal noises." Three or four of them, she recalled, grabbed at her thighs and shoulders, trying to pull her off the tandem bike as it passed. She had been terrified, she told Lederer.

When Moore cross-examined Dean, his questions suggested that her fear came from something other than any physical threat. "So you were terrified," he said, "by the fact that they pulled their hoods up?"

"I was terrified at the number of them, the fact that we were going toward them, that they were pulling their hoods up," she replied. "I was terrified."

"You are constantly referring to 'them,' " said Moore. "And by 'them,' you mean the young people that you saw on that night?"

"A large group," said Dean.

"Have you ever been at a basketball match or a baseball match?" he asked.

"Yes."

"Are you terrified . . . by crowds of people?"

"No."

The Supporters began to perk up as they realized where Moore was going. "You mentioned that they were dark-complexioned; am I correct?"

"They seemed to be," said Dean.

"Did that terrify you?"

"Yes."

"You are terrified by large groups of dark-complexioned people?"

"I am terrified," she explained calmly, "by large groups making sudden movements and doing things to cover up their faces."

"And especially," said Moore, "if they are dark-complexioned people; am I correct?"

"Not necessarily."

Now Moore was ready to move on to the next stereotype. "Did you form an opinion as to why they were trying to grab at you?"

Lederer's objection to the question was overruled. "Yes," said Dean.

"And what was that opinion?" asked Moore.

"Probably the fear that a lot of women may have," she replied. "I did not think that they were going to just knock us over and leave us alone. That was my opinion."

"Your fear," Moore suggested, "was that they were trying to rape you. Was that your fear?"

"My first fear," she said, "yes."

"And what was that fear based on?"

"Things that you hear, the dangers of being a female in New York . . . being in the park too late that night. Many things."

"And do you think that these people that you saw, this group of dark-complexioned people, do you think they have a greater propensity for violence than other groups of people?"

Again, Lederer's objection was overruled.

"No," said Dean, "not necessarily greater."

"So you were not of the opinion that they were trying to get you and Gerry," continued Moore. "You thought they were just trying to get you; am I correct?"

"Yes," she said. "I mean, I thought, I was a woman and my very first opinion was they would beat up Gerry and knock him out and possibly rape me."

With that the Supporters erupted in laughter that was so loud, so openly derisive of the witness, that Galligan warned them he'd clear the courtroom if it was repeated.

———

In the eyes of the Supporters, Moore was doing a masterful job. The Cuffees thought so, too.

THE DEFENSE ATTACKS

Grace Cuffee's four daughters and one son remained a close-knit family, despite her separation from her second husband, Paul Richardson. The forty-eight-year-old Ms. Cuffee, relying on disability benefits since suffering a stroke seven years earlier, lived quietly in Schomburg Plaza with Kevin. His older sister, Connie, and stepsisters, Angela, Crystal and Valerie, often came by for Sunday dinner. They were not a radical clan but their collective political consciousness was quickly being raised as a result of the trial. The black press, the local activists they knew as neighbors and the Supporters at the courthouse were all having some influence on the family.

The decisive factor in the Cuffees' decision to switch lawyers now, however, was not politics but their judgment that Diller's approach to Kevin Richardson's defense was anemic. Moore's dramatic opening had impressed the Cuffees as much as Diller's dull speech had disappointed them. For three days they watched Moore challenge the DA at every turn. They listened nightly to the spirited sidewalk press conferences at which Moore argued that Lederer's case was built on a foundation of straw. He had not only vowed to vigorously cross-examine the Jogger, but planned to put on an alibi defense, too. It was obvious to Richardson's family that Kharey Wise was represented by a fighter, while Diller, they thought, was simply going through the motions.

At about 10:00 P.M. on Wednesday, the third day of trial, Diller got a call at home from Angela Cuffee, telling him he was fired. Vernon Mason, meanwhile, was sending out a press release, announcing that he was coming into the Jogger case to represent Richardson.

The Cuffees were taken aback on Thursday morning when Galligan not only refused to permit Diller to withdraw but denied his request for an adjournment until Mason was available. Mason, who had a jury deliberating in Brooklyn and could not appear before Galligan until Friday, had not told the family he would need the judge's permission to take over the case.

At the end of Friday's session, having kept Mason waiting around the courthouse for most of the day, Galligan dismissed the jury and let the radical lawyer say his piece. Mason proceeded to lambast Diller, who sat in silent humiliation at the defense table. It was bad enough, said Mason, that Diller had "poisoned the jury pool" by releasing his client's videotape to the press, but that was only the first sign of his incompetence. Diller had failed to conduct an investigation, said Mason, had failed to hire experts, had refused to line up character witnesses and had not informed the family of his strategy, if indeed he had one.

Lederer and Galligan raised the concern that there was a potential conflict of interest between Mason's representation of Antron McCray on appeal and Richardson at trial. My clients, said Mason, have waived the conflict. Then Mason asked the judge, whom he had called a racist in this courtroom barely a month earlier, for a staggering accommodation. It would be necessary to declare a mistrial, said Mason, for several reasons: He needed time to try a second case in Brooklyn for which jury selection had just opened; he needed time to investigate Richardson's case himself; and furthermore, he could not possibly come into a case with a sitting jury when he had not participated in its selection.

Galligan refused to permit Mason to enter the case, citing case law that gave him discretion over a change of counsel in midtrial. The Cuffees, bitterly disappointed but not yet ready to give up hope, continued to consult with Mason over the weekend.

In chambers the following Monday Diller pleaded with Galligan to let him quit. The family, he told the judge, had become very hostile. They expected him to stop representing Richardson immediately. If he didn't leave, said Diller, they said they would try their case in the media, "with their antagonism of me as the centerpiece."

"What else is new?" asked Galligan. "How is that different than any of the other cases that preceded here, using the media as a focus of the defense?"

It was not just the family who were hostile, said Diller, but strangers among the Supporters, as well. "I'm very concerned with my personal safety," he said.

"Now, Mr. Diller," said Galligan, "I'm not going to do indirectly what I refused to do directly. . . . This is nothing more than an attempt by this family to do what I refused to do on Friday." The judge ordered Diller to continue his representation of Richardson.

Lawyers on both sides of the case, and Galligan himself, had sporadically received death threats over the past eighteen months. Now Diller believed he had a genuine reason to fear bodily harm from the angry Supporters. Lederer noted her own predicament. "Just for the record, Mr. Diller, I'm threatened every day when I come in and leave," said the prosecutor. "Four times a day."

Minutes later, out on the sidewalk, a spokesman for the Cuffees, Lamont Radcliff, read the assembled press corps a list of forty complaints about Diller's handling of the case. As far as the family was concerned, Radcliff said, Mason was now Kevin's lawyer. Acting on Mason's advice, Grace and Angela Cuffee then went into the courtroom and told the judge they would not testify on Richardson's behalf. This meant Diller would be without witnesses when the time came to put on a defense.

The hard-core supporters of Kharey Wise were relieved. Schomburg Plaza's few experienced political activists, to whom Moore was a valued colleague, had been fearful that Galligan would grant Mason's mistrial motion, thus killing the growing momentum they perceived in Moore's performance. "Kevin should get the lawyer he wants," said William Perkins, president of the Schomburg tenant association, "but not at Kharey's expense."

So Moore pressed ahead, stretching his defense of Wise from that point on to encompass Richardson's interests whenever possible.

———

Lederer again put Dr. Robert Kurtz on the stand to testify to the extent of Harris's injuries. As he had in the first trial, Kurtz explained that the victim sustained five major lacerations of the head, in addition to several smaller cuts that overlay skull fractures. It was from these lacerations that Harris lost nearly three-quarters of her blood as she lay in the cold woods.

On cross-examination Moore stubbornly pursued a futile effort to get the surgeon to agree that, by the time the victim had reached Metropolitan Hospital, any threat to her life had passed. In seeking to minimize Harris's injuries, Moore abandoned elementary logic, provoking open laughter from several jurors. "The lacerations, in and of themselves, were not life-threatening, were they doctor?" asked Moore.

"They certainly were," Dr. Kurtz replied. "Taken together they created a life-threatening blood loss."

"Well, apart from the fact that they bled profusely," continued Moore, "did the lacerations, in and of themselves, threaten in any way the life of Paula Harris?"

"I can't say it any other way," Kurtz insisted. "With her in her circumstances, they did threaten her life because she lost so much blood from them that she almost died."

Instead of dropping that line of inquiry after having lost the point, Moore continued. "The life-threatening conditions arose from the fact that . . . the bleeding was not stopped, isn't that correct, and not from the nature of the injury?"

Kurtz became exasperated. "The nature of a scalp laceration," he said, "is that it will bleed copiously. . . . That's what it does."

Moore showed the doctor a photo of the left side of the victim's head, depicting several large lacerations, some still bleeding through stitches. "Wouldn't you say that's a lot of blood?" he asked.

"Absolutely not," replied Kurtz. "A lay person would look at this and say that's a lot of blood. But a physician would look at this and say it's piddling."

"It's piddling?" Moore asked.

"Yes."

"So you consider that the injuries to her were piddling?" said Moore triumphantly.

"That's not what I said," the doctor responded with obvious disdain. "You asked me if the amount of blood on her face was a lot of blood, and I said, no, it isn't."

The examination continued in this fashion, with Moore suggesting that the doctor had done no more than replenish the blood supply of a patient who was no longer in danger at the time. But his attempt to denigrate Dr. Kurtz's role failed miserably, with the surgeon ultimately lecturing the attorney in his final answer. "None of these things is really important," said Kurtz. "What is important is that she was in danger of dying, and she was transfused and ventilated, and had the various intensive surgical care techniques applied to her to save her life."

Moore grudgingly returned to his seat.

———

Between the two trials Moore had publicly threatened to put Harris through an extensive cross-examination regarding the details of her sex life. It was a legitimate area of inquiry, he told the press, because of the presence of her boyfriend's semen on her tights and the failure of DNA tests to link any defendant to the crime. If Moore's intention had been to throw a scare into Harris with this talk, he was too late. Having met the challenge of appearing in the first trial, she had the confidence to do it again.

When Harris walked unsteadily to the witness stand on the morning of Friday, November 2, the jurors and spectators were again transfixed, but this time the gallery was not as crowded. In the city's newsrooms, and therefore in the public mind, this trial was considered a replay of the first, with identical guilty verdicts expected. Several organizations, including *The New York Times*, didn't have a reporter in the courtroom every day. The press corps, which had filled five rows of seats daily during the summer, now occupied only two benches.

Lederer carefully guided Harris through a reiteration of her original testimony. When the prosecutor finished, Moore rose and, in a manner more polite than any he had thus far displayed, launched a half-hour of cross-examination.

Moore began with the suggestion that, despite the lasting effects of her injuries, Harris was not as debilitated as the prosecution had led the jurors to believe. In response to Moore's questions, Harris testified that she was working eight to nine hours a day at Salomon Brothers, performing the complicated, demanding tasks of a vice-president in the corporate finance department. She was jogging five to six times a week "as part of my rehabilitation," she said, and she walked up and down four flights of stairs in her apartment building daily. "I view that as part of my rehabilitation, also," she volunteered.

Next Moore moved to establish the probable time of the assault. A neighbor had testified that he had seen Harris leave their apartment building on East Eighty-third Street at about 8:55 on the night of the attack. It would take her perhaps ten minutes to reach the park entrance at Eighty-fourth Street and Fifth Avenue. On the map beside the witness stand Moore traced what she had said was her usual route up the park's East Drive and through the 102nd Street Crossdrive. At Moore's request, Harris estimated the distance between the entrance and the scene of the crime: less than a mile. She would have reached that point, she now said, in five to seven minutes.

Moore seemed pleased with her answer. It put the time of her abduction between 9:10 and 9:15 P.M., approximately a half-hour before Loughlin was attacked at the reservoir seven blocks to the south. This was the chronology Lederer had advanced in the first trial but had since abandoned. Moore now had testimony from the Jogger herself dispelling the contention of both Wise and Richardson that the rape was committed after the reservoir assaults.

He turned to the Boyfriend Theory. Harris had testified that her last memory of Wednesday, April 19, was a phone conversation at 5:00 P.M. in which she canceled a dinner date for that evening with a friend named Michael Allen.

"Would you describe him as a very good friend?" asked Moore.

"What do you mean by 'very good friend'?" she asked.

"Well, had you dated him on prior occasions?"

"No."

"Had you been intimate with him?"

"No," said Harris, as Lederer was rising to object.

"Now, you don't recall, do you," asked Moore, "whether Michael ever did come to your house that evening?"

"No, I do not," she replied.

"And also, you would have no recollection as to whether Kevin O'Reilly was in your apartment when you went home that evening; am I correct?"

"I have no recollection," she reminded him, "but I don't believe that he was because he was out of town on Tuesday night and he was to get back on Wednesday. He was out West on business and I remember that the time he was going to get back would be in the evening."

"Okay," said Moore. "But you don't recall if he perhaps came a bit earlier than he had indicated to you, do you?"

"No, I do not."

"Now, Ms. Harris, you had indicated that Kevin O'Reilly knew the route that you used to run; am I correct?"

Lederer's immediate objection was sustained but the jury knew from the witness's earlier testimony that the answer would very likely have been "yes." Under Lederer's questioning Harris had testified that passing through the crossdrive was her usual route, that she had discussed it with several friends, and that she and O'Reilly had gone running in the park after having sex on the morning of Sunday, April 16.

The shape of Moore's theory was coming into focus. Some in the press corps had been told by confidential sources that Harris and O'Reilly were in the midst of a breakup during the weeks preceding the crime. Moore seemed to be suggesting that perhaps O'Reilly, having somehow learned of his girlfriend's date with Michael Allen, had ambushed her on the crossdrive and nearly beaten her to death. Or maybe it was Michael Allen? Or how about her former roommate, Patrick Garrett, whom she was supposed to meet at ten o'clock that night?

"While you were in Metropolitan Hospital," continued Moore, "do you ever recall saying to a nurse—do you ever recall calling the name of a boyfriend?"

Lederer jumped to her feet to object and requested a sidebar conference. At the bench she demanded that Moore provide a factual basis for the question.

"We have a nurse from Metropolitan Hospital," said Moore, "who will testify that she heard Ms. Harris calling the name of a friend and saying, in effect, 'John, you are not going to do that to me anymore.' "

"And when did this supposedly occur?" asked Galligan.

A couple of days after she was admitted, said Moore.

This drew a scornful reaction from Lederer.

"Who is this nurse?" Lederer demanded. "Was this someone in charge of her care? Is this a document in the medical records? Is this somebody who had any connection to her care at all?"

Moore did not divulge the nurse's name. A friend of hers, he said, had told his private investigator about the incident.

Galligan said he would allow Moore to ask the witness if she had any recollection of saying anything at the time in question. "If she says no," said the judge, "that's the end of it; period."

Moore asked Harris if she recalled "saying certain things" three or four days after being admitted to the hospital.

"No," she replied, "I was still in a coma."

After you came out of the coma, he continued, in early May, do you remember saying anything in the presence of nurses?

"No," said the witness.

Harris, who had been calmly watching the defense lawyer throughout the questioning, glanced at Lederer in momentary alarm when Moore said, "Let me refresh your recollection." The prosecutor shot up to object and Galligan immediately cut off Moore.

Moore dropped the hospital scenario but he wasn't ready to give up the suggestion that Harris had suffered violence at the hands of an acquaintance. "Prior to April 19," he asked, "did you have any altercations with Kevin O'Reilly?"

Lederer's objection was sustained.

"Prior to April 19, were you ever assaulted by any male friends of yours?"

Objection sustained.

"What was your relationship with Kevin O'Reilly?"

"He was my boyfriend."

"I understand that," said Moore, "but were there altercations in the relationship?"

Objection sustained.

"How would you describe the relationship?"

Objection sustained.

"Prior to April 19, Ms. Harris, do you recall going to a doctor—"
Objection sustained.

Moore turned to Galligan and said, "I haven't asked the question
yet."

"I'm not going to let you ask the question," the judge replied.

Moore then took the examination into new territory. He asked Harris
whether she had undergone any therapy to restore her memory.

She had taken a class in the hospital on general memory techniques,
she answered, but had never made any specific attempts to regain a
memory of the night of the crime.

Moore then elicited a response that impressed the jurors greatly and
would benefit his client during deliberations. "What happened to you
on the evening of April 19 . . . was a very traumatic event; isn't that
correct?"

"Yes," she said, "it was."

"And therefore you would naturally have an interest in seeing that
those who committed it are convicted, am I correct?"

"Yes."

"Wouldn't it also cause you some concern if the wrong people,
people who did not do that to you, were convicted?"

Harris answered without hesitation, "Yes."

"Therefore," he continued, "you have an interest then in making
sure that your memory is restored, so that you would be able to identify
those people who committed the crime; isn't that correct?"

Lederer's immediate objection was sustained before Harris could
answer.

"So is it your testimony then, Miss Harris, that between April 20,
1989, or right after the event, and up to the present time, that you have
not sought a memory reconstruction?"

Again Lederer's objection was sustained. "She has answered the
question," said Galligan.

But Moore would not let go. "Is that correct?" he asked again.

"She has already answered it once," repeated the judge.

"Thank you," said Moore, taking his seat at the defense table.*

*These questions echoed an effort undertaken by Vernon Mason and Reverend Al
Sharpton during the previous trial. Stating that the Jogger "claims selective amnesia,"
the pair had filed a friend-of-the-court brief seeking Judge Galligan's permission to
"provide experts to cure the Jogger's memory problem." If her memory were restored,

The next day's newspapers were as critical of Moore as they were admiring of the Jogger. Harris had maintained her composure throughout the cross-examination and Moore was less harsh than expected. Still, he was widely criticized. An editorial in the *Post* charged that his questions had been "designed further to humiliate" the victim. Virtually every press account debunked Harris's supposed hospital outburst, many quoting Dr. Kurtz saying that such an episode was impossible because Harris had a respirator tube down her throat for thirteen days after the assault.

Most of the press corps concluded that Moore had fabricated the story. But those reporters, consumed with their mandate to capitalize on each day's hottest testimony to the exclusion of all else, did not delve very deeply into their clip files to check out Moore's contention. Perhaps they would have if the lawyer had been accurate about the date of Harris's supposed flashback.

Back on May 23, 1989, the *Post* had run a story by Peter Moses reporting that the Jogger "had a terrifying outburst" on May 21, more than two weeks after she came out of the coma. The Jogger was "thrashing around in bed and looking in anger at the people crowding her," wrote Moses. Attributing the account to an anonymous source who was in the room at the time, Moses quoted the Jogger as having said: "Leave me alone. You're the ———— who did this to me." When two nurses attempted to restrain her, the Jogger reportedly cried: "Don't hold me down. You did this before. Leave me alone." The story also quoted Kurtz saying, "If it happened, I don't know how to interpret it."

The *Daily News* ran a story the next day calling the veracity of the *Post* account into question. After examining a nurse's notes and dis-

---

Mason had argued, the Jogger's testimony "could indeed be exculpatory." Permission was not granted.

The kind of memory therapy Colin Moore was talking about might have been appropriate if Paula Harris's amnesia had been the result of a psychological defense mechanism. But most neurologists who considered the case were of the opinion that Harris's memory loss resulted from physical trauma. When the brain is damaged during a beating such as the one she sustained, several experts agreed, it is not capable of storing any memory of that trauma. In other words, she did not forget what had happened that night because the memory would be too painful. Rather, her brain had been incapable of recording the events in the first place.

cussing the events with staff on the scene, Kurtz told the *News*, "The report cannot be substantiated." The doctor acknowledged, however, that the Jogger had been "agitated and did require sedation" on the evening in question.

Moore never did produce his witness at trial.

CHAPTER 17.

MELONIE'S BLUES

HOMICIDE DETECTIVES MCKENNA AND TAGLIONI, ON LOAN TO THE DA, were still looking for potential witnesses, people to whom Kharey Wise might have bragged about the rape. A week into the second trial, on Saturday, October 27, they went to Jesse and Joyce Ann Mason's apartment at Schomburg Plaza. Among those living in the Masons' home were two friends of Wise: Joyce's nephew, sixteen-year-old Ronnie Williams, and her brother, nineteen-year-old Corey Jackson.

Joyce Mason's sister, Melonie Jackson, happened to be at the apartment. Jackson, who was twenty-nine, told the detectives about a conversation she'd had with Wise in July of 1989. She had been visiting her sister's apartment when Wise had called from Rikers Island. She told the detectives that Kharey said he had never raped that woman in the park, he just touched her legs.

When Lederer heard about Jackson she thought the detectives had happened on the perfect witness. Here was a credible, adult friend of Wise who could corroborate precisely what he said on videotape. Jackson, however, told the detectives she would not testify. She could be subpoenaed, of course, but that was no guarantee that she'd be cooperative. Lederer asked the cops to bring her in for a chat.

At 11:00 o'clock one night Detective Taglioni arrived at Lederer's office with Jackson. The women talked for a long time. It was clear to Lederer that Jackson cared for Wise and did not want to do anything to hurt the teenager. Moreover, she was an unemployed, single mother and was afraid of antagonizing her community by cooperating with the DA. Jackson's sister, for one, would consider any cooperation she gave the prosecutors a betrayal. If Jackson refused to testify under subpoena, however, she could be jailed for contempt of court, so she had little choice.

The women reached an understanding. "You know, I've seen you on TV," said Jackson, "and from what I hear about you, and what I read about you, everybody says you're a real bitch. . . . But you're really not so bad."

Lederer took the defense lawyers by surprise on the morning of November 7 when she gave them a copy of Jackson's statement to Detective McKenna only minutes before putting her on the stand. Colin Moore tried to prevent Jackson from testifying with an objection based on the *Rosario* rule, which required the state to turn over any prior statements made by its witnesses at the start of the trial. But Judge Galligan accepted the DA's argument that she had not even known of the witness's existence until the trial was well under way.

Once Lederer had Jackson on the stand, she was not so sure putting her there had been a smart move. After identifying Wise, whom she had known for ten years, Jackson bowed her head. When the prosecutor began asking about the phone call from Rikers Island, Jackson's answers were so sparse that Lederer worried she might not even be able to elicit the critical testimony.

"What did you say to Kharey Wise when you spoke to him on the telephone?" asked Lederer.

"I said, 'Hello, Kharey. How are you?' " said Jackson. "He goes, 'I'm fine, Mel.' "

"Did you say something else to him at that time?"

"Yes, I did."

"What did you say to him?"

"I said, 'Kharey, I don't believe what I have been hearing. I don't believe you had sex with that woman, or whatever you want to call it.' "

"Did he say something to you when you said that to him?"

"He said, 'Mel, I didn't have sex with her.' " Jackson stopped there.

"What else did he say to you then?" prompted Lederer. Jackson didn't answer. She was crying. "What did he say to you after that, Miss Jackson?" repeated Lederer.

" 'Mel, Mel, I didn't have sex with her, I didn't have sex with her.' "

Lederer didn't let her concern show, but if she didn't get the rest of the conversation out of Jackson she had done her case more harm than good by calling this witness. "Did he say something else to you then?" the prosecutor calmly asked.

"Yes, he did."

"What did he say to you?"

"O, God," sighed Jackson, before delivering the quotation that she knew would so hurt her young friend. " 'Mel, I didn't have sex with her. But the only thing I did was held her legs.' "

"Did he say anything else to you about what he had done to the woman in Central Park?"

"He just touched her legs," repeated Jackson, corroborating what the jurors would hear when they watched Wise's videotape.

———

As Moore began his cross-examination, Lederer feared that he would be able to turn Jackson's considerable affection for Wise to his advantage. She worried, said Lederer later, that he would ask such questions as: You love him like a brother, don't you? Have you ever known him to commit violence? You don't think he should go to jail, do you? Isn't he easily manipulated?

Instead of befriending the witness, however, Moore attacked her mercilessly and Jackson only seemed to gain strength in response to his insults. If this tactical mistake were not bad enough, Moore also had the witness repeat Wise's incriminating statement three times.

Jackson testified that she told Wise, "Believe me, Kharey, I love you and I care about you," and when Moore openly scoffed at this remark she said to him, "I don't believe you can laugh." Soon after that Judge Galligan had to admonish both lawyer and witness for shouting at each other.

As Moore angrily pressed for more details of the phone conversation, Jackson quoted Wise as saying he "fondled" the woman's legs, then she switched back to "touched."

The attorney seized on this inconsistency. "What was it?" he loudly demanded, "He held her legs, fondled her legs, touched her legs? What did he say?"

"He said, 'I held and fondled her legs,' " she replied. It was the only point Moore scored, but it was important because several jurors accepted the lawyer's implication that the word "fondled" was too sophisticated for Wise's limited vocabulary. Furthermore, the fact that Jackson had not uttered the word on direct examination might be taken as an indication that she was fabricating the quotation.

Finally, Moore assaulted Jackson's integrity, asserting that she had been paid to testify. Then he asked, "Why did you wait a year and a half before coming forward with this information?"

"I have no idea," she said.

"Maybe it's because you're manufacturing it. . . . You're making it up," continued Moore. "You want the publicity . . . to be the star witness in this case. Isn't that what you want?"

"No."

"What do you want?"

"I don't know," Jackson softly, sadly replied.

"You want to convict an innocent person," shouted Moore. "Is that what you want?"

Lederer's objection was sustained. When it was all over, the prosecutor found herself admiring Jackson's courage immensely. "She had nothing to gain," said Lederer later, "except the sense that she was doing what was right."

———

Jackson's testimony was followed by that of John Freck, one of four detectives who went up to Schomburg Plaza on the night of April 20 to pick up Yusef Salaam. They had encountered Salaam, along with Kharey Wise and Eddie de la Paz, in the hallway.

When Wise identified himself to the detectives he pronounced his first name as "Corey," which is what he was called by most of his acquaintances. The cops had been looking for a "Corey," based on the statements of several kids they had interviewed, so they took Wise and de la Paz with them to the Twentieth Precinct. The pair rode with Freck and his partner, while Salaam rode with the other team of detectives.

In the car on the way to the stationhouse, Freck testified, Wise and de la Paz both said they had not been with the gang in the park the previous night. "They were with them earlier," said Freck, repeating what the boys had told him, "but they left and got haircuts."

In his summation, Moore would later incorporate this testimony into his alibi defense. But he never offered any corroborating testimony from the barber who supposedly gave Wise a haircut on the night of April 19. Moore's investigator never interviewed the barber.

Quite by accident, however, the barber had spoken to an alternate juror from the first trial. This alternate was getting a haircut in East Harlem shortly after that trial when conversation turned to the Central Park case. (Freck had not testified in the first trial, so the juror had never heard of the haircut alibi.)

I was a juror in that case, he offered.

You know, replied the barber, a couple of those kids came in that night and said there was some trouble in the park. They asked me to tell the cops they had been here earlier, so they'd have an alibi, he added.

But, according to the juror, the kids hadn't been there and the barber had refused to lie for them.

John Hartigan, the fatherly homicide detective who had managed to get crucial admissions from Santana, Richardson and Wise, was the state's next witness. No single detective played a more pivotal role in the Central Park case, one of the last investigations of Hartigan's twenty-five-year career. Since retiring from his approximately $50,000-a-year job in July 1989 he had been working as an investigator for an insurance company in New Jersey.

Hartigan testified that he and his partner, Scott Jaffer, had arrived at the Central Park Precinct at about 10:00 A.M. on April 20. They walked into the youth room, where Richardson was being interviewed by two young detectives, Carlos Gonzalez of the Central Park squad and John O'Sullivan of the Sex Crimes Squad. Also present were Detective Sergeant Robert Fiston and the suspect's mother, Grace Cuffee.

Hartigan noticed a scratch under Richardson's left eye. He made eye contact with Gonzalez and nodded in Richardson's direction, pointing to the corresponding position on his own face. Gonzalez picked up the cue and asked Richardson how he got scraped. At that point Hartigan and his partner stepped outside.

A few minutes later, Hartigan testified, Gonzalez and O'Sullivan came outside with Ms. Cuffee. Hartigan introduced himself and urged her to get her son to cooperate. "I told Ms. Cuffee this was the opportunity for her son to tell the truth," Hartigan said. He told Mrs. Cuffee that the Jogger might die, so her boy had better explain that

scratch under his eye now, because later could be too late. "I told her
. . . they could take scrapings from underneath her fingernails," said
Hartigan. "If it matched the skin of her son, that would be the physical
evidence."

What was Ms. Cuffee's response to that? Lederer asked him.

"She said she wanted to learn the truth also," answered Hartigan.

When the questioning resumed, Hartigan testified, Gonzalez went
to work on Richardson. Hartigan recounted the crucial part of the
interrogation for the jury.

First, Gonzalez told Richardson, you said you scraped your face
when you fell running from the cops. Now you're telling me you were
accidentally scratched by the patrolman who tackled you. I'm going to
get the officer who arrested you, said Gonzalez, and ask him if that's
what happened. If he says no, then I'll know you've lied to me twice
already.

At that point Gonzalez stood up and walked across the room, ostensibly on his way to find Officer Robert Powers. As he got near the door,
he was stopped by Richardson's voice. "Alright. It was the girl. She
scratched me when we had the fight."

It was that admission, coming at about noon on April 20, approximately fifteen hours after the rape, that gave the cops their first break.
Earlier that morning the detectives had interviewed Lamont McCall
and Clarence Thomas, neither of whom said anything about the female
jogger. But now Richardson, the third suspect interviewed, was providing the first link between the gang and the attack on Paula Harris.

In addition to implicating Santana and Lopez in the rape, which he
described in detail to Gonzalez and Hartigan, Richardson gave up
names of boys who were not yet in custody, including Michael Briscoe
and Antron McCray. By the time he finished writing out a statement
in his own hand, Richardson had accused Briscoe of beating Harris into
unconsciousness and McCray of "having sex with her."

Richardson's written statement, which Hartigan read to the jury,
concluded with a sentence the boy added at the suggestion of Angela
Cuffee: "I was the one that didn't rape her."

Diller's cross-examination of Hartigan did not blunt the impact of his
client's statement, but it did lay the groundwork for a coercion defense
and pointed up some of the inaccuracies in the boy's story. Richardson,
for example, described Harris as wearing gray shorts and a white tank

top, when in fact she wore black tights and a long-sleeved shirt. Richardson had told Hartigan the Jogger was running from west to east
when "we started chasing her down the road." All of the other evidence, Diller noted, indicated she was running in the opposite direction. "I assumed she made a U-turn and started running away from
them," explained Hartigan.

Questioning Hartigan and Gonzalez, Diller abandoned the polite
attitude he had shown the victims and medical experts. He became
more aggressive and more accusatory. He waved his arms as he paced
and shouted at the cops. When Hartigan said that Richardson was told
simply to tell the cops what he'd done the previous night without
specifically being asked about Central Park, the lawyer shouted: "It
happened in Times Square?" This newfound militancy pleased the
Cuffees, who were still comparing Diller's performance unfavorably to
Moore's.

Diller hammered at the notion that the detectives had taken advantage of a naive family. "Did you explain to Mrs. Cuffee that there
appears to be a serious problem," he asked, "and she may want to
consider engaging an attorney for her fourteen-year-old?"

"No."

Next Diller suggested, as had his colleagues in the first trial, that the
incriminating statement was obtained through false promises. "Now,
you never told Mrs. Cuffee: 'Listen, you're tired; you're here all day.
We just have to take a statement from Kevin and you and Kevin can
go home'?"

"I never said that," replied Hartigan.

Diller raised his voice, pumping it full of disbelief. "You never said:
'All that Kevin has to do is tell the truth and the truth will set him
free'?"

"I never said that," repeated the detective.

Midway through Richardson's April 20 interrogation, Grace Cuffee,
who had not recovered from the effects of her stroke, had told the cops
she was ill and had to go home. Angela Cuffee had taken her mother's
place as Richardson, under Hartigan's guidance, wrote out his incriminating statement.

"You never gave Angela Cuffee any of the [Miranda] rights?" asked
Diller.

"I never did," said Hartigan, "no."

"Did you ever go over with Angela Cuffee what her purpose of being
there was?"

"No."

"Did you ever tell Angela, 'You're substituting for your mother. Why don't you speak to Kevin'?" asked Diller.

"No," said the detective, "I never did, no."

Finally, Diller questioned whether such terms in Richardson's statement as "male," "female," "unconscious" and "roadway" were not more likely suggested by the detectives than chosen by a fourteen-year-old. But Hartigan insisted that the boy wrote the statement in his own words.

The next day the jury got a chance to judge the credibility of Richardson's words when the prosecutors played his videotape.

___

Kevin Richardson, seated between Diller and Wise at the defense table, watched his thirty-minute videotape impassively. He barely moved a muscle and his uninterested expression never changed. It was as if he were watching a stranger.

If the jurors suspected that the teenager's calm demeanor was calculated to impress them as a mark of innocence or self-discipline, they were about to learn otherwise. The boy seemed equally detached on the videotape as he answered Lederer's questions, insisting that he was a bystander at events that did not appear to upset him.

"Why did you go to the park that night?" asked Lederer.

"I just, like, wanted to get away from the block," said Richardson. "I wanted to walk around."

"Well, what was everybody wandering around the park for?" asked Lederer. "What were they going to do?"

"I guess, beat people up."

"Okay," replied Lederer, "and you were part of that group that was walking around?"

"Yes."

For the most part Richardson avoided using the first-person plural, repeatedly referring to the gang as "they" rather than "we." They beat up the bum, they tried to knock the couple off the tandem bike, they beat up a male jogger at the reservoir, they raped the lady Jogger. He consistently portrayed himself as a follower who periodically urged his friends to halt the assaults but could not muster the courage to walk away.

The beating of the male jogger, said Richardson, took "nine minutes," with McCray doing most of the damage with "this little steel bat . . . not a bat, like a pipe or somethin'." After that, he said, the gang resumed walking down the West Drive.

"What were you doing?" asked Lederer.

"Nothin'."

"Well, what were you looking to do?" she pressed. "Why were you going with these guys?"

"I don't know," he said. "I was just followin' them."

Richardson's sister, Connie, sat on the aisle in the first row of Supporters, watching the television monitor as her brother described the assault of Paula Harris.

"Raymond had her arms," said Richardson, "and Steve had her legs. He spread it out. And Antron got on top, took her panties off."

The jurors were stunned, not only by the event he described but by the teenager's deadpan manner. Ivette Naftal slumped down in her chair, as if recoiling from Richardson's videotaped image. Steve Gilliam, a big man with the build of an athlete, looked upset and anxious. As Richardson described McCray, Santana and Lopez raping the unconscious Jogger, Sonia Ramon, her front-row seat in the jury box putting her closest to the television screen, dropped her head in dismay.

The camera moved in for a closeup of the boy's left cheek as he tried to explain the scratch on his face. "Everybody was around her . . . I came over there and I was, like, tryin' to stop them," he said. "And I got in the way. She kind of, like, scratched me a little bit."

"Didn't you tell the police earlier today that you had tried to grab her?" Lederer asked. "And that was when you got scratched?"

"No. Not like . . . feelin' her up," said Richardson. "Tryin' to stop it."

"Well," said Lederer, "you grabbed *her* arm when you wanted to stop it?"

"Yes," he replied.

Describing his arrest, Richardson told Lederer that the patrolman who caught him (Powers) had punched him in the face with a closed fist. "How many cops hit you?" she asked.

"One."

"Are you okay?"

"Yeah," he said without a trace of complaint in his voice. "Because it ain't really hurt. It was like, just hittin' me."

Lederer came back to this point later in the interview. "That scratch that you have on your face . . . that's got nothing to do with anything about the police?"

"No," the boy confirmed.

One advantage for the prosecutors in trying Richardson with Wise was the minimal amount of editing this pairing required in Richardson's tape. Since he mentioned Wise only four times, the jury only heard the beeping tone four times during the long and chilling narrative. The only incriminating information deleted was Richardson's contention that Wise punched or kicked Loughlin and was present at the rape scene. Richardson did not attribute to Wise any role in the rape.

"Did you have intercourse with her?" Lederer asked Richardson on the tape.

"No," he replied, calmly as ever.

"If we do a DNA test . . . are we gonna get a match?"

"No," he said, soon adding: "I didn't do nothin'."

When the tape finished playing, a recess was called. As the solemn jurors walked by the defense table, where Richardson slumped in his chair, they resembled nothing so much as a procession of mourners passing an open casket.

During his direct examination on November 7 and 9, Detective Hartigan had testified about the interrogations that led to Wise's series of increasingly self-incriminating statements, two written and two videotaped. After each session with the teenager, Hartigan testified, he had either personally interviewed other suspects or talked to detectives who had done so, and was amassing a growing battery of hearsay evidence against Wise. The more he learned about the events of April 19, said Hartigan, the more convinced he became that Wise was lying about his involvement. Each time the detective had confronted the teenager with new information that indicated he had lied, Wise had changed his story, adding by stages to his own level of guilt.

After hearing Judge Galligan's standard instruction that a defendant's words cannot be considered as evidence against his codefendant, the jury listened to Hartigan read Wise's two written statements. In the first Wise admitted going into the park with the gang and witnessing the assault of Antonio Diaz and the harassment of Gerry Malone and Patricia Dean. When a police cruiser came along the boys scattered, Wise said, and he ran out of the park and home to Schomburg Plaza. The next day his friend Yusef told him "they jumped a guy at the reservoir" and that they had grabbed "a lady jogger" and beat her up. Yusef and Al Morris also told him, said Wise, that Lopez and Richardson had raped the woman. (In the edited version of the statement Hartigan was reading, the phrase "a guy" was substituted for Richardson's name.)

In his second written statement, nine hours after the first, Wise stated that he had not left the park as early as he claimed. He had been running through the woods when he heard a woman screaming for help. Running toward the voice, he came upon the rape scene. He hid behind a tree, he said, and watched as Santana, McCray and Lopez beat up the Jogger. Again, he stated that Lopez and "a guy" raped her while Santana and McCray fondled her breasts and legs. After those boys left, said Wise, his friend Eddie de la Paz, who seemed to have appeared out of nowhere, ventured from behind the trees to look at the body. "Eddie ran up to her and called me," Hartigan read from Wise's statement, "and I looked at her body, which was all black and blue."

Moore's cross-examination of Hartigan, while by no means flawless, was his most effective piece of work. The only difference between the first and second statements, the lawyer suggested, was that in the second Wise claimed to have witnessed the events that he had described in the first as having been related to him by Salaam and Morris on the day after the rampage. The teenager had made the second admission out of expediency, Moore argued, due to considerable pressure applied by Hartigan and also because of intellectual deficiency. By thus raising the issue of Wise's mental competence, Moore hoped to get the psychiatric evidence before the jury that Galligan had ruled inadmissible.

Back on the first day of jury selection Moore had told the judge he intended to introduce psychiatric evidence demonstrating that Wise was not capable of understanding his *Miranda* rights. This evidence consisted of school records that included the results of an IQ test in which Wise had scored 64 on the verbal section and 87 on the performance section, for a full-scale IQ of 73. (Psychologists interpret such a score as an indication of below-average intelligence, if not mild retardation.) The records also indicated that Wise, while in the eighth grade, had the reading and math skills of a second-grader. Sylvia Troy, a school psychologist, noted that Wise, fourteen years old at the time of the test, did not know "how many things are in a dozen."

DA Tim Clements had quickly filed a brief seeking to block introduction of the records on several grounds. First, Clements had noted, Moore was woefully late, as the defense is required to notify the prosecution of an intention to introduce psychiatric evidence within thirty days of filing a plea. Second, he argued, the school records did not constitute expert testimony that addressed the *Miranda* issue with any degree of scientific certainty. Indeed, Moore was offering a psychiatric evaluation written in March 1987 as a means of establishing Wise's state of mind when he waived his rights two years later.

Moore would have had a better chance to put a psychological profile into evidence if he had followed proper procedures: getting a new evaluation done that specifically supported his defense and notifying the DA within the time frame prescribed by law. There was even some precedent that could have bolstered his argument, cases in which state trial judges had ruled, for example, that defendants with IQs of 83 and 68 were not capable of waiving their *Miranda* rights. Given Galligan's earlier refusal to allow Mickey Joseph to introduce psychiatric evidence, however, it was not certain Moore would have succeeded even if his efforts had been more competently pursued. In any event, Galligan ruled in Clements's favor.

So at trial Moore suggested through his questions to Hartigan that Wise had not comprehended what he was getting himself into when he succumbed to the will of the police. "Didn't he appear to have some difficulty understanding what you were saying?" asked the lawyer.

"No," said Hartigan.

"This 16-year-old kid," Moore continued, "didn't once ask you, 'What does that mean?' "

"No, sir," said Hartigan.

Moore wondered aloud why Hartigan had written out Wise's statement while Richardson had written his own. "You never asked him to write it down?"

"No," said the detective.

"And that was because you knew that Kharey could not write; that Kharey did not know how to write well, isn't that the reason?"

"No, sir."

"Isn't it because you had come to the conclusion that he had some difficulty in understanding?"

"No, sir."

Hartigan could deny these points all day but the jury was getting Moore's message. The lawyer also brought an animosity to this examination that pleased the Supporters no end. At one point Moore said to Hartigan, "You were very busy?"

"Yes," replied the detective.

"Getting statements out of 14- and 15-year-olds!" declared Moore scornfully.

When Moore challenged the accuracy of something in Wise's second statement, Hartigan explained that he had written what the boy claimed had happened. "So," said Moore sarcastically, "if he told you Jesus Christ came out of the sky, you would write that down?" The Supporters murmured their approval of the remark, although they were more subdued than they'd been earlier in the day, before Galligan had angrily expelled one of their number from the courtroom.*

As Moore pressed his long examination of Hartigan he managed to emphasize that other teenagers—including Santana, Lopez and de la Paz—had been accompanied by parents when interviewed by this detective, while his client, only a year older than his friends, was alone. And Hartigan's episodic questioning of Wise, noted Moore, consumed a total of about eight hours between 12:30 A.M. and 3:30 P.M. on April 21. Eventually Moore got to his critical point.

Under Lederer's direct examination, Hartigan had testified that he visited de la Paz at Schomburg Plaza to see whether the boy would corroborate Wise's assertion that they had watched the rape together. When he got back to the precinct, said Hartigan, the DA was taping her first interview with Wise. When the session ended, Hartigan took Wise into a room that contained a large holding cell. They stood in the space beside the cell to talk. Wise slumped to the floor, Hartigan had said, when he was told that de la Paz denied having been with him in the park.

They were both sitting on the floor outside the empty cell, Hartigan had testified, as he tried to convince Wise that a jury would not believe his story. Put yourself in the position of the jurors, the detective had told Wise. They are, after all, regular people like you and me. "If you heard a person come in and tell three different stories, and you heard

---

*Frank Yancy, a former prison guard, had let out a loud exclamation— "Ooohhh!"—when Hartigan gave Moore an answer that Yancy considered incredible. The judge immediately had the jury taken out of the room and ordered the court officers to remove Yancy. On his way out Yancy said to Galligan, "This is a racist court; very racist. You don't want no black folks in here; you don't want no justice." Then, in the favorite phrase of Reverend Al Sharpton's followers, Yancy warned: "Without justice there can be no peace."

Yancy was the second Supporter thrown out during this trial. Two weeks earlier Galligan had ejected Bruce Kareem, whom he spotted sitting in the gallery wearing a black T-shirt with large, white lettering on the front that said: "My Brother Antron McCray Is Innocent."

other people telling that you were implicated in that crime, would *you* believe what you are saying?" It was then, the cop had testified, that Wise said he wanted to tell the DA the truth, a decision that resulted in his second, and more damning, videotape.

As he cross-examined Hartigan, Moore knew his defense would stand or fall on his ability to convince the jury that this episode amounted to coercion. "You braced him against the cell block," he accused.

"He wasn't braced," replied Hartigan, "he was leaning against the cell block . . . the bars."

Moore said, "In other words, he's being tried by a jury now. . . . Isn't that the image [you were] conjuring, he's now in court?"

Hartigan agreed. Moore expressed doubt that this threat of trial, by itself, would have led Wise into self-incrimination. "I guess," said Hartigan, "it was the realization of what was happening that he finally, he told me he wanted to tell the truth."

"Oh, I see," said Moore with an exaggerated show of sarcasm. "This is like St. Paul on the road to Damascus! . . . He just got hit with the urge to confess everything to you, right?"

"If you want to say that, yes," replied Hartigan.

Moore then posed questions to make the point that his client had used the same ill-conceived strategy in his second video as he had in his second written statement, that is, the belief that he would satisfy the cops if he admitted taking part in events to which he had already admitted being a witness. Moore was laying out the heart of his defense: that, as the interrogations continued, growing ever more intense, Wise finally admitted to being a principal actor rather than merely a spectator.

"Do you remember almost at the end of the video," asked Moore, "that [Wise] said that all of the detectives came in my face, arguing with me, cursing at me, hitting at me?"

"Yes," said Hartigan, who then corrected the lawyer's phrasing: "He said, 'hitting on me.' "

"And weren't you in fact the one arguing with him," asked Moore, "and hitting on him and cursing at him? Weren't you doing those things?"

"I never hit him and I never cursed at him," said Hartigan.

"After the pressure you had put on him," Moore asked, "this young man would have told you whatever you wanted him to tell you, isn't that a fact?"

Lederer's objection was sustained.

"You wanted him to tell you that he was involved in the rape of Paula Harris," said Moore, turning up the volume for this series of questions. "That's what you wanted, isn't it?"

"I wanted him to tell the truth," said Hartigan.

"This was your version of the truth, right?"

"That's what I believed to be the truth," said the detective.

Moore, his deep voice spilling over with righteous indignation, asked: "And you, 52 years old, cross-examined a 16-year-old, and you got what you wanted, right? You got what you wanted?"

"Justice," said a confident Hartigan, "got what it wanted."

"Where is the Manhattan North Homicide Squad located?" asked Lederer when she got a chance to question Hartigan again.

"East 119th Street," he said, locating his office in the heart of Harlem.

"Have you ever had occasion to hear certain slang expressions used when you've conducted interviews in that area?" she asked.

Moore's objection was sustained.

"What does the expression 'hit on' mean?" asked the prosecutor.

"Pestering me," replied Hartigan, "bothering me."

This was a weak attempt to dismiss Wise's allegation of physical abuse. To many people the expression may have most commonly signified an unwanted sexual advance, usually an attempt by a man to pick up a woman. But the suggestion that in Harlem it carried a connotation of more general verbal nuisance was ludicrous.

Moore was to be frustrated in his efforts to corroborate Wise's allegation of having been beaten. Detective Robert Nugent, who testified a few days after Hartigan, denied Moore's accusation that he had slapped Wise across the face three times. A medical examination at Rikers Island on April 23, conducted at the lawyer's request, turned up no evidence of a beating. Moore tried to introduce a record of the examination anyway, so the jurors would know of his complaint to jail officials, but that effort was blocked by the DA's objection. And, of course, the hearsay rule would have prevented Moore from introducing the pertinent lines from the poem Salaam had read at his sentencing:

I told the cops the truth like this
and then—boom!

They smacked my man up, Kharey Wise,
in the next room.

Moore won his only significant procedural battle during a bench conference on November 15. The prosecutors, nearing the end of their case, wanted to subpoena Shabazz Head, a teenager with whom Wise had a conversation on the sidewalk in front of Schomburg Plaza no more than eight hours before being picked up by the police. A week after that Head told the cops he had asked Wise: Did you hear about what happened to that girl last night in Central Park? To which Wise replied, according to Head: Yeah, that was us; we did that.

The prospect of this testimony alarmed Moore, who strenuously objected on the grounds that he had not previously been given a copy of the witness's statement to the police, which had been in the state's possession for nineteen months. Galligan demanded an explanation from the prosecutors for this apparent breach of the *Rosario* rule.

Lederer, quoting the state Criminal Procedure Law, told the judge she was only required to turn over prior statements of witnesses she *intended* to call from the outset of the trial. "I can only say to this Court, and I represent as an officer of the court," she said, "it was not my intention at the commencement of this trial to offer this witness." It was not until opening day, the prosecutor explained, when Moore belatedly notified her of additional alibi witnesses, that she began to consider calling Shabazz Head to defuse such a defense. "It was not until the end of October," said Lederer, "that I first met this person and, in the presence of his grandmother, had a conversation about his testifying." The prosecutors were still not certain Head would cooperate, even if threatened by the court with a contempt citation.

The judge said he accepted Lederer's word on the matter, but he was not inclined to let her slip a witness through such a narrow loophole. "The difficulty with that argument," said Galligan, "is that it can always be made and never refuted. Therefore the district attorney can always hold these [statements] until a point in time when they want to turn them over and they can always make that argument."

The prosecutors were stung when Galligan upheld Moore's objection, refusing to let them put Head on the stand.

Kharey Wise's first videotape, a detailed, ninety-minute dialogue with Lederer, stunned the jurors, who watched it in the hushed courtroom on November 14. In that interview Wise had essentially followed the scenario of his second written statement. There were, however, two major changes in his story by the time Lederer halted the taping: Santana had been added to the list of rapists and Richardson (his identity protected at trial by the high-pitched beeping tone on the soundtrack) had been accused of hitting Harris with a rock.

The latter revision from Wise probably hurt the state's case more than it helped. Lederer had only managed to squeeze the information out of Wise after a long series of questions, each pressed with more insistence than the last, about the source of the Jogger's head injuries. The exchange followed Wise's viewing of a gruesome photo of Harris's broken skull and Lederer's warning that "this may be murder." Wiping away tears, Wise finally agreed that mere fists could not have caused such damage; it must have been a rock. A moment later he was accusing "BEEP" of having swung "a small, hand-rock" against the side of the victim's head.

When it had become apparent to Lederer that Wise was about to capitulate, she had said to him: "I don't want you to think you *have* to say that." The remark failed to preserve the DA's credibility, however, as jurors might well doubt that the teenager believed he had a choice. Steve Gilliam, Eric Roach and Victoria Bryers were among those jurors who thought Lederer had pushed too hard to win this prize.

The rape scene, as described by Wise on that first video, was no less chaotic than Lederer had depicted it in her summation at the previous trial. Things were moving fast, with various youths grabbing at legs and breasts even as a cohort forced intercourse on the pinned victim. Santana, according to Wise, wanted to orally sodomize the Jogger but reconsidered. "The condition she is in," said Wise, quoting Santana, "she might bite my stick."

On the second videotape, screened for the jury two days later, Wise was a pathetic figure. Whereas he had been animated during the first session, scurrying for explanations with which to dodge Lederer's insinuating inquiry, this time he was obviously tired and scared. A large medallion in the shape of Africa dangled from a long cord over his red-and-white-striped sweatshirt. His legs constantly bounced as he revised his story, promising the prosecutor "the whole truth and nothin' but the truth."

On this tape Wise not only incriminated himself—confessing to kicking the bum and a male jogger, and holding Harris's legs while Lopez raped her—he also accused people he had not mentioned in his first video. McCray, for example, was now at the rape scene, Briscoe had kicked the Jogger, and Salaam joined Wise in "playing with her legs." This picture of a more crowded rape scene than Wise had previously described matched the prosecution's version of events. He had now incorporated nearly all of the defendants into his story, though Richardson's name was again replaced by the beeping tone when Wise listed those who had "fucked" the victim.

Wise's narrative also included projections of his imagination. He told Lederer what the Jogger was thinking. In reference to Richardson's role, for example, Wise said: "She thought it was a punch but it was a rock that hit her." (This was reminiscent of the first tape, on which he described Harris getting a look at Lopez's knife: "She thought her life was through.") He also went off on odd tangents, such as the significance behind certain nicknames of the Schomburg boys.

Wise's vivid description of the rape scene horrified the jurors, despite the large quantity of sensational testimony they had already seen and heard. As the youths beat the woman senseless, said Wise, as they hit her with rocks and bricks, as Lopez slashed her legs with a knife, he and Salaam stood by and watched. "Yusef was laughin'," he told Lederer, "and he got a way of laughin' . . . My expression toward that, I felt kind of bad." It was the violence that upset him most. "I can imagine anyone rapin' a woman," he continued. "If I have to rape a woman, I'm gonna rape her. But I can't beat her up."

Wise spoke vividly about Lopez, Santana and "BEEP" attacking a man in a dark van only moments before their capture. "I guess it was money or jewelry," he told Lederer. "Somethin' was in there that they wanted real bad." The jury had heard no evidence of such an assault. Perhaps the anecdote was based on fragments Wise had heard from someone who had escaped when the plainclothes policemen jumped out of a van on Central Park West and chased the gang. It sent Wise off onto another tangent. "I thought about it," he said, "and a guy up by my way got shot for messin' with a undercover cop in a bread truck. I thought about this van . . . I left the man in the van alone."

Then there was an unlikely story of a jogger at the reservoir who had supposedly struck back at his attackers. "He beat up half of everybody that was with us," said Wise.

Some who listened suspected that Wise might occasionally be parroting the police. One speech in particular, near the end of the tape, had the ring of a homily a veteran detective might deliver to a teenager needing just a little encouragement to make a confession.

"We went to the park for trouble; we got trouble. A lot of trouble," said Wise slowly, calmly, like a penitent who has cleansed his soul of a great, burdensome sin. "That's what they wanted and I guess that's what I wanted. If I was doin' it, that's what I wanted, too. I can't apologize, because things is too late. Now what we gotta do is pay up for what we did. And you can't; we can cry and everything, but that still won't solve no questions."

The impact of the tape was devastating. Juror Ivette Naftal covered her eyes at one point and shook her head slowly. Stephanie Samoy sat in the back row with tears in her eyes. When the VCR was finally wheeled away, Eric Roach buried his face in both hands for a minute.

Lederer rose and told the judge, once again, "The People rest."

CHAPTER 18

HOSTILE WITNESSES

"WHEN I WENT BACK INSIDE, I HEARD THEM CURSING AT MY SON AND saying to my son, 'You know you effed her! You little M.F.!' And I heard this lady say, 'Why don't you tell? You don't want to go to jail for no one else. Because you the one going to end up being effed and they going to be free.'"

Grace Cuffee, wearing a royal blue blazer with white beret and matching pocket square, shook with sobs as she described Kevin Richardson's interrogation. "And he saw me. He called my name. And I went over to him and I said, 'We going home.' And—" She broke off there, in tears.

"Would you like a recess, Mrs. Cuffee?" asked the judge.

"Yes," she said, wiping her eyes as Galligan told the jury to take a break.

One of the court officers put a chair out in the hall so Ms. Cuffee would have a place to sit during the recess. As she struggled to regain her composure, she was consoled by her daughters.

Three weeks had passed since the Cuffees, on Vernon Mason's advice, had refused to cooperate with Richardson's attorney. But the family then decided that Howard Diller was better than no lawyer at all. Over Lederer's objection, Galligan had agreed to let the defendant's mother testify, despite the fact that she had been attending the trial and listening to the testimony of the state's witnesses.

As it was described by Ms. Cuffee, the scene at the Central Park Precinct on the morning of April 20 bore little resemblance to the episode related by detectives Hartigan and Gonzalez. She had been asked to step outside and there had been a conversation in the driveway, as Hartigan testified, but the circumstances were quite different in the mother's version. The detective who urged her to cooperate had put his hands on her shoulders to keep her focused on him. When she turned away to look through the window into the youth room, said Ms. Cuffee, she was alarmed to see a lot of cops surrounding her son.

"I wasn't hearing what [the detective] said because I was looking in the window," she told the jury. "And I turned from him, and he turned my shoulders back. And that's when I knocked his hand off my shoulder and I ran back inside the youth room."

There were about a dozen cops badgering the boy, Ms. Cuffee said, and in some ways her good cop/bad cop description of the interrogation seemed more credible than the orderly, businesslike process the detectives had described. It made sense, for example, that a detective would use the old "Why should you take the fall for those guys?" line to get a scared kid talking.

But Lederer scored some points on cross-examination by establishing that the Cuffees had continued to cooperate with the investigators even after Richardson was arrested. Several hours after the interrogation Angela Cuffee drove around the neighborhood with a detective, pointing out boys who had been named by other suspects as part of the gang. And later, in rebuttal, Lederer elicited testimony from a policeman who asserted that the window through which Ms. Cuffee claimed to have seen a crowd of cops badgering her son was either painted or covered over with an opaque material at that time.

Al Morris and Raheim Fladger, two teenagers from the Schomburg crew, came to court on November 20 in response to Colin Moore's subpoenas. He expected the teenagers to testify that they had gone into the park with the gang on the fateful night but left, with Kharey Wise, before the Jogger was attacked. That, at least, was what Morris had told the cops at one time. Moore wanted the testimony in evidence to bolster the alibi that his client was back at Schomburg Plaza before the rape occurred.

The jury heard no such testimony. The mothers of both teenagers had taken the precaution of hiring an attorney to accompany them and their sons to court. At a bench conference, Dominic Porco told the judge that his clients would take the Fifth Amendment rather than answer Moore's questions. Galligan agreed, however, to let Moore make a record of his effort, out of the jury's presence. As a result, the press and spectators heard, for the first time, from members of the gang who had never been indicted.

Morris, eighteen, sat in the witness chair with his attorney standing by his side. Moore began by asking whether he knew Kharey Wise.

Porco whispered in his client's ear for a moment and Morris slowly said, "I refuse to answer the question."

Moore asked the youth where had had been at 8:00 P.M. on April 19, 1989.

Again Porco whispered in his client's ear. "I refuse," said Morris, his voice trailing off at the end of the phrase so it came out sounding like: I refew.

Moore asked whether the witness had gone into Central Park that night with Kharey Wise.

Porco quickly grabbed his client's arm, lest he should speak before being told what to say. After listening to another whisper, Morris again said, "I refew."

Seeking to cut this process short—and presumably to get the Fifth Amendment invocation into the record as well—Galligan interrupted Moore. "I assume your refusal is based upon the fact that the answers might tend to incriminate you. . . . Is that right?" the judge asked Morris, quickly adding as he pointed to Porco: "Talk to him first."

Morris again listened to his lawyer before saying, "I stand on the Fifth Amendment."

The judge asked whether he would refuse to answer all further questions about that date.

"Yes," replied Morris.

"Okay," said Galligan, "you can step down."

The scenario was repeated with Fladger.

A throng of outraged Supporters accosted the two teenagers as they walked toward the elevators with their mothers. "Pigs," someone shouted. "You just sold your souls to the devil," said another Supporter.

Angela Cuffee was crying. "Our boys are going to jail," she screamed at her neighbors, "and you say nothing?"

Lederer was also disappointed that the pair did not testify. "I would have had a great time cross-examining those kids," she said in an interview months later. Lederer believed there was much more to tell the jury about their activities that night. There was Clarence Thomas's statement that it was Morris who originally suggested to the gang: "Let's go to the park and start some trouble." Morris had also made conflicting statements to the police, initially claiming that he left the park alone after the bum was attacked. And Lederer would certainly not have failed to remind the jurors that both Wise and Richardson had said on videotape that Morris was at the rape scene.

Lederer would have welcomed an opportunity to try to get either Morris or Fladger to incriminate himself on the witness stand. If something more than they had previously told the cops came out at trial, "perhaps it would have risen to a level where I would have had cause to take a blood sample from them," said Lederer later. "I don't know what that would have said to us, in the end, about that unmatched semen."

Moore kicked off the alibi defense with Clara Chew, who lived in a three-bedroom apartment at Schomburg Plaza. In April 1989 Chew was caring for her fourteen-year-old granddaughter and three foster children: a two-year-old, a three-year-old and Lisa Williams, fifteen, who was Wise's girlfriend. Chew testified that Wise had come to the apartment with Lisa at 9:05 P.M. on April 19. They left after five or ten minutes, she said, and returned at 9:35. Wise then remained in the apartment until 11:00 P.M., Chew said.

This was a less than airtight alibi, since it failed to account for the estimated time at which the attack on the Jogger took place. The prosecution's theory, which Moore had adopted, was that the wilding spree lasted roughly from 9:00 to 10:00 P.M. While Lederer had decided not to pinpoint the Jogger attack at this trial, Moore used the DA's original chronology in his cross-examination of Paula Harris, which placed her assault between 9:15 and 9:30, immediately before the reservoir muggings.

Chew's granddaughter, Lashon Rush, testified to roughly the same circumstances, except that she said Wise left the apartment alone and did not return until 9:45 P.M. Then Robert Moore, a heavyset young man who worked as a security guard at Schomburg in the spring of 1989, took the stand. Peering through dark sunglasses and chewing gum as he testified, the guard said he had seen Wise in front of the building at 9:00 P.M. on April 19.

Colin Moore should have foreseen the damage Lederer was about to inflict on his case through cross-examination of these witnesses, each of whom had been visited by a team of homicide detectives in the preceding weeks. Lederer established, for example, that Chew had originally told the cops Wise had been in her apartment from 8:30 to 11:00 P.M., which would have put her at odds with the testimony of the other alibi witnesses. Then the DA showed the security guard logs from his company that indicated he had not worked on April 19. Robert Moore claimed he had simply not signed in on that night. She also confronted him with having originally lied to the cops about his identity and telling them he did not remember on what date he had seen Wise. (According to the later testimony of Detective Arroyo, the guard had told the cops he regretted having become involved with the defense team: "He made mention that he had given an inch and they had taken a yard.")

Most damaging, however, was Lederer's cross-examination of four-teen-year-old Lashon Rush, Mrs. Chew's granddaughter. "Before you saw Kharey Wise in your apartment on that night, you were in front of [Schomburg]. Isn't that true?" asked the prosecutor.

"Yes."

After establishing that Rush saw Wise out on the sidewalk with Yusef Salaam and Eddie de la Paz, Lederer asked: "Do you remember telling the police that you saw them go into the park together?"

"Yes," said the girl. Moore, seated at the defense table, shook his head in disbelief.

"And they were with other people at that time, weren't they?"

"Yes."

Lederer then asked a series of questions about a conversation Wise later had with Lashon and Lisa when he arrived at the apartment. The prosecutor had already established, with a question put to Chew, that Lisa had told police Wise did not show up until 10:00 P.M. "Do you remember asking him where Yusef was?" she asked.

"No," said the girl.

"Did Kharey tell you on that night that they got busted—"

"Objection!" shouted Moore.

"—that they were in the park bugging, acting stupid?" continued Lederer.

"No," said Lashon, after Galligan overruled the objection.

The alibi defense survived all of this impeachment, however, thanks to Nomsa Brath, a community activist and black nationalist who was a former resident of Schomburg Plaza. As a cofounder of Motherlove, a support group for the families of the defendants, it was Brath who had recommended Moore to Wise's mother. After establishing Brath's credentials as a nurse, tutor, tenant organizer and pioneer in the movement to remove asbestos from the public schools, Moore asked her about the night of April 19, 1989.

She was coming back to Schomburg from an errand shortly after 9:30 P.M., Brath testified, when she saw Wise in front of the building and stopped to speak with him. "There had been a rather spectacular, moving incident that took place at the complex that day," said Brath, "where a young man had attempted to commit suicide. And the police had come in to Kharey's house to get [the man] and try to keep him from jumping off the terrace. Kharey had intervened and gone outside, talked to the young man, and grabbed him by his legs and brought him into the apartment, thereby, you know, not allowing him to commit suicide. . . . I wanted to compliment him."

The prosecutors had tried to prevent Moore from introducing Wise's alleged rescue of the potential suicide on the grounds that it could not be documented. Indeed, press reports at the time stated that the man Wise had coaxed off the terrace was not a jumper at all but a burglar fleeing from the police. And Lederer noted in her objection that the police department had no record of a suicide attempt. Nonetheless, Galligan ruled for the defense.

The prosecutor could not shake Brath's credibility. The jury would later calculate that, while Wise might have been able to get back to Schomburg from the rape scene by 9:35 or shortly thereafter, he could not possibly have been present for the reservoir assaults ten or fifteen minutes later.

On the morning of November 21 Moore called Kevin O'Reilly, Harris's boyfriend at the time of the crime, so he could ask: "Were you aware of the fact, when you gave the sample of blood, that you were a suspect in this case?"

After sustaining the prosecutor's objection, Galligan instructed the jury to disregard the question. Most of the questions Moore asked O'Reilly during his brief examination remained unanswered because of Lederer's frequent objections. Moore was asking them in an attempt to reinforce the jealous-boyfriend motive.

O'Reilly, a vice president in the equity trading department at Salomon Brothers, testified that he had returned to New York from Kansas City at 8:15 or 8:30 P.M. on April 19, 1989.

"Were you aware of the fact, Mr. O'Reilly, that Paula Harris had a dinner date with Michael Allen?" asked Moore.

Objection sustained.

"Were you aware of the fact that Pat Garrett—"

Objection sustained.

Moore believed O'Reilly had not visited the Jogger at the hospital until several days after her admittance. This, he had told the judge at the bench, implied some conflict in the relationship. Galligan refused to let him probe the topic but Moore asked the witness about it anyway. "After Sunday, April 16, when was the next time that you saw Miss Harris?"

Objection sustained.

After hearing again about O'Reilly and Harris's lovemaking and jogging three days before the rape, the jury listened as Moore's final question also went unanswered.

"You don't know for a fact whether she had intercourse with someone else [after] Sunday, April 16, do you?"

Objection sustained.

Moore accomplished little with his questioning of O'Reilly, a tall, handsome, thirtysomething man, except to indirectly repudiate the incongruous allegation that he was black. The source of this disinformation, which had been embraced by many Supporters, was *The Daily Challenge,* an obscure black newspaper that had printed an editorial during the first trial asking: "Who allowed the Central Park case to become a racial issue? Did District Attorney Robert Morgenthau's office know all along that Paula Harris's boyfriend was black? Why was this information held back? Had this information been made public would the outcry from the city's white community have been different? Who would have been their audience without a racial angle? That's the real public crime in this case."

A framed copy of that editorial hung in the anteroom of Vernon Mason's office.

Moore's decision to put Dr. Vernard Adams on the stand blew up in his face. Lederer had used Adams, a deputy medical examiner for New York City, in the first trial to explain to the jury how each of the Jogger's injuries was most likely caused. In the second trial the prosecutors had decided not to call the doctor. The photos of the injuries, coupled with the testimony of other medical experts, were sufficient, they reasoned.

What Moore wanted from Adams was simple. Wise had said on his videotape that Lopez had slashed the Jogger's legs with a knife. Moore knew, based on the record, that Adams would testify that none of her injuries was caused by a knife. The doctor therefore offered authoritative evidence, reasoned Moore, that his client's tape was not worthy of belief.

To Lederer, however, Adams's appearance meant something else. As soon as he walked into the well on the morning of November 21 the prosecutor knew she was going to get a rare opportunity to completely turn a defense witness around on her opponent.

One by one, Moore showed the doctor the full set of thirty glossy pictures of the Jogger's wounds, asking him to explain the probable cause of the injuries. After the witness did so, Moore would ask: "Is that inconsistent with a sharp instrument such as a knife?" Each time the doctor answered, "Yes."

On cross-examination, Lederer displayed the photos on the big easel and guided the doctor through a reprise of his testimony from the first trial. The jury listened carefully as Adams described injuries that, while not consistent with a knife, could have been caused by a brick, a pipe, a zipper and fists. Some of the scratches on her legs were also the results of having been dragged across rocky terrain, he opined. The Q&A was rapid, smooth and relentless. After all, Lederer and Adams had been through this together several times since she summoned him to the Twenty-fourth Precinct on the morning of April 21, 1989, to examine the first snapshots of Harris taken by a detective at the hospital. She had wanted to be fully informed about the nature of the victim's injuries during her videotape sessions with the suspects.

Now, as Adams covered the familiar ground once more, Lederer held up the rock she had put into evidence weeks earlier, the rock on which another expert had found head hairs similar to the Jogger's. "Could the use of this rock," asked Lederer, "applied with force to the head, have caused the injuries that are depicted in these photographs?"

"Yes," said the pathologist.

Rather than return the rock to its paper bag in the evidence cart, Lederer placed it on the shelf attached to the railing of the jury box. There it sat—close enough for the jurors in the front row to see the faint bloodstains—for the duration of this long cross-examination.

When Lederer finished taking Adams through the Harris photos, she turned to those of David Lewis and John Loughlin. Moore objected on the ground that a witness may only be cross-examined on matters that are within the scope of the direct examination conducted by the attorney who called the witness. "All of what's been brought out on the direct," said Moore at a bench conference, "has to do with the [injuries to] Paula Harris. I think introducing Loughlin or Lewis is beyond the direct."

Technically Moore had a point. But Galligan chose not to observe the procedural limits too strictly, instead applying the principle that turnabout is fair play. "She is making him her witness for those," he told Moore. "The objection is overruled."

———

A defiant Delores Wise could barely compose herself long enough to answer Moore's simple questions while she was on the stand. She stared at Lederer, her eyes ablaze with hatred. The prosecutor returned an equally hard gaze.

Ms. Wise mentioned, in response to one of her lawyer's early questions, that her son was in a special education program. Lederer rose to cut off this apparent effort to introduce the barred psychiatric evidence. "Objection," said the DA.

"Shut up!" snapped Ms. Wise, before the judge had a chance to speak.

Moore had put the defendant's mother on the stand to bolster his alibi defense and the allegation that his client had been beaten. Ms. Wise said that Kharey was coming out of an elevator opposite their apartment when she got home from church at 9:35 P.M. on April 19. She also testified that his face was swollen both when she saw him at arraignment on April 23 and a few days later at Rikers Island.

"After you saw Kharey," asked Moore, "where did you go?"

"When I saw him come out the elevator," she replied, "I took my fingers and I clupped him upside the head."

"Why did you do that?"

"Because he knows he's supposed to be upstairs before that."

"So that was a form of punishment?" asked Moore, trying to put the best face on this incident.

"No," said Ms. Wise coolly. "That's what I usually do when I see him and I know there's somethin', he did somethin'. I clup him upside the head."

"What he did wrong was what," asked Moore, "being late?"

She nodded. "He should have been there since about 8:30."

Moore next had his witness describe her odyssey of April 21. Five months pregnant, she traveled from the Central Park Precinct down to central booking in lower Manhattan and back up to the Twenty-fourth Precinct, looking for her son. She finally found a cop who told her the teenager was under arrest. "I axed him what for," she testified, "and when he told me, I fainted."

"What did he tell you?" asked Moore.

"That Kharey had raped a lady in the park."

When she came to, Ms. Wise asked a detective if she could see Kharey. "He said: 'Why would you want to see a scumbag like him,' " she testified, her anger momentarily disappearing as she began to cry softly. "And I explained to him, he was my kid, and he was very slow, and he doesn't understand whatever you talkin' to him."

Ms. Wise never did get a chance to see her son that day. "I walked on home," she testified. "I was in a daze. I just didn't take a cab. I walked."

Having cross-examined Delores Wise at the pretrial hearing, Lederer was prepared for extreme hostility. So, apparently, were the bureaucrats who coordinated trial security. Nine armed guards were assigned to Galligan's courtroom that afternoon.

The prosecutor began by pointing out inconsistencies between Ms. Wise's trial testimony and her prior statements. On the stand the witness denied having told Moore, back in May 1989, that she didn't get home until 10:00 P.M. on April 19. She also denied having more recently told Moore's private investigator that she got home at about 9:45 P.M.

The first of several outbursts that punctuated Ms. Wise's testimony came early in this line of questioning, when Lederer confronted her with statements she had made to reporters. "Isn't it a fact that you told a reporter for the *New York Times*," said the prosecutor, "that you didn't get home that night until 9:45?"

"I never spoke to the *Times*," said Mrs. Wise. "I hate the *Times*. . . . It's a prejudiced newspaper."

When Lederer produced a clipping from the paper, the witness refused to look at it, drawing the first of several warnings from Galligan. "If you want to testify here, you're going to follow the directions of the court," said the judge.

Lederer next brought up remarks Ms. Wise had made to a reporter for WABC-TV at the Twenty-fourth Precinct. Isn't it true, she said, that you told Kathy Wolff that Kharey was in the park that night?

"I don't know how you all did this thing," she replied in a voice laced with both wonderment and foreboding, "but Jesus is going to undo this thing."

Galligan instructed her to answer the question.

"She's tryin' to trick me," complained Ms. Wise, "like she tricked those doggone kids." With that she began to rise and announced: "I'm going home."

Galligan immediately declared a recess and dismissed the jury. He then warned the witness he would strike her testimony if she failed to follow instructions.

"Okay," replied Ms. Wise, "let me go home." She then turned on Lederer again. "This is my kid!" she shouted. "He's facing 57 years! You made this thing up!"

The judge granted Moore a few minutes to calm his witness in privacy. When she returned to the stand Ms. Wise promised to follow orders. But a moment later she was staring at Lederer again and suddenly hissed: "Snake!"

Galligan, exhibiting more patience than his reputation gave him credit for, issued a final warning to Ms. Wise before having the jury brought back. By the time Lederer rose to resume her cross-examination the crew of court officers ringing the room had been increased to thirteen.

Relying on records from the Board of Education and Bureau of Child Welfare, Lederer confronted Ms. Wise with evidence of her son's extensive truancy in 1982 and her own request that he be placed in a residential school. Asked to confirm this information, Ms. Wise said, "Let me say somethin'. Let's get to the park."

"Isn't it a fact," Lederer pressed, "that you told his school that you felt that within three years you might not have control over him, and that he could get into problems which might put him in jail?"

"That's a lie," said Ms. Wise contemptuously. When the DA asked her to look at the records herself, she demanded: "What does this have to do with the park?"

"No, no, no," Galligan admonished her, "don't ask questions!" Exasperated, the judge announced that he was striking her testimony.

As she left the courtroom Ms. Wise turned to Lederer and shouted: "Wait 'til you see what Jesus is gonna do to you!"

Galligan ordered the jury to disregard the testimony in its entirety. "Don't let it form any part of your determination in this case," he instructed the panel. It was unlikely, however, that the spectacle of Ms. Wise's performance could be wiped out of the jurors' minds by judicial fiat. "When you saw her," said alternate juror Robert Lind after his dismissal a week later, "you saw where Kharey Wise was coming from, and it was not a pretty picture."

———

"You seem a bit reluctant to look at the videotape," said Moore with Kharey Wise on the stand. "Why is that?"

"I don't like it. It broke me," the witness answered. "I let life break me. I didn't want to say that."

"Did they force you to say it?" asked Moore.

"Yes," replied Wise, "that's why I don't watch it."

Most defense lawyers in the Central Park trials were terrified of their clients' videotapes, and shuddered every time those images appeared on a television screen. But Moore had decided to attack the state's case at its strongest point. If Wise's two tapes were the most potent weapons at the DA's disposal, they also presented his lawyer with opportunities to sow reasonable doubt in the jury box. Moore's determination to exploit the implausible portions of the videos, and to highlight his client's obvious revulsion on seeing the tapes, was his smartest tactical decision.

Another reason to put Wise on the stand was Moore's inability to put on a credible coercion defense without his client's testimony. Unlike the other defendants who'd made videotapes, Wise had no relatives who could testify to having been tricked or deceived by the police. So, under Moore's questioning and with several interruptions to look at selected bits of videotape, Wise uncomfortably discussed his long night and day of interrogations.

It all began, he testified, with a cop asking: "Did she look good?" From then on, said Wise, all the detectives wanted to talk about was the rape. They scoffed at his denials, insisting that they already knew of his involvement from other suspects. After Hartigan took the first statement (in which Wise said his friends had told him on April 20 that Lopez and Richardson had raped the Jogger) he left the teenager alone with Nugent, who screamed at him for more than an hour, called him "a fuckin' liar" and slapped him across the face three times, Wise testified.

Wise's story did not seem farfetched. The detectives were dealing with an adult, unprotected by parent, guardian or lawyer. The notion that two tough, white New York detectives might intimidate and slap around an uncooperative black rape suspect did not require a great stretch of the imagination.

Wise claimed that he decided to cooperate because the cops promised he could go home if he told them what they wanted to hear. "I said, 'I seen somebody hittin' her. I seen somebody hittin' her,'" he testified. When Nugent asked who was hitting the Jogger, Wise told him it was Steve Lopez and Raymond Santana.

"Why did you say Steve and Raymond were hitting her?" asked Moore.

"Because that night all he was talkin' about was Lopez and Raymond," answered Wise.

This suggestion that his client had gone along with the scenario given him by the police became the pattern of Moore's examination. Wise admitted going into the park but said he left with Al Morris before the violence began. Consistent with his testimony at the pretrial hearings, he claimed every incriminating detail in his statements was either dictated by the detectives or suggested to him by their questions. In other words, he had been totally framed.

Moore did not stop at accusing the cops of improper conduct; he wanted the jury also to focus on Lederer's behavior. Wise testified that he was drowsy, hungry and scared when he sat down to make the first video. When you described the beating of "the lady," asked Moore, you based that on what the detectives had told you?

"That," said Wise, "and the photos Miss Lederer was showing me; the pictures of her."

Moore then produced the snapshot of the Jogger's broken, bloody head with which Lederer had so upset Wise during the taped interview. "Do you remember seeing this photograph?" asked Moore.

Wise took a quick glance and turned away, wincing.

"Look at it," said his lawyer. "How did you feel, Kharey, when you saw this photograph?"

There was no answer as Wise squirmed in his chair.

"Look at it," urged Moore. "How did you feel when you saw it?"

In a high whine, seeming on the verge of tears, Wise said: "I felt upset. It's a rough scare."

Moore followed up with two more photos, drawing similar reactions. Then he played the portion of the first videotape in which Lederer questioned Wise insistently about the head injuries, saying they could not have resulted from punches or a knife. "What did you feel when she told you it could not come from punches?" he asked.

"She got me scared," said Wise.

"Did you feel you had to change your story?"

Lederer's objection was sustained.

"You told her it was from a rock," said Moore. "Why did you tell her that?"

"That's what the detectives was tellin' me to say," he whined, "by a rock."

It was during the conversation outside the cellblock, said Wise, that Hartigan finally convinced him to incriminate himself in the rape. "He started talkin' about Eddie, tellin' me, you know, Eddie wasn't there, he say he wasn't with you. Then he said, you know, the jury ain't gonna buy what you just said. You got to put yourself in this."

"If you did that," asked Moore, "what would happen?"

"I'd go home."

Moore next showed portions of the second video to Wise, who claimed each damning admission it contained was a lie. "I never seen none of this stuff I was saying," he insisted.

What happened when the second video session ended? Moore inquired.

"I axed [Hartigan], can I go home," said Wise. "He said the only place I'm going is to jail."

"And what happened?" asked Moore. "Did you go to jail."

Wise seemed to consider the answer painfully obvious. "I'm here now," he replied.

Cross-examination of Wise required a very different approach from the one Lederer had taken with Yusef Salaam. For one thing, Wise's story was more complex and harder to sort out. He was offering an alibi, for instance, yet he admitted having gone into the park with the gang. In addition, while Salaam had refused to acknowledge even the simplest facts in the state's case, Wise was conceding a lot. The probable cause for his arrest, for example, was not in dispute. Nor were the structure and progress of his interrogations, or the gist of his cellblock discussion with Hartigan.

While Lederer had no compassion to spare for Kharey Wise, she rightly suspected that some jurors did. She could not afford to be as overtly antagonistic as she had been toward Salaam. But Lederer was only prepared to back off so far; she was not about to relinquish control of her examination to a defendant, no matter how sympathetic.

Although she was not permitted to put Shabazz Head on the stand, Lederer still had a means of getting Wise's alleged April 20 conversation with him into evidence. "Do you remember being with Eddie de la Paz and seeing Ronnie Williams and Shabazz Head at about 3 o'clock on that afternoon?" she asked.

"I don't recall," said Wise.

"Isn't it true that you told Ronnie Williams at that time that the police were looking for you, and when he asked you why, you told him it was because you had raped and beaten a woman in Central Park?"

"No," said Wise, "not true."

As the prosecutor continued her very logical inquiry its overriding theme became clear: If the detectives had dictated Wise's statements, why were they not more coherent, more accurate and, most important, more incriminating?

"The police told you to say that you were hiding behind a tree?" asked Lederer.

"Yeah."

"That's what they wanted you to say?"

"Yeah," said Wise, "so I could go home."

"They didn't make you say that you had gotten on top of her and raped her by putting your penis inside of her, did they?"

"They could have."

"Did they?"

"They could have."

"Did they?"

"They could have."

"Did they?"

"They could have."

Wise's answers were repeatedly confirming Lederer's point. If "they could have," why didn't they? If they were framing him, in other words, why wouldn't they have made him say he raped her?

"Did the police make you say that you hit her in the head with a pipe?"

This startled Wise. "Hit who in the head with a pipe?" he asked.

"The female Jogger," said Lederer.

"Did I hit her with a pipe?" he asked.

Now she had him confused. "Did the police make you say that in that statement?"

"Say what?" he asked suspiciously.

"That you hit her in the head with a pipe?" Lederer's tone remained even, giving the witness no clue to what might be the right answer.

"That's what it says there?" asked Wise, pointing to his second written statement.

"Did the police make you say that?" repeated Lederer.

"That's what it says there?" he asked again.

But he wasn't about to get the answer from the DA. "Did the police make you say that?"

"If it's there," said Wise, "yep."

But the jurors knew that it wasn't there. Again, he had only succeeded in shoring up her theme: Why wasn't it there?

Lederer kept this technique running a while longer. "Did they make you say it on the video?" she asked.

"On what video?"

"Either video."

"What?"

"That you struck her with a rock or a brick or a pipe?"

"That's what it says?" asked Wise incredulously, his voice rising now with something close to panic. "That's what I said?" The prosecutor remained silent, waiting. Wise opted for consistency: "Yes, they did."

It was the wrong answer again. He had never said anything about striking the Jogger himself, with his hands or with any weapon.

Lederer pressed a series of detailed questions about the contents of the videos, hammering her theme home. If Wise had agreed to cooperate with the cops, why had it been necessary to go back and make a second videotape at all? If the detectives had dictated everything on the first tape, as Wise maintained, why did it include his denials of such things as joining in the assault of the bum? If Detective Sheehan had taken him to the rape scene and told him to wipe some of the Jogger's blood on his shirt, as Wise claimed, why did Sheehan then accept the kid's refusal to do so?

By the time this line of questioning was exhausted, Wise's hatred of the prosecutor was beginning to show. Although Lederer wanted the jury to see the anger of which she believed Wise capable, there was a risk in getting him too upset. She knew from cross-examining both Delores and Kharey Wise at the pretrial hearings that the teenager was likely to mimic his mother's behavior. Lederer was scoring points and she did not want Wise's testimony stricken. The challenge was to push him to the edge without hitting his breaking point.

The prosecutor began to ask about Wise's truancy, going back as far as 1985, and his apparent fondness for hanging out in the park. "Were you in Central Park . . . when you were supposed to be in school?" she asked.

"Central Park?" he replied. "Maybe."

"You were playing hooky?" she asked.

"No."

"You weren't in school?"

"The reason why I wasn't in school," said Wise, "I had been threatened not to come back to school."

"And that was the reason you didn't go to school in April of 1989? April 5th, 6th, 7th?"

"Yeah," he said.

"You didn't go to school every day in that month, either, did you?"

"I was threatened," he repeated.

Lederer ran down the whole month, asking about two or three dates at a time. "I was threatened," he insisted, tacking a challenge to the end of each answer: "Go ahead."

She did. "In the last week of March, isn't it true that you missed four days of school?"

A growing irritation had begun to harden his voice. "I was threatened . . . to bring them my lunch money . . . with my life!"

When Lederer brought up another week in 1985, Wise shouted plaintively: "I don't remember all that! I don't remember all that!"

The prosecutor produced a record of his truancy to refresh his recollection. Wise would not take the document from the court officer, who placed it beside him on the railing around the witness stand. "What does this have to do with my case?" demanded Wise.

Galligan ordered him not to ask questions, but Wise persisted. "I'm sayin', though, come on, man," he complained. "I'm tired of hearing this!"

As the prosecutor tried to ask another question and Galligan admonished Wise to keep quiet, his complaints grew louder, until he suddenly snapped.

"What does this have to do with my case?" screamed Wise, again and again as Galligan tried to silence him.

"I don't care. Come on, man," shouted Wise, spitting on the truancy record before jumping to his feet. "Shit, man, come on!"

As Wise spun away from the stand, as if to descend the few stairs into the well, a court officer immediately blocked his path. Galligan hurriedly declared a recess and ordered the jury removed.

As the panel filed past the witness stand, the outraged defendant yelled at the judge, at the jury, at the gallery, at the world. "I'm facing 57 years over this, man! She bringin' up 1985? I was 12 years old back then, man! What this have to do with Central Park? What this have to do with Central Park?"

The last few jurors were passing in front of Wise when he picked up the truancy record and waved it in the air. "I want the jury to see this! The reason why I wasn't in school—because I was threatened not to go back to school."

The panel was gone by the time he turned, in disgust, to Lederer. "People puttin' guns to my head," he said, sneering at the DA, "that's why!"

After warning Moore that he would strike his client's testimony if this outburst were repeated, Galligan had the jurors brought back into the room. When they were all seated Wise surprised them by saying, calmly and steadily, "Jury, I apologize for what I said. Alright? Sorry."

The cross-examination proceeded quietly for a few minutes, until Lederer attempted to turn on the VCR. "I can't look at that," Wise announced.

"You don't have an alternative," said the judge.

"I can't look at that, Judge Galligan," said Wise firmly. "They broke me already. I can't do nothin' more about that. I can't look at that."

The judge summoned the lawyers to the bench and told Moore he would strike the testimony if Wise refused to watch the video. Lederer, wanting very much to preserve this Q&A, quickly offered to change course. "I can do some other things, if you want, and come back," she suggested.

The judge sent Wise to the defense table so Moore could explain the danger of another outburst. As he ambled across the well, his arms held far away from his sides, Wise looked older than his eighteen years.

He was short, five feet five inches, but huskier than when the videos had been made nearly two years before. On his way back to the stand after a conference with his lawyer, he was fighting back tears.

Eventually Lederer worked her way back to the videotape, playing the clip in which Wise, punching the air with both fists in rapid succession, described how Lopez and Santana had thrashed Paula Harris's face. The prosecutor asked a series of eleven questions that suggested this bit of detail was too spontaneous to have been directed by the detectives. Wise tried to dodge each question, claiming the cops had "somehow" made him make those gestures, until Galligan finally ordered him to give the prosecutor a direct answer.

"The police didn't make you do that punching, did they?" asked Lederer.

"No," he conceded, nearing the end of four hours of testimony. "I did it myself."

Having put on the stand Grace Cuffee, a few character witnesses and Paul Richardson, his client's father, Howard Diller thought his defense was complete. But as the trial neared its conclusion, he found himself having to call Angela Cuffee, too, against his better judgment. Diller believed the young woman's acerbic attitude toward Lederer at the pretrial hearings had hurt her own credibility and, by extension, her brother's case. He also knew the prosecutor had since developed evidence that would negate the value of any testimony Angela Cuffee could offer about the circumstances of Kevin Richardson's confession.

But Lederer had Diller in a difficult situation. The DA had asked the judge to include a missing witness charge in his instructions to the jury if Richardson's stepsister were not to testify. Lederer was on solid ground; Cuffee was a material witness to her brother's interrogation; she had signed his written statement, which the defense was claiming had been coerced. In a missing witness charge, the judge would instruct the jury that it could infer from the sister's failure to testify on the defendant's behalf that her testimony would have been detrimental to his case.

Galligan had agreed. Nevertheless, he surprised all the lawyers by saying he would permit her last-minute testimony if she wished to give it, in spite of the fact that she had sat through much of the trial and heard a great deal of the testimony of other witnesses. Colin Moore urged Diller to accept the judge's offer. But Diller knew better than to do so.

At the pretrial hearing Angela Cuffee had denied signing a page of notes on which Hartigan had written details of the Jogger assault as he listened to Richardson's confession. (The detective had wanted her to sign the notes to substantiate that the details had been provided by Richardson.) Lederer had sent numerous examples of her handwriting to the police lab for analysis and was prepared to offer expert testimony that the signature on the page of notes was indeed that of Angela Cuffee.

But Cuffee could not afford to change her testimony now. She would have to continue to deny that the signature was hers, not only to support the defense that the cops had dictated Richardson's statement, but also to avoid a possible perjury indictment, based on her having made a prior contradictory statement under oath.

To Diller the missing witness charge was less damaging than exposure of Cuffee's testimony as unreliable, which would undercut his coercion defense. But Moore took matters into his own hands. He told Angela Cuffee of the judge's offer. She then went to Diller and demanded that he put her on the stand.

When Lederer showed the witness the page of notes bearing her name, Angela solemnly declared: "As God is my witness, that is not my signature." The next morning the DA's handwriting expert would give the jury a slide show demonstrating his research, explaining, in effect, why he was scientifically satisfied that Angela Cuffee was a liar.

As the hapless Diller had feared, his witness also alienated several jurors with her antagonism toward Lederer. "You weren't in Central Park on the night of April 19, were you?" asked the prosecutor.

"No," snapped Cuffee, "were you?"

Lederer concluded by suggesting the witness had a callous attitude toward the victim. "Did you care about what had happened to that woman?" she asked.

"Of course," said Cuffee. "I'm a woman."

"Did you care about who had done that to her?"

"I knew Kevin didn't do it," she answered.

"Isn't it a fact," pressed the DA, "that when you saw Officer Reynolds at the 82nd Street precinct you said to him, 'Why are you making such a big fucking deal about this? All he did was rape her; he didn't murder her'?"

"You've got to be crazy," said Cuffee, staring angrily at Lederer. "Of course not. I never said anything like that."

"I have nothing further."

CHAPTER 19.

SPLIT DECISION

——

"IT WAS A CASE OF THE POWERFUL AGAINST THE POWERLESS," SAID Colin Moore, setting the tone for a long summation in which he pleaded repeatedly with the jury to prevent a racist miscarriage of justice.

When "the horrible crime" that had been visited upon Paula Harris was discovered, Moore charged, the black and Latino boys who had been randomly grabbed by patrolmen on Central Park West became the perfect fall guys for a white Establishment seeking retribution. Within hours, the full weight of the forces that drove the media, the police department, mighty Salomon Brothers and City Hall had come crashing down on "poor and powerless" families of East Harlem. "From the very inception," he declared, turning to point at the defendants, "these young men did not have a snowball's chance in hell."

Comparing the NYPD to "Nazi storm troopers," Moore characterized the investigation as rife with corruption from top to bottom. A key architect of this massive frame-up, he argued, was Detective Hartigan. "After Kharey makes his first statement," said Moore, running through the chronology of his client's interrogations, "Hartigan leaves. Because he has a lot of other business to do. He has other kids to beat up and get confessions from."

In Moore's scenario the DA's office happily furthered the conspiracy. "Miss Elizabeth Lederer, the director, comes in," said Moore, "with the production of the movie entitled 'The Confessions of Kharey Wise.' So now, everything that they coached him to say, they are ready now to put it on the video screen."

As he punctuated his summation with soundbites from Wise's videotapes, Moore was the only defense lawyer at either trial to effectively highlight the leading nature of Lederer's questions and the apparent willingness of his client to concur. Wise says on his first tape, for example, that he does not know Raymond's last name; but when Lederer asks, "Is that Raymond Santana?" Wise says, "yes." Every time the DA poses an open-ended question, argued Moore, Wise tells her he does not know the answer. "Any time the answer is suggested . . . then he says yes." Such behavior is consistent, added Moore, with "a young kid who is in a situation of captivity. . . . It is a hostage syndrome."

The defense lawyer was midway through his summation when court recessed for the day. As Moore stepped into the crowded hallway he was greeted by a throng of Supporters, whose cheers and applause bounced off the tile walls and were heard in every courtroom on the east side of the seventh floor.

The next morning Moore underscored a fact that had worried Lederer ever since she had agreed nineteen months ago to let Wise make a second video. The prosecutor has given you two written statements and two videotapes, Moore reminded the jurors, all of which conflict with each other in important respects. "Which one are you supposed to believe?" he asked. The DA wants you to accept the portions of Wise's statements that incriminate him, said Moore, and reject those parts that do not. But you know by now, he said, that Wise is not credible and you must therefore reject all of his statements. "And that leaves you with no evidence."

In conclusion, Moore reminded the jurors that Harris herself had told them she did not want to see an innocent person go to jail. "Follow the admonition of Paula Harris," he solemnly urged the panel, "and acquit an innocent man."

"Mr. Moore has argued to you that this is a racially based prosecution. That is simply not true," Lederer told the jury. "It is an insult to your intelligence for someone to suggest it, and it would be a violation of your oath to judge this case on racial grounds."

The prosecutor ran through a long list of black and Latino teenagers who were questioned by investigators and released without having been arrested. "This case is not about white and black and Hispanic," she said, "it's about right and wrong and what happened in Central Park."

Lederer seemed more relaxed, more confident than she had been during her closing argument in the first trial. Much of what she said this time—the vivid descriptions of the wilding, the weapons and the pain inflicted on innocent victims—was an echo of the earlier speech, delivered in a similarly dry monotone. When she focused on the specific defenses offered by Moore and Diller, however, Lederer became animated and energetic, imploring the jury to see the evidence as she did.

She dismissed Moore's suggestion that his client had been coerced, playing a video clip to demonstrate the casual, earnest manner in which the teenager told his story. Then the prosecutor reminded the panel of Wise's demeanor on the witness stand. "You saw him hostile, assertive, refusing to look at evidence," she said, "absolutely in contrast to Mr. Moore's picture of a pliant, fearful youth ready to please his captors."

Lederer mocked Wise's insistence—on tape and to Melonie Jackson—that he had done nothing but fondle the Jogger's legs. "He still doesn't get it," she said. "He still doesn't understand that he helped others rape her." Under the acting-in-concert theory, she explained, Wise was certainly guilty of rape.

With the crime scene photos displayed on the big board behind her, Lederer addressed Moore's claim that there was no proof of rape. She reminded the jury that Richardson had said that McCray penetrated Harris, and that both Richardson and Wise had said that Lopez had done so. Furthermore, she noted, hair similar to the victim's had been found not only on Richardson's clothing but on Lopez's, too. She urged the jurors to consider the evidence not in isolated pieces but in its totality. That approach, she promised, would lead to the inescapable conclusion that these defendants were the Jogger's assailants. "There is no other explanation."

The DA made short work of Richardson's defense. She rejected the notion that Ms. Cuffee had been misled, insisting that the policemen had warned her that her son was implicated in a rape, and possibly a murder. The usually restrained prosecutor almost shouted: "What's wrong with the police telling Grace Cuffee, 'We think your son should tell the truth?' What's wrong with telling the truth? When is it wrong to tell the truth?"

In conclusion, Lederer revisited the theme employed by Moore, her most formidable opponent. Yes, she said, this is a case of the powerful against the powerless. But Moore, she suggested, had reversed those roles. "On the night of April 19," said Lederer, "no one in the city was more powerful than Kharey Wise, Kevin Richardson. . . . And look at how they wielded their power. Look what they did to their victims."

The jury got the case on November 30, after listening to Judge Galligan's complicated instructions for a couple of hours. The panelists spent the first four days of deliberations tediously retracing every detail of the wilding spree on the big map of Central Park. Then they began considering the evidence against Kevin Richardson.

Howard Diller's brief closing argument, which had been delivered before Moore's, had not given the jurors much to think about. Diller had been under orders from his client's family not to concede, as he had in his opening statement, that the boy was in Central Park that night. This left him unable to argue credibly his theory that Richardson had been a bystander and, since he shared no intent to commit the crimes, could therefore not be found guilty under the acting-in-concert theory. Instead, Diller had offered the jury a summary of a coercion defense that centered on his contention that the detectives had deceived the Cuffees and thereby violated his client's rights.

It was not the kind of argument that could be expected to seize a prominent place in the jury's collective psyche. Indeed, the lower counts in the indictment—assault of the male joggers, robbery and riot—were dispatched with relative ease as the panel applied the acting-in-concert principle to convict Richardson of each charge.

The jurors considered that part of the case overwhelming for several reasons. First, Richardson had been caught in the park and had made a spontaneous remark in the squad car about seeing McCray "do the murder." Second, his sister was present for his written statement, as was his father for the videotape session, crippling the coercion defense in the eyes of most jurors. Third, there was the videotape, which not only closely followed the statement Richardson himself had written earlier but contained a description of the reservoir assaults that was too detailed to have been supplied by the detectives.

The panel's consensus dissolved, however, when it came to the charges related to Paula Harris. At this point Steve Gilliam, a thirty-year-old bill adjuster for American Express, demanded evidence beyond Richardson's own words before he'd agree to convict on the rape, sodomy and attempted murder counts. Gilliam took the presumption of innocence seriously. A stubborn and confident black man from East Harlem, he didn't just theoretically embrace the principle that a defendant is innocent until proven guilty; he locked his long arms around it in a bear hug. He was a defense lawyer's dream, determined to burden the prosecution with the highest possible standard of proof. Two black women, Christine Rudisel and Bernadette Heron, proved to be Gilliam's most staunch allies.

The jury's other African-American, twenty-seven-year-old Eric Roach, led the fight for conviction with Stephanie Samoy, an Asian-American, and two whites, Ralph Pollock and Christine Rathgebar. Other conviction advocates and a few swing voters were less vocal during the next three days of debate.

A series of remarkable contradictions that would ultimately stand as the record of these jury deliberations began to emerge at this stage. Nobody doubted the veracity of Richardson's video, yet those who accepted it as damning in relation to the reservoir assaults did not consider it sufficiently incriminating when it came to the rape scene. "Steve and Bernadette said in their hearts they knew the kids were guilty," recalled Roach in an interview later, "but they needed evidence."

Those who were reluctant to convict Richardson justified their position by challenging the acting-in-concert principle, which was now subjected to widely differing interpretations. Perhaps the literal application endorsed by the conviction advocates drove Gilliam and his allies to the opposite extreme; the defendant can be convicted, argued Pollock and Samoy, simply because of his presence at the scene with the gang that committed the criminal acts.

Gilliam and Rudisel countered that such a reading of the judge's instruction was too general. They demanded specific proof that Richardson's actions satisfied all three elements of the law: knowledge of the crime, intent and assistance in commission of the crime. The acquittal camp would only be satisfied by physical evidence that corroborated the teenager's statements.

Attempted murder was the first high count on which the conviction advocates prevailed. The jury listened to a readback of the testimony of Detective Robert Honeyman, the crime scene specialist who had found, near the base of a big tree seventy-five feet north of the 102nd Street Crossdrive, the rock that had been used to crack the Jogger's skull. Other experts had testified that blood on the rock was "consistent" with the victim's blood and that hair on the rock was similar to her head hair.

Because of the editing of the videotapes, the jurors had never heard Wise say it was Richardson who wielded the rock. Like their predecessors in the first trial, however, several jurors made the logical assumption that Richardson's name had been deleted from Wise's tapes and vice versa. Gilliam was *not* one of those jurors.

He was more inclined to accept the kid's guilt on the higher charges, however, after going out to the courtroom to watch Richardson's video again. "When he said, 'We chased her down,'" said Gilliam, quoting Richardson's tape in an interview after the trial, "that really disturbed us. . . . I said: 'What gives you the right, some teenager that can't blow his nose yet . . . to chase somebody down?' That made his intentions clear."

Meanwhile, the leaders in the conviction camp were arguing that the use of the rock, the extent of the Jogger's injuries and the fact that she had been left for dead provided sufficient evidence for an attempted murder conviction. When another vote was taken, Richardson stood as the only defendant at either trial convicted of that charge.

The sodomy conviction was won not as a result of the semen found in Harris's rectum but by the photographic evidence. The acquittal voters became convinced that sodomy had been committed when they were shown a photo depicting abrasions and bruises on the Jogger's knees.

It was on the rape charge that Gilliam and his allies dug in their heels. They discounted Moore's argument that a rape never occurred but they contended that the acting-in-concert theory was not enough to convict Richardson. Gilliam was troubled by the prosecution's failure to get a DNA match. The credibility of Richardson's video, on which he claimed to be "way in the back" of the group watching as the rape was committed, also helped the defendant. Even Richardson's contention that he got scratched when he grabbed the Jogger's arm in an attempt to stop the rape seemed plausible to Gilliam. "That could have been true," said Gilliam, "that he actually went over and said . . . 'This is just too much. Let me go try to help the lady.' "

The head hair found in Richardson's underwear and the pubic hair on his shirt—both similar to samples taken from Harris—weakened the resolve of those in the acquittal camp, but it was not enough. Unlike fingerprints or DNA, hair samples cannot be conclusively matched to an individual. So the conviction advocates began looking for more physical evidence.

Nothing else would do. There was no need to attack the testimony of the defense witnesses because nobody on the panel had found them credible. While many jurors were sympathetic to Grace Cuffee, they rejected Diller's argument that the police had conned the woman. She had waived her son's rights out of either hope or ignorance, they reasoned, not as a result of promises, threats or deception. And nobody believed Angela Cuffee's testimony about the detectives' dictating the details of Richardson's statement. Last, the testimony of several character witnesses to the defendant's exemplary reputation was considered irrelevant to what had happened in Central Park on the night in question.

The lack of blood on Richardson's clothing and the obvious explanation that semen would be present in an adolescent male's underwear worked against those arguing for conviction. By the seventh day of deliberations, however, that group had nine votes and they were determined to win over their last three colleagues. A meticulous inspection of Richardson's clothing turned up what they needed. Dirt on the inside of his dungarees shook Heron and Rudisel and began to sway Gilliam, too.

Finally, Ivette Naftal turned Richardson's underpants inside out and found what appeared to be dirt and grass stains. She reached across the table, holding the underpants out in front of Gilliam. "Richardson said he fell in the mud with his pants on," she said. "But he has mud on his underwear, not his pants!"

Gilliam offered no argument. His reluctance to convict had always been rooted in a commitment to the principle that the state must conclusively prove its case; not in any deep belief in Richardson's personal innocence. This latest discovery undermined the credibility of Richardson's videotaped denials, and now that the pattern of circumstantial evidence was becoming overwhelming, Gilliam's doubts no longer seemed reasonable to him. Whether or not Richardson had raped Harris, he reasoned, the kid had pulled his pants down, so he must have had the intent required to satisfy the acting-in-concert law. The panel was finally unanimous in voting guilty on the rape charge.

Naftal's inspection of the underpants was a lucky break for the prosecutors. Their experts had not tested the stains and had offered no testimony about their origins.

As the deliberations dragged on, Galligan's courtroom and the adjacent hallway began to look like a refugee camp. Winter coats and scarves were piled everywhere. The large Cuffee family, with assorted aunts, in-laws and infants, took meals and naps on a hallway bench as they awaited the verdict. Kevin Richardson carried a Bible during deliberations and his mother occasionally convened a group prayer. Delores Wise would drop by, sometimes with Kharey's baby brother in a stroller. The Supporters came and went, debating racial politics and the lasting influence of slavery on American institutions, or hurling abuse at the passing prosecutors and journalists. The size of the press corps fluctuated, as the courthouse regulars were joined by reporters anticipating an imminent verdict. On one slow day Galligan delighted the front-row sketch artists by sending out from chambers drawings he had made of some of them.

There was a constant shifting of people between courtroom and hallway. Lawyers, Supporters, reporters and detectives tried to guess what was going on in the jury room. Their conversations sometimes shed light on the various prisms through which New Yorkers viewed the Central Park case.

Elombe Brath, a former Schomburg resident who had testified as a character witness for both teenagers, was a graphic artist at WNBC-TV who had long been active in the black nationalist movement. Brath looked at the case from a political perspective that was not atypical of the Supporters. He believed the alibi defense alone was sufficient to acquit Wise. A rejection of the testimony of the alibi witnesses, including that of his wife Nomsa, would be a demonstration of contempt for the defendants' community, said Brath.

And surely there was contempt among some of the cops who had worked on the case. One afternoon a reporter was telling a detective that he found it hard to understand how teenagers could commit such a violent rape and then calmly discuss it a few hours later with a video camera whirring across the table. "In that race," said the white detective, "in that society, rape is no big deal. It's only a big deal when she doesn't get her five dollars."

On December 4, the fifth day of deliberations, the hallway was abuzz with news of a verdict in the case of a racist murder in Bensonhurst, Brooklyn. Two white men, who had been prosecuted under the acting-in-concert law, had been acquitted of the murder of Yusuf Hawkins, a sixteen-year-old black. When Detective Taglioni passed a group of reporters, one asked whether he'd heard the Bensonhurst verdict. "It's good news," said the white policeman. "It's about time one of these cases went our way."

The day the Bensonhurst verdict came in, Howard Diller received a phone call in which he was threatened with death if Richardson were acquitted. Diller was more accustomed to antagonism from the Supporters, whom he referred to as "terrorists." After six weeks of trial, he was desperate to see it all end. "If I don't at least get a movie contract out of this," he had said on the eve of summations, "I'll be very distressed."

On the seventh day of deliberations a peculiar verdict came out of a courtroom down the hall from Judge Galligan's. A defendant had been convicted of second-degree murder but was acquitted of possession of the murder weapon. Galligan's crew of court officers shook their heads on hearing this latest confirmation of the axiom that anything can happen in a jury room.

"If we don't get a rape conviction," said Detective McKenna two days later, "we lost the case." A reporter asked whether a conviction on attempted murder, technically a higher count, would not be considered a victory. No, said McKenna, it had to be a rape conviction. Taglioni nodded in agreement.

Out on the sidewalk one evening Delores Wise took the opportunity of a radio interview to send a message to Paula Harris. "She knows, and her boyfriend knows, that he beat her up before and he'll do it again," she said. "He's a dog!" For her own protection, said Ms. Wise, Harris should turn her boyfriend in to the authorities. "Next time, he'll kill her."

The first thing Steve Gilliam had done as deliberations started was ask his fellow jurors to throw out the testimony of witnesses whom they could agree were not credible. Eight days later the panel consequently began debating a case against Kharey Wise that no longer included the evidence provided by Melonie Jackson.

This would prove a major blow to the prosecutors, who had expected Jackson's testimony to go a long way toward clinching the case. If Wise's confession had been dictated by the police, why would he repeat it to a friend three months later?

But several jurors had been swayed by Colin Moore's efforts to impeach Jackson's credibility. Gilliam said, for example, that he doubted Wise would have used the word "fondling" and he wondered why Jackson had not come forward sooner. Gilliam also accepted Moore's contention that, since Wise was only permitted to use the jailhouse phone for six minutes at a time, Jackson must have lied when she claimed to have talked to the defendant for approximately fifteen minutes.

Gilliam, however, was ignoring a number of related facts. First, Jackson had explained that she was testifying under threat of a contempt citation, *not* because she belatedly decided to cooperate with the DA. Second, she only used the word "fondling" because of Moore's badgering, after having repeated Wise's statement without using that term at least three times. Third, Jackson had explained that their conversation was interrupted when Wise had to let somebody else use the phone. He called back a few minutes later, she said.

Even so, Gilliam found enough support on the panel to have Jackson's testimony discarded. This episode demonstrates the illogical approach that some jurors who were inclined to acquit Wise brought to the debate. "I believe he said that to Melonie Jackson," said Victoria Bryers, a U.S. Coast Guard petty officer, after the trial. "I really don't think he knows what he did. . . . Kharey Wise had been told so many times that he fondled her legs that he believed it. . . . But we didn't know what to believe, so we had to throw it out." As Moore had hoped, his client's total lack of personal credibility was his best defense.

It is also clear, however, from interviews with three jurors who worked to acquit Wise of the most serious charges, that there was a hidden agenda at work. The panel knew that Richardson, as a juvenile, faced a maximum ten-year prison term and that Wise, according to his own outburst on the witness stand, faced more than fifty years. This subject was not openly discussed and there were certainly other important factors working in Wise's favor. But to people like Gilliam and

Bryers—who considered Wise a bystander to the crimes of which
they'd already convicted Richardson—this disparity of punishment
represented a huge injustice.

The major thrust of Moore's theory—the racist conspiracy angle—
had ostensibly been rejected. Gilliam and Roach said after the trial that
they resented Moore's persistent appeals to their racial loyalty and the
Boyfriend Theory was never seriously discussed. Both jurors considered
ridiculous Moore's suggestion that they ignore the evidence and suc-
cumb to race paranoia.

It was true that the jurors most reluctant to convict Richardson—
Gilliam, Rudisel and Heron—were black, but so was Roach, one of the
leading conviction advocates during those deliberations. And when it
came to the case against Wise, the acquittal camp was enlarged by the
addition of two steadfast whites—Bryers and Morris Siebold.

It is impossible to say, however, that Moore's racism defense did not
have unspoken (or at least unconscious) impact. Robert Moreland, a
black alternate juror, told *Newsday* after his dismissal: "Sure there was
prejudice on the part of the police, even if they didn't think there was.
It's part of the society we live in." Jurors of both races might be
expected to agree with that assessment.

Working from the bottom of the indictment up, the jury had little
trouble applying the acting-in-concert theory to convict Wise of riot.
The robbery and assault charges related to the attacks of Loughlin and
Lewis were another matter.

The panel agreed that Nomsa Brath, whose testimony placed Wise
at Schomburg Plaza after the rape but simultaneous with the reservoir
assaults, was the only credible alibi witness. Approximately half of the
jurors also considered Wise's first videotape more credible than the
second. On the first tape Wise claimed he had left the park after
watching the rape from behind a tree, never having gone south to the
reservoir. Eventually even those jurors who believed the second tape,
in which Wise admitted kicking one of the male joggers, agreed to
acquit him of the reservoir charges.

The fractious debate over the second videotape consumed much of
the five days the jury spent deliberating Wise's fate. The jurors came
into the courtroom over and over to watch both tapes, doing so in a
manner that taxed the patience of their large, mystified audience.
Because the judge would not permit the jurors to take notes during

playbacks, they watched the tapes in ten-minute segments. After viewing a portion of tape they returned to the deliberation room, where each juror wrote down the points he considered pertinent. The panel also used this painstaking method for long readbacks of testimony.

Ralph Pollock, a sixty-year-old retired restaurant consultant, accepted the second videotape unconditionally and considered it grounds to convict Wise of every charge. At the other extreme was Morris Siebold, fifty-nine, a security guard who argued that the second tape must be rejected in its entirety because Wise had been beaten by the police. As the rest of the panel lined up between these two poles, the discussion focused on the issues of coercion and credibility.

Roach, a data processor for a law firm, had, like Siebold, switched to the acquittal camp when deliberations turned from Richardson to Wise. He was troubled by the many mistakes (for example, the knife-slashing of Harris's legs) and flights of fancy (for example, the attempt to rip off the van) in Wise's account.

Although he also thought the behavior of the police amounted to coercion, Roach was curiously willing to excuse their conduct. Regarding his belief that Detective Nugent had slapped Wise, for example, Roach later said: "I don't fault any police officer for doing his job." And he believed that Detective Hartigan had simply told Wise the truth when he had warned the suspect that a jury would not believe his first tape. But it was this truth, Roach maintained, that had led Wise to incriminate himself falsely.

Gilliam was one of those who harbored an enormous amount of sympathy for Wise. He had been impressed by Moore's denigration of Hartigan's testimony. Among other things, Gilliam was troubled that the detective had chosen the cellblock as the locale for a heart-to-heart talk with the impressionable youth. Indeed, Gilliam considered Hartigan's own description of the episode nothing less than an admission of coercion. In an interview after the trial, he subtly misquoted the detective as having said to Wise, "You have to make your story believable."

Several jurors accepted Moore's accusation that Lederer had tried too hard to implicate Wise by showing him the gruesome photos of Harris's injuries and urging him to agree with her about their cause. Bryers wondered why Lederer had abruptly cut off the interview when, near the end of the second tape, Wise had begun to talk about "another jogger" who came along after the rape. The DA, thought Bryers, was trying to protect the credibility of the statement. "He was just rambling," she said, "he made no sense whatsoever."

Other jurors, including leading conviction advocates Rathgebar and Samoy, were unable to shake those who refused to trust the second videotape. Every time the jurors watched the tape somebody found another source of doubt about its veracity. Even swing voters who had been early supporters of the Richardson conviction, such as Naftal and James McNulty, were growing suspicious. Naftal was troubled that Wise's admissions of guilt so blatantly contradicted his first video; the second story was just *too* different.

By the twelfth day of deliberations, Wise stood convicted of nothing but riot. The jurors were exhausted and the leaders of each faction despaired of winning over their opponents. The panel agreed to declare itself hung if it could not reach a verdict on the remaining charges by the end of the day. With that last line drawn in the sand, the quest for compromise began.

Given the rationale that had been used to convict Richardson of attempted murder, there was no hope of finding Wise guilty of that crime. To convict Richardson the panel had agreed that the life-threatening blows to Harris's head had been delivered with the rock just off the crossdrive. Wise claimed to have stumbled upon the rape scene as he ran along the bottom of the ravine. By then, said the acquittal advocates, those who intended to kill Harris had already done the worst of the damage.

The conviction advocates turned their efforts to assault, of which there were two counts in the indictment. For the same reason that they failed to get a guilty verdict on attempted murder, they could not win a conviction for intentional assault with a weapon: Wise had come along after the fact. The second count, alleging "depraved indifference to human life," offered more room for negotiations. A defendant can be convicted of this count, the judge had explained, if he engaged in "reckless conduct" that created "a grave risk of death" and resulted in serious injury.

To the acquittal voters who believed most of Wise's first videotape, on which he described watching the others slap and punch Harris, this charge seemed appropriate. "He did nothing to stop it," Gilliam later explained. "He walked off and left her," said Bryers, "and he felt she was going to die." Thus, Wise was convicted of first-degree assault.

A compromise on the sex crimes proved harder to reach. There was no way that jurors who doubted the veracity of the second videotape would convict Wise of rape or sodomy. Having decided to reject all of his self-incriminations beyond the first video, they considered Wise merely a spectator at the rape scene.

The discussion turned to the lesser charge of sexual abuse, the subjection of someone to sexual contact by forcible compulsion, which the conviction advocates considered better, at least, than a hung jury. This count was acceptable to those swing voters who were still struggling with reasonable doubt. Wise had at least admitted "playing with her legs" on the second videotape. To the acquittal leaders who refused to consider that tape, however, another justification for this compromise had to be found.

The result was a tortured convolution of the acting-in-concert principle, derived from a misreading of Galligan's charge to the jury. Explaining the verdict later, three jurors maintained that the judge instructed them to apply the acting-in-concert law differently to sexual abuse than they did to the rape and sodomy charges. To be convicted of rape or sodomy, claimed these jurors, the defendant must have personally participated in those acts. But to be convicted of sex abuse, they added, he only had to be at the scene.

This was a rationalization of the jury's compromise. The application of the acting-in-concert principle does not change from crime to crime, nor had Galligan given the jury any instruction remotely resembling this explanation. It was, however, a means to end. "If we didn't compromise on something," said Bryers, "we never would have gotten out of there."

The conviction advocates, exasperated by nearly two weeks of debate that often seemed devoid of logic, refused to discuss the deliberations in the weeks following the trial. Even the swing voters were unhappy with the results. "They were well-intentioned people," said foreman McNulty of those in the acquittal camp, "but they had no understanding of the law."

At 1:15 P.M. on Tuesday, December 11, the jury brought its verdict into a courtroom where order was supposed to be assured by a crew of fifteen armed court officers. Wise and Richardson sat nervously at the defense table beside their silent attorneys. The extended Cuffee family, their arms locked together in solidarity, filled nearly two rows of seats, with dozens of other Supporters crammed throughout the gallery. Delores Wise was absent.

Lederer and Tim Clements were impassive as Galligan's clerk ran down the indictment, asking McNulty for the jury's verdict regarding Kharey Wise on each count.

Attempted murder?

Not guilty.

Rape?

Not guilty.

Sodomy?

Not guilty.

Sexual abuse?

Guilty.

Assault of Paula Harris?

Guilty.

Robbery?

Not guilty.

Assault of John Loughlin?

Not guilty.

Assault of David Lewis?

Not guilty.

Riot?

Guilty.

The Cuffees sighed with relief, sharing the assumption of most that the panel would go no harder on Richardson than it had on Wise. But their hope evaporated a moment later as McNulty began to tick off the verdict on Richardson.

Guilty of attempted murder, guilty of rape, guilty of sodomy, guilty of robbery and guilty, guilty, guilty, guilty again. With convictions on eight counts, Richardson became the only defendant at either trial nailed for every applicable crime in the indictment.

By the time McNulty finished, Grace Cuffee was prostrate on the hardwood bench, clutching her heart and struggling for air. Angela Cuffee was on her feet. "How can they do that?" she yelled. "Why him? He didn't hurt anybody! He never hurt anybody in his life!"

As if in response to her cry, many Supporters rose, screaming "white racists" and "white justice" as Galligan called for order. They focused their wrath on Lederer, who stood at the prosecution table facing the gallery, with detectives McKenna and Taglioni at either side. "Bitch, you're mine!" the defendant's brother-in-law, Lee Richardson, shouted at Lederer. "You're mine, bitch! You hurt my mother!"

Paramedics were administering oxygen to Ms. Cuffee as Angela tried to get her stepbrother's attention. "Kevin, it's all right," called Angela, her face dripping with tears. "Don't worry about it. We love you. Kevin, do you hear me? Don't worry about it. It's all right; it's all right; it's all right."

But Kevin wasn't all right. He and Wise appeared terrified as they embraced each other and wept.

Galligan ordered the room cleared and told the court officers to take the defendants away. As Wise was escorted through the side exit he turned to call Lederer a "bitch" and issue a final warning. "God will get you," he promised. "You'll pay for this."

The Supporters took their rage into the hallway. Bruce Kareem pounded on an elevator door. "I told you I'm fucking the jury up," he declared, adding, in a reference to Eric Roach: "The light-skinned juror in front is through!" Said Frank Yancy: "Whoever really raped that woman, I hope he rapes 100 more white motherfuckers."

Out on the sidewalk Lee Richardson hoisted a huge concrete block over his head, threatening to throw it at a group of television camera-men before cooler heads convinced him to drop it on the curb. Other Supporters menaced Lederer, who was briskly walking up the block at the center of a knot of bodyguards, with threats and epithets such as "lying whore."

As disappointing as the Wise verdict was, the prosecutors managed to find some consolation. At least, thought Lederer, Wise didn't beat *all* the sex-crime charges and, as an adult, he still faced some heavy time. If the judge imposed maximum sentences on each count—assault, sex abuse and riot—and ordered that they be served consecutively, Wise would get a term of eight and one-third to twenty-six years.

Galligan's reputation as "Father Time" led nearly everybody on Centre Street to expect as much. When he conducted the sentencing hearing on January 9, 1991, however, Galligan again proved less pre-dictable than his critics imagined.

After rejecting motions to set aside the verdict argued by Moore and Vernon Mason (whom the judge now permitted to replace Diller), Galligan afforded the defendants the customary opportunity to address the court.

Richardson stood and turned to face the gallery, hands clasped at his waist, his big body trembling from top to bottom. "I'm sorry for what happened to the people," he said, "but you got the wrong person."

Richardson could not repress the tears as he began to thank his family.

"Be strong, brother," shouted a Supporter.

"I'm innocent," he said weakly, "but, you know, the judge railroads black and Hispanic people. . . . I didn't do these crimes. . . . Don't worry, I'll never stop fighting. . . . I love you all."

"We love you," cried Angela Cuffee. Two Supporters stood and yelled "Freedom or death!" before court officers ordered them to be seated.

Wise managed to keep from crying during his brief remarks, but it was obviously a struggle. "I thank you all for supporting me," he said to the gallery. "Only the good Lord knows what happened . . . I'll be back." He made a peace sign with his fingers, put them to his lips, and blew a kiss to the Supporters. Delores Wise was not in the courtroom.

Describing the Central Park wilding as "cowardly, mindless, mob-induced madness," Galligan imposed the same sentence on Richardson that he had four months earlier on McCray, Salaam and Santana: five to ten years, the maximum on these crimes for a juvenile.

The judge's preamble had indicated that he also intended to grant Lederer's request to incarcerate Wise for the maximum period possible. "Wise's strident and ardent behavior at the time the verdict was rendered," said Galligan, "and his belligerent and offensive conduct as a witness, speak volumes about who he is. Indeed, it goes a long way to understand his conduct in the park."

The judge then pronounced the maximum term on each count. But he stunned his audience with an order that Wise's sentences be served concurrently rather than consecutively. This, explained Galligan, was due to "the minimal difference between his age and those of his co-defendants."

Thus was Kharey Wise, at age eighteen, sentenced to five to fifteen years. Kharey Wise, who had sat across a narrow table from Lederer twenty-one months earlier and said, "This is my first rape." The only defendant who might have grown to middle age in prison would be eligible for parole before he turned twenty-two.

When the judge finished his short sentencing speech more than a dozen Supporters jumped to their feet, chanting: "Malcolm X! Freedom or death! We will win! Freedom or death!"

Galligan angrily surveyed his courtroom, often during the past two years the scene of pandemonium. Some bright yellow signs that a handful of Supporters were holding above their heads incensed the judge. "We Know Where You Live," declared the bold, black lettering.

"Take those people into custody!" Galligan told the court officers. "That man who just held up that sign," shouted the judge, pointing out a culprit for the confused guards, "take him into custody!"

Moments later a short, stocky black man named Rahin Howard, twenty, was in the well, looking up at the furious judge. "What does that mean, 'We know where you live'?" demanded Galligan, standing behind the bench.

Howard did not seem afraid. "That means that you and anybody else that's had something to do with this trial, trying these boys that are innocent . . . I'm not alone," he said. "You take it any way you want. . . . What we are saying is: the streets are ours. They belong to us, you know . . . I'm saying, we know where you live."

"All right," replied Galligan, "I'm going to hold you in contempt of court. I'm going to sentence you to jail right now."

Moore and Mason intervened, asking the judge to forgive the protest on the grounds that the black community was deeply upset by the Central Park case. But Galligan, who had received more death threats than he cared to count since this case had been dropped into his lap, was not dissuaded.

"I am perfectly aware of the community's feelings about this case," said Galligan. "This has nothing to do with that. . . . If we, as judges, sit in court and allow people to come in and intimidate the court, then we don't belong here. That is as simple as it is." And Galligan sentenced Howard to thirty days in jail.

Before putting on her coat and walking down the center aisle, Lederer asked the court officers if she could take one of Howard's signs. "We Know Where You Live." Back at the office, the prosecutor hung it on the bulletin board behind her desk.

CHAPTER 20

THE TRIAL THAT
NEVER WAS

ELIZABETH LEDERER WAS NOT LIKELY TO FORGET KHAREY WISE'S DE-
scription of the argument between Steve Lopez and Yusef Salaam
about whether to kill Paula Harris.

Lopez had apparently been incensed that the victim had shown
disrespect for the gang by daring to fight back. The dialogue, which
Wise had described as taking place after the boys finished "sex abus-
ing" the woman, went as follows.

Salaam: "Yo, Steve, let her go, man! You know, we don't want no
dead body on our hands. . . . Let her live."

Lopez: "No, man, no. She wants to scratch Kevin, man. She wants
to scratch!"

Salaam: "So what, man? What you gonna do? You gonna kill her?"

Lopez: "I wanna do something."

Salaam: "Come on, man. By now, we got cops out here lookin' for
us. Come on! They got half our people! . . . Don't kill her. Bad enough
you rapin' her! Don't kill her, man!"

At that point Lopez had said something that Wise did not hear,
something that had scared Salaam enough to prompt his immediate
departure. "Come on, Polo," said Salaam, addressing Wise by his

306

nickname, "we're outta here!" The pair walked away, Wise had said, leaving Lopez and Kevin Richardson alone with the unconscious woman.

The recollections of Kharey Wise were not Lederer's only confirmation of Lopez's propensity for violence. Shortly after the crime Barry Michael Cooper reported in *The Village Voice* that Lopez was among the leaders of a crew of Schomburg boys who had broken windows and mugged several tenants of Los Tres Unidos, a neighboring project. Then there was the rebuttal testimony of Detective Victor Cornetta at the second trial. Cornetta testified that he had asked Wise why the gang had beaten the Jogger so badly. "He said it was Steve Lopez," said Cornetta. "That while he was on top of her, while he was doing her, he got sick of looking at her face and he had picked up a brick and raised it over his head as though to hit her. And that's when Kharey Wise turned away."

Cornetta's story corroborated what Raymond Santana had said about Lopez yelling, "Shut up, bitch!" while hitting Harris twice in the face with a brick. But these nuggets were no more likely to help Lederer nail Lopez than the knowledge that McCray, Santana, Wise and Richardson had said on tape that he participated in the rape.

The Lopez case, which was crippled from the start by the absence of self-incrimination, had withered further in the twenty months since his indictment. Now, with a date to take the last rape defendant to trial on January 30, only three weeks after the Wise-Richardson sentencing, Lederer was running out of time. Her personal conviction about the centrality of Lopez's role wasn't going to win the case. The question was not: What happened in Central Park on April 19? The question was: What proof could Lederer offer, within the narrow confines of the rules that govern a trial, that would convince twelve jurors that it had happened the way she believed it happened?

Jesse Berman was looking forward to going to trial. Confident of his courtroom skills, he would welcome the scrutiny that had exposed the weaknesses of his colleagues. And it was a sweet irony that his guy was simultaneously the defendant the DA most wanted to put away and the one against whom she had the weakest case.

Lopez had shrewdly avoided incriminating himself of anything on videotape. He had admitted witnessing the assaults of Diaz, Lewis and Loughlin but had denied having participated, just as vehemently as he had denied ever having seen a woman in the park. The evidentiary value of Lopez's video was further weakened when Berman, after negotiations with Tim Clements, won the DA's agreement to delete the prejudicial portions on which Lederer told Lopez his story was not credible because he had been implicated by other suspects.

As far as the other evidence was concerned, both sides knew the state would never get most of it in front of a jury. The videotapes of the teenagers who had already been convicted could not be used against Lopez for two reasons: First, he had a Sixth Amendment right to cross-examine his accusers and, second, the allegations on those tapes were hearsay except insofar as they incriminated the speaker. As for the allegations concerning Lopez's activities at Los Tres Unidos, they couldn't be introduced at trial unless Berman made his client's character an issue. And, finally, Berman could probably have Wise's remark to Detective Cornetta excluded as hearsay.

But Berman was not inclined to get overly optimistic. There was one troubling aspect of the case about which he knew little and could do less: the testimony of accomplices. Several kids had made statements implicating Lopez to one degree or another, and there was no telling how much more they might be willing to reveal in exchange for some sort of deal. Berman was getting sketchy reports from his colleagues in the defense bar about the DA's efforts to shore up her case.

Orlando Escobar, under indictment for robbery, assault and riot in connection with the beating of Loughlin, refused to make any deal. The word on the street was that the prosecution had offered Escobar probation with no jail time if he would agree to tell a jury what he had told the cops: that Lopez had participated in the beating of Loughlin. But emotions in East Harlem had run higher with each new Central Park verdict, and Escobar's mother was afraid of the consequences if her son were tagged as a sellout.

The same issue prevented Clarence Thomas from testifying against Lopez. Thomas had always denied the allegations of other defendants that he had been at the 102nd Street Crossdrive (McCray, in fact, had named him as one of the rapists). He had told the prosecutors, however, that Lopez had kicked the bum and had later said, "Let's get a woman jogger." That evidence would help, but the only way to get it was to threaten Thomas with contempt of court if he refused to testify. Thomas's lawyer hinted that the boy's mother might sooner see her son jailed for contempt than known on the streets as a rat.

Then there was Tony Montalvo, who was under indictment for the beating of Antonio Diaz. He could link Lopez to that crime, but even the talkative Montalvo had always denied having been at the rape scene.

Lederer had refrained from putting Jermain Robinson on the stand at the earlier trials because she did not want Berman to get a preview of his testimony. But the actual damage Robinson could inflict was limited. Robinson could place Lopez at the reservoir—in fact he had told the DA that Lopez was struck by a flying piece of tree branch when somebody broke it over Loughlin's back—but he did not witness the rape.

The thing that really worried Berman was the amount of information he did *not* possess. His client had always sworn that he was not at the rape scene, but what if Montalvo, Robinson or others should testify that Lopez had bragged to the contrary before the heat had come down? And what had Lederer learned during her interview with Jomo Smith, the only suspect to make a videotape who was never charged with a crime? Above all, Berman feared the unidentified Mystery Witness, whose testimony Lederer had described at arraignment as placing Lopez "between the victim's legs."

The prosecution's rape case against Lopez disintegrated when the Mystery Witness refused to honor his earlier promise to cooperate. The publicity that accompanied six months of trials, the incessant allegations in the black media that the prosecution was a racist lynching, the agitation by the Supporters, all weakened the teenager's resolve. In the racially tense atmosphere that now prevailed throughout the city, the Mystery Witness had become uncooperative, his stories full of inconsistencies, his memory fading.

This left the DA with nothing that could link Lopez conclusively to the rape. Hair had been found on his shirt that was consistent with Paula Harris's head hair. But that was hardly proof of rape, and Berman was sure to argue that it could have been transferred to Lopez from the clothing of another defendant at one of the police stationhouses. Yes, there was a bit of blood on Lopez's underpants, but it could not be linked to the victim or to anybody else in the case.

Lederer's last hope was to convince one of the convicted teenagers to testify. The jury still wouldn't see that defendant's tape, but his availability for cross-examination would permit him to incriminate Lopez with his testimony.

The only youth Lederer might be able to turn was Raymond Santana. There was no love lost between Lopez, who had gone to the park with his Schomburg pals, and Santana, who ran with the Taft crew. And Santana was now the only rape defendant whose case was not in the hands of a militant advocate. At Lederer's request, Peter Rivera went to see his former client in jail to find out whether he'd be willing to testify against Lopez.

It was a long shot. Santana was now a ward of the state Division for Youth and thus beyond the authority of the DA or Judge Galligan. As a result, Lederer could not promise to have his sentence reduced in exchange for testimony against Lopez. The best she could do was offer to write a supportive letter to the parole board when Santana became eligible for early release.

Even if this incentive were not weak, it was unlikely Santana would cooperate. The Mystery Witness would have been safer on the streets with the label "Informer" on his back than Santana would be behind bars if he were to sell out Lopez.

All of this left the prosecutors with a decent case against Lopez for robbery, the reservoir assaults and riot. But without a reasonable expectation of winning convictions for the crimes related to the Jogger attack, could Lederer justify putting Paula Harris and the other victims through the rigors of a third trial? She thought not. After nearly two years, what Paula Harris needed most was the chance to retire from the role of "Central Park Jogger."

Berman got the first call about a plea bargain on Monday, January 28. Lederer told him that her rape case against Lopez was weaker than the case regarding the reservoir assaults. There are several kids, she said, who are prepared to testify against your client about the robbery and beating of Loughlin. The good news for Berman in this message was the unspoken acknowledgment that Lederer had lost the Mystery Witness.

The next day Berman spent three hours discussing Lederer's offer with Lopez and his mother. Steve could plead guilty to one count of robbing Loughlin, he explained, in exchange for a sentence of one and one-half to four and one-half years. Berman believed there was a fifty-fifty chance of beating the charges related to the reservoir assaults at trial. If they went to court and lost, however, Lopez faced a sentence of three and one-third to ten years on the robbery count, considerably stiffer than the deal Lederer was offering. Then there was the risk that Paula Harris's testimony might convince a sympathetic jury to convict Lopez on the higher counts, too, despite the lack of evidence. Berman had tried too many cases to trust a jury.

His clients sent him back to the DA with a counteroffer: a sentence of one and one-half to three years. But Lederer, who disliked having to make this deal at all, refused to come down any further. With the eight months he had served while awaiting bail in 1989, if Lopez took the plea she was offering he would be eligible for parole after ten more months in jail. Even if parole were denied, he'd be out in twenty-eight months (for a total of three years) with good behavior.

As jury selection opened on Wednesday, January 30, Lederer and Berman huddled in the private corridor behind Galligan's courtroom. Inside, a pool of hundreds of potential jurors was filling out questionnaires about the case. The Lopez family, said Berman, has decided to accept your offer, provided that Steve remains free on bail until sentencing. Lederer agreed.

A few minutes later Lopez, now seventeen years old, was standing in front of Galligan, pleading guilty to one count of first-degree robbery.

"On April 19, 1989, were you in Central Park?" asked the judge.

"Yes," said Lopez.

"Were you there with a number of other individuals?"

"Yes."

"And at that time did you and they, acting together, forcibly take property from a male by the name of John Loughlin?"

"Yes."

"Did you or one of the others working with you at the time use, or threaten the use of, a dangerous instrument?"

"One of the others," said Lopez.

"But they were working towards the same thing that you were doing, is that right?"

"Yes."

"What was the instrument?"

"A pipe."

The fact is, it wasn't a pipe at all. "Pipe" was a misnomer that had become part of the symbolic vocabulary of the Central Park case. A pipe is hollow. The weapon Lopez was talking about, the weapon that had been used, depending on whose tape you credited, by Salaam, McCray or Richardson, was a bar, a solid iron bar about 14 inches long, wrapped in black tape from end to end.

It was the bar Eddie de la Paz had given Salaam after taking it from Wise's apartment, where its purpose was to secure the door not only against burglars but also against an outcast brother. It was the bar Montalvo had refused to take, or perhaps had discarded, when McCray offered it to him at the end of the wilding spree. It was the bar that had broken Loughlin's head open. And it was the bar that a group of angry boys between the ages of thirteen and seventeen had used, along with a rock, a brick and their bare hands, to pound the promise out of Paula Harris's future.

Afterword

*"No person shall be . . . deprived of life,
liberty or property without due process of law."*
—FIFTH AMENDMENT, U.S. CONSTITUTION

STEVE LOPEZ, STANDING AT THE DEFENSE TABLE WITH JESSE BERMAN, declined to say anything when given the customary opportunity to address the court at his sentencing. His father, displaying an angry scowl, and his mother, quietly but steadily crying, watched from the gallery as Judge Galligan sent their eldest son to a juvenile detention center, where he would serve his one-and-a-half- to four-and-a-half-year sentence.

Galligan described Lopez as "one of the most vicious perpetrators among a cowardly group that went on a sadistic, brutal rampage." The judge, who had approved the plea bargain, then told the small group of spectators, "It is ironic that the rights of due process prevent me from imposing a tougher sentence."

Among those who watched the court officers lead the seventeen-year-old away was a white man with a large button on his lapel: "Justice for the Jogger."

It is now one year since that sentencing hearing, three years since the night of the Central Park wilding, and one still wonders whether the Jogger got justice, or whether justice isn't simply too much to expect.

In the current conservative political climate, it has become fashionable to attack the courts for a supposed failure to avenge the victims of violent crime. But it is fairness, not vengeance, that gives the American criminal justice system its strength. The U.S. Constitution, and all of the criminal procedure laws that derive from it, cannot restore any victim to the status she enjoyed before she became a target of criminals. Perhaps the best those laws can do is make it difficult for the state, with its enormous, discretionary powers of prosecution, to punish the wrong person.

Amid all of the political noise about courts coddling criminals, it is easy to overlook some fundamental facts that distinguish America's criminal justice system from the kangaroo courts of totalitarian states. We should first keep in mind that a trial is an infrequent event. In most jurisdictions, the great majority of defendants plead guilty to one of the offenses they have committed. (In New York, for example, only one of every ten felony indictments goes to trial.) Trials occur when a defendant, for one reason or another, decides to put up a fight. It may be hard for the media, the public, police, prosecutors and even judges to accept, but sometimes a defendant makes that fight because he's not guilty. It is that wrongly accused person, as rare as he might be, that the system is designed to protect. The possibility that such a person could be brought to trial is the very reason that the prosecution's burden of proof must be so heavy.

In ivory towers on law school campuses across the country, wide-eyed students are taught that a trial is a search for the truth. Those who choose to practice in the criminal courts, however, will soon learn otherwise. They will learn that a trial is a contest of credibility, their own and that of their witnesses, with evidence, not truth, at its core. The winner of the contest is the lawyer who convinces a jury that his interpretation of the evidence makes more sense than that of his opponent. In many cases, what may or may not have actually happened at the crime scene, or in the interrogation room, will never objectively be known.

In the Central Park case, for example, there were so many contradictions among the defendants' accounts that it is impossible to know conclusively what occurred. In an interview more than a year after the last trial, Elizabeth Lederer explained how those discrepancies, particularly concerning the opposing chronologies of the assaults as described by different defendants, affected her strategy. "You weren't there. I wasn't there," she said in reference to the night of April 19, 1989. "You work with what the defendants say to you. . . . I don't think it's my job to go in and say, 'This is what happened.' I mean, I can tell you, 'This is what the evidence says happened . . . and I find this compelling, or this to be a very persuasive argument. . . .' But I can't tell you [what happened], despite what I might personally think." A prosecutor, in Lederer's view, is at the mercy of the evidence, much of which may come from the mouths of the defendants. Two defendants may disagree about the details of the crime, but that fact doesn't necessarily mean one is not guilty.

The credibility contest is played according to a lengthy compilation of narrow rules, and the judge who interprets and applies those rules plays a huge role indeed. But all along the way there are opportunities for other players to affect the outcome of the contest, too, and their conduct helps determine whether a defendant gets a fair trial. In this way, a verdict is influenced by a great many people, only twelve of whom are voting jurors.

Here is a partial list of the people who had key roles in the Central Park case: Lederer, Galligan, Colin Moore, Thomas McKenna, Yusef Salaam, John Hartigan, Kharey Wise, George Louie, Ron Gold, Bobby McCray, Harry Hildebrandt, Linda Fairstein, Sharonne Salaam, Mickey Joseph, Angela Cuffee, Steve Gilliam, John Loughlin, Howard Diller, Steve Lopez, Bobby Burns, Vernon Mason, Pedro Sanchez, the Mystery Witness and, of course, Paula Harris.

Different decisions, different testimony, different opinions on the part of any one of those people may have led to significantly different results. The record shows, however, what those people did and what they said. We should not be surprised that the record is imperfect, that it seems to satisfy nobody fully.

Lederer, now the deputy chief of the Career Criminal Bureau in the Manhattan DA's office, believes she presented as strong a case as any prosecutor could have and says she feels "positive" about the outcome. Given the distance of time, however, she admits disappointment with the results regarding Wise and Lopez. Lederer also regrets that the case did not spur New York's legislature to expand the category of crimes for which juveniles can get heavy sentences.

Tim Clements is practicing law with old friends in a small negligence firm in Cleveland, his hometown. We recently discussed the Wise verdict and the explanation offered by the acquittal voters, who claimed the acting-in-concert principle is applied differently to sexual abuse than to rape. That, Clements agreed, was simply a rationalization of what was a typical compromise verdict. "There is no way under the law to justify it," he said. "If he's guilty of sex abuse, he's guilty of rape."

Jesse Berman is angry that Lopez, having served the minimum one and a half years on his sentence for the robbery conviction, was denied his first chance at parole. But under New York's so-called "good time law," one third is automatically taken off the maximum sentence as a reward for good behavior. As a result, Lopez, will probably be released after having served three years. Berman logically believes his client, a first-offender, would have drawn less time, or none at all, if his offense hadn't been tied to the Central Park case. He is adamant about reminding interviewers that Lopez was not convicted of any offense related to the assault of the Jogger.

At this writing, William Kunstler has filed the only appeal for a Central Park defendant. In a sparse, thirty-five-page brief, Kunstler argued for reversal of Salaam's conviction on three grounds: that Galligan should have granted Kunstler's request for a hearing on whether Pedro Sanchez's discussion of news reports during deliberations tainted the verdict; that Salaam should have been given a separate trial because the playing of his co-defendants' videotapes was prejudicial to him; and that Salaam's oral statements to Detective McKenna should have been suppressed. He might also have argued that Bobby Burns's representation of Salaam was incompetent, but he decided not to, said Kunstler, because he didn't want to publicly criticize a black lawyer. (A claim of ineffective assistance of counsel is extremely difficult to win in New York, where strategic blunders such as those committed by Burns, no matter how grievous, are not considered valid grounds. Still, the argument should have been made against the odds.)

Vernon Mason and Colin Moore, who spoke with conviction about a miscarriage of justice having put their innocent, young clients in jail approximately eighteen months ago, still have not filed their promised appeals. But both lawyers have been busy. In 1991 Mason and Moore ran for seats on New York's expanded City Council, and both lost. During the campaign, a car accident in Crown Heights, Brooklyn, in which a Hasidic Jew ran over and killed a seven-year-old black boy, sparked riots in which another Hasidic man was murdered, allegedly by a group of black youths. Moore represented the parents of the dead child, Gavin Cato, and played a leading role as a spokesman for the larger black community in the negotiations with City Hall that followed the riots.

Meanwhile, the less political defense lawyers, Burns, Mickey Joseph, Peter Rivera and Howard Diller, have returned to their modest practices.

Jermain Robinson served eight months of his one-year sentence and is free again.

Michael Briscoe also did his time and was released, but he has since been arrested twice on drug-selling charges.

Antron McCray, Raymond Santana, Yusef Salaam, Kevin Richardson and Kharey Wise are all still in custody. Each will become eligible for parole after serving the five-year minimum on his sentence, less the credit he gets for time spent in pretrial detention.

Paula Harris is still working for Salomon Brothers. And on the streets of East Harlem, where I discussed the case recently with several residents who were *not* among the hallway Supporters, lots of people still wonder whether her boyfriend did it.

—April 25, 1992

Cast of Characters

The First Trial

DEFENDANT	FAMILY[1]	DETECTIVES[2]	LAWYERS	CONVICTIONS	SENTENCE	PROSECUTORS
Antron McCray, 15[3]	Bobby and Linda McCray	Harry Hildebrandt, Carlos Gonzalez	Michael "Mickey" Joseph, C. Vernon Mason	Rape, assault (4 counts), robbery, riot	5 to 10 years	Elizabeth Lederer, Arthur "Tim" Clements
Yusef Salaam, 15	Sharonne Salaam, "Big Brother" David Nocenti, Marilyn Hatcher, Vincent Jones, Aisha Salaam	Thomas McKenna, John Taglioni	Robert "Bobby" Burns, William Kunstler	Rape, assault (4 counts), robbery, riot	5 to 10 years	
Raymond Santana, 14	Raymond Santana, Sr., Navidad Colon	John Hartigan, Humberto Arroyo, Michael Sheehan	Peter Rivera	Rape, assault (4 counts), robbery, riot	5 to 10 years	

The Second Trial

DEFENDANT	FAMILY	DETECTIVES	LAWYERS	CONVICTIONS	SENTENCE	PROSECUTORS
Kevin Richardson, 14	Grace Cuffee, Paul Richardson, Angela Cuffee	John Hartigan, Carlos Gonzalez, Michael Sheehan	Howard Diller, C. Vernon Mason	Attempted murder, rape, sodomy, assault (3 counts), robbery, riot	5 to 10 years	Elizabeth Lederer, Arthur "Tim" Clements
Kharey Wise, 16	Delores Wise	John Hartigan, Robert Nugent, Michael Sheehan	Colin Moore	Assault (1 count), sexual abuse, riot	5 to 15 years	

The Plea Bargains

DEFENDANT[4]	LAWYERS	CONVICTIONS	SENTENCE	PROSECUTORS
Michael Briscoe, 17	Alton Maddox, Joseph Klempner	Assault (1 count), and unrelated drug charge	1 year	Elizabeth Lederer, Arthur "Tim" Clements
Orlando Escobar, 16	Stephen Pugliese	Attempted robbery	6 months jail, 4½ years probation	
Steve Lopez, 15	Jesse Berman	Robbery	1½ to 4½ years	
Antonio Montalvo, 18	Richard Wojszwilo	Attempted robbery	1 year	
Jermain Robinson, 15	Elliot Cook, Natasha Lapiner	Robbery	1 year	

[1] Only relatives who played key roles at trial are listed.
[2] Only detectives who provided significant testimony at trial are listed.
[3] Ages are given as of April 19, 1989.
[4] Charges of assault and unlawful assembly against Clarence Thomas, 14, and Lamont McCall, 13, were adjudicated in Family Court. Those records are not public.

Chronology

1989

APRIL

19: The night of the Central Park wilding, during which a female jogger is raped and severely beaten. Several cyclists and male joggers are also assaulted.
- Raymond Santana, Steve Lopez, Clarence Thomas, Kevin Richardson and Lamont McCall are picked up at about 10:30 P.M.

20: McCall, 13, is released with Family Court summons.
- Antron McCray, having been implicated by Richardson, is brought in for questioning at about 11 A.M.
- Prosecutors Linda Fairstein and Elizabeth Lederer arrive at Twentieth Precinct to assist detectives at about 8 P.M.
- Yusef Salaam and Kharey Wise are picked up at about 10 P.M., also having been implicated by other boys.

21: Lederer begins videotaped interviews with suspects at Twenty-fourth Precinct at about 1 A.M. She is soon joined by prosecutor Arthur "Tim" Clements, who will assist her for the duration of the case. Video sessions continue all day and into the next.
- Michael Briscoe and Jermain Robinson are arrested.

23: Criminal Court arraignments at approximately 1 A.M.

24: Grand jury convenes.

25: Residents of Schomburg Plaza, where four defendants live, hold prayer vigil at Metropolitan Hospital for the comatose rape victim, known only as the Central Park Jogger.

26–28: Salaam, Richardson, Santana, Lopez, McCray, Wise, Briscoe, Robinson indicted.
- Thomas released with Family Court summons.

321

MAY

3: The Jogger comes out of coma.

10: The Central Park case is assigned to Acting Supreme Court Justice Thomas G. Galligan.
    • Howard Diller releases video made by his client, Kevin Richardson.

JUNE

7: The Jogger is released from Metropolitan Hospital, to continue rehabilitation at Gaylord Hospital in Connecticut.

SEPTEMBER

25: New York *Newsday* obtains a set of the videotapes and prints extensive excerpts. Clips from the videos subsequently appear on television newscasts.

OCTOBER

5: Jermain Robinson pleads guilty to robbery, agrees to cooperate with prosecutors.

10: Start of pretrial hearings to determine admissibility at trial of defendants' videotapes and incriminating written statements.

NOVEMBER

14: The Jogger is released from Gaylord Hospital.

27: The Jogger returns to work at Salomon Brothers investment bank.

28: Defense lawyers are given results of DNA tests that fail to link any of the defendants to the rape. Of several semen samples tested, the only one that can be identified was taken from the Jogger's tights. It is her boyfriend's semen.

29: Pretrial hearings end.

1990

JANUARY

11: Tony Montalvo and Orlando Escobar are arrested for alleged participation in the Central Park wilding. They are charged, respectively, with the assault and robbery of a pedestrian, known as "the bum," and a male jogger.

CHRONOLOGY

FEBRUARY

23: Judge Galligan rules that the videotapes may be played at trial.

MARCH

4: Briscoe arrested on charge of selling angel dust. Pleads guilty soon after to that charge and one count of assaulting a male jogger in Central Park.

16: Judge Galligan approves prosecution's request to put McCray, Santana and Salaam on trial together, holding cases against other defendants in abeyance.

JUNE

13: Jury selection for first trial begins.

25: Opening statements.

JULY

16: The Jogger testifies.

AUGUST

1: Salaam testifies

18: Verdicts returned.

SEPTEMBER

10: Galligan agrees to prosecution request to try Wise and Richardson together, holding case against Lopez in abeyance.

11: McCray, Santana and Salaam sentenced.

OCTOBER

11: Jury selection begins for second trial.

22: Opening statements.

NOVEMBER

2: The Jogger testifies.

7: Melonie Jackson testifies.

26: Wise testifies.

DECEMBER

11: Verdicts returned

20: William Kunstler, representing Salaam on appeal, is held in contempt of court for telling Judge Galligan he is "a disgrace to the bench."

1991

JANUARY

9: Wise and Richardson sentenced.

30: Lopez, an alleged ringleader of the gang of wilders, pleads guilty to one count of robbery on first day of jury selection for his trial.

MARCH

13: Lopez sentenced.

Index